Praise for *Sandstorms:*

"As the younger brother of Paul and Alexander. . . . Theroux doesn't disappoint those who like their wit to be laced with acid observation, and he's mordantly funny about the opportunist Westerners who look upon Saudi Arabia as a cultureless money pit, when that judgment might be made as easily about their own system."
> —Christopher Hitchens, *Conde Nast Traveler*

"Peter Theroux's delightful memoir about his experiences in the Middle East is must reading. This account of an American abroad is as entertaining as it is informative, and Theroux provides shrewd insight into a part of the world that affects us all and about which we still know so little. It's a book to savor, and ponder."
> —Haynes Johnson, author of *Sleepwalking Through History*

"Peter Theroux is bound to loosen the blinders many of us wear when reading about the Middle East. . . . Theroux does very well, writing with the freshness of a lively observer, combined with a thoughtful perspective gained through his fluency in Arabic and his conversance with Arab literature and history."
> —*Denver Post*

"A tangy blend of good-natured cynicism and curiosity. This memoir is brimming with vivid sketches of life in a volatile, often contradictory, ever-intriguing culture."

—*Booklist*

"Theroux studied Arabic, studied the history and politics of the area and disabused himself of the mischievous misconceptions of the Arabic people that are rife in the United States. . . . A welcome addition to the small reliable library of Middle Eastern studies written by authors from the West."

—*The Pittsburgh Press*

Sandstorms

. . . There was an Orient like a child,
Imploring, crying for help;
The West was his infallible master—
But this map has changed;
The cosmos is ablaze
Gleaned from its ashes,
The Orient and the West
Share one tomb.
>   Ali Ahmed Said
>   *The West and the Orient*

People who use a "Q"
without a "u" after it are playing by
rules we can't even begin to understand.
>   Will Durst

By the Same Author

The Strange Disappearance of Imam Moussa Sadr
Cities of Salt, by Abdelrahman Munif (translator)

Sandstorms

Days and Nights in Arabia

Peter Theroux

W. W. Norton & Company New York · London

Printed in the United States of America.

The text of this book is composed in Bembo, with display type set in Legend.
Composition and manufacturing by the Haddon Craftsmen, Inc.
Book design by Charlotte Staub.

First published as a Norton paperback 1991

Library of Congress Cataloging-in-Publication Data

Theroux, Peter.
  Sandstorms : days and nights in Arabia / Peter Theroux.
    p. cm.
  1. Arab countries—Description and travel. I. Title.
DS49.7.T48 1990
953.05'3—dc20   89–28609

ISBN 0-393-30797-2

W. W. Norton & Company, Inc., 500 Fifth Avenue, New York, N. Y. 10110
W. W. Norton & Company Ltd., 10 Coptic Street, London WC1A 1PU

3 4 5 6 7 8 9 0

For my brothers and sisters:

Eugene, Alex, Paul, Ann Marie,
Mary and Joseph

Contents

Prologue

Much of my seven years in the Middle East was spent researching the unexplained disappearance of Imam Moussa Sadr, leader of Lebanon's Shia Muslims, in Libya in 1978. When I began to follow reports of his captivity or murder (or, periodically, his imminent reappearance) in the Arab press, the case struck me as a curiosity, and I thought of the Imam as an Arab Jimmy Hoffa or Lord Lucan. I could not resist the challenge to investigate and report the Sadr affair formally, and the more I uncovered the more I was aware of an almost bottomless fund of ambiguity and complexity in Sadr's personality and his career. He was the most complicated man in Lebanon, which says quite a lot.

After leaving the Middle East, I spent nearly a month in Paris interviewing former Iranian President Abolhassan Bani Sadr (no relation), former Prime Minister Shahpour Bakhtiar and others about the Imam. Almost everyone concerned told me the same thing: "No one had mixed feelings about Imam Sadr; people either loved or hated him." But everyone—especially the people who pronounced that sentence—had mixed feelings about Sadr: they loved and hated him.

Eventually I began to wonder whether the real "story" was not the disappearance of Moussa Sadr, or even his life, but rather the times and places that make such mysterious people and events possible. In looking more closely at the seven years I spent in the Middle East, I decided that the times and places I came to know in that period were the only thing that I could write about with any certainty, and this book is the result of that conviction. In the end, the informal process of earning a living, playing tourist, and trying to satisfy my curiosity about the Arab world helped me more than any research could to reach a comfortable understanding of it. My aim here is to try to pass that on.

P.C.T.
September 1989

Sandstorms

1

Aliens in Arabia

$\mathcal{A}$t the time I did not realize that the donkey ladies were terrorizing all of Riyadh; I thought I had a scoop.

My friend Hamdan did not want to see me that night because the house was in an uproar, but hospitality prevailed and he buzzed me through the high iron gates. Stevie Wonder's *Secret*

Life of Plants was blasting from the sons' wing of the house. Old Abu Hamdan was praying loudly, his mother was shrieking into the telephone, his sisters were weeping in the television room. *It* had happened to two of their girlfriends: they had been strolling down the block and were attracted by the sound of music from the Festival Palace in this flat Arabian suburb of Suleimaniya. The girls peeked in to see almost a hundred elegant unveiled women dancing to tribal wedding music.

"Come in—join us!" called one of the tallest and lightest-skinned women—a princess, surely.

The girls pulled off their veils and were about to start dancing when one of them grabbed her friend's elbow.

"Look at their legs!"

All the women had the legs and hoofs of donkeys.

The girls snatched their veils and ran out of the ranch-style palace, through the marble courtyard and gardens, to the side-walk where a little yellow taxi was parked under the fizzing amber streetlights.

"Get the police! And get a sheikh—there's a party of demons in the Festival Palace!" screamed the girls.

"How do you know they were demons?" asked the driver placidly. Skepticism was, of course, natural in a taxi driver here, in this no-nonsense capital of Wahabi Islam (despite his language's macabre riches: *ghoul, efreet,* and *genie* being only a few of the Arabs' gifts to English—actually, *macabre* is another).

"They were dancing, and had donkey legs!"

"Like this?" The driver lifted the hem of his thobe, the ankle-length white shirt Saudi men wear, to reveal his hirsute donkey hoofs.

The girls ran screaming home and phoned all of their friends.

"When did this happen? I just drove by the Festival Palace and it was dark—no one was there."

"That's just the point—it was a demon party." Hamdan sighed impatiently. Did I think that demons would leave a forwarding address? He was a medical student and valued logic. "I don't know when it happened—some friends of those girls were just talking to Johara."

The donkey ladies, who were to haunt Riyadh for years, stayed with me because this was the first urban myth I ever heard in Saudi Arabia, and the last that didn't involve foreigners. Saudi Arabia was thinly populated and fabulously wealthy, so that most of the work was done by hired help from abroad. Many were Arabs or Muslims but most were neither, with the result that native Saudis could hardly make themselves understood in their own language once they stepped outdoors. Riyadh, once a cozy and isolated village, had now become a towering (and sprawling) Babel of Indian barbers, Swiss bankers, Thai nannies, Filipino chauffeurs, American military advisors, Korean construction workers, and tens of thousands of other quacking, sunburned, homesick, menacing, money hungry, constantly carping infidels.

After the donkey ladies, sighted by uncounted dozens of anonymous Riyadhi women ("What were they doing walking around by themselves?" was a common reaction among local men), came the Thai (or Filipina or Sri Lankan) maid who asked her employers, on their way out for dinner one evening, if she might eat their new baby. "Of course!" smiled the soon-to-be-bereaved lady of the house. The denouement—the horrifying smell, the broiled and dismembered tot, the screams—made this by far the most popular Saudi folktale of the early 1980s.

And then there were the Korean truckers who ran over a

stranded Saudi motorist (or Pakistani hitchhiker) and lugged the dead victim home to hide the evidence. They decided to eat the body, but the game was up when they got violently ill and had their stomachs pumped at the Military Hospital. The police later found, or so the story went, big bones, a messy torso, and the half-eaten head in the freezer of the Koreans' communal kitchen in their work camp outside the city limits.

The royal government unknowingly stoked Central Arabian xenophobia and appeared to give credence to these grisly legends with a crime-deterrent TV special featuring the reenactment of a double murder of a Lebanese Muslim couple by two of their Filipino servants. It aired six times the day after both servants were publicly executed in Riyadh, on both television channels after the local news, the *News in English* and the *News in French*.

Mr. and Mrs. Aitarouni, the victims, were played by two young Saudi men; the murderers, bedecked in handcuffs, ankle irons, and clanking chains, shuffled through the actual murder house demonstrating, for a wobbly hand-held camera, how they had bludgeoned the husband (here the Saudi, reading the daily *Okaz* in a La-Z-Boy recliner, dropped his newspaper and slumped over, and his headcloth rolled off) and stabbed the wife. One of the killers provided the chilling narration in English ("Apter Meester Aitarouni pell down, I tell Cesar to bash the pipe for his forehead and he smash all of it. . . .").

The queasy punchline to the whole event was that the murderers were so slight, button-cute, and effeminate. Horrified viewers were thinking: if *they* could do *that* . . . ?

Not that the country was *not* being plundered and cannibalized—it was, though chiefly at the corporate level. There certainly was something to the atrocious myths the Saudis embroi-

dered over sweet tea on their rooftops: the criminal and cannibal-
istic threads that ran through the stories said a great deal, I
thought, about the virile menace of the horde of aliens who fed
their children, drove their cars, managed their money, trained
their army and those of their worst enemies, sold them cigarettes,
entertained them, and reported their news. American expatriates
scowled at what they considered Saudi intolerance, but it was
hard for me to imagine the same situation, transferred to the U.S.
bible/oil belt—so similar to central Arabia—leading to anything
but uprisings on a massive scale.

Of all the alien confrontations—between invaders, traders, patriots, crusaders, colonialists, missionaries, slaves, and masters—in
history, these Middle Eastern ones were the most bizarre. The
Saudi Arabians had never been colonized but had now imported
and were employing their tormentors. The Israelis were surely
the world's first oppressed imperialists. Iran and Iraq, culturally
almost twins, were locked in a desperate war. America, the superpower with the greatest interests in the region, had much the same
lucrative, hazardous role it had played in the Latin America of the
1950s: investor, deal-maker, co-conspirator.

I drove home slowly from Hamdan's, through the *toz,* the
opaque rusty mist that shrouds Riyadh when the desert wind
whips up the powdery orange sand of the Nejd, that hid the grim
high walls whose top surfaces were set with broken bottles or
strung with bare lightbulbs. None of these streets had names—
most were too new, and eventually the Emirate of Riyadh would
abandon a project to name them—it was too colossal a project for
the labyrinthine city (people had their own folk-names for the
streets, anyway: Pepsi Street, Chicken Street, even—in the case of
the tiny lane I lived in—Peter Street). Ugly breezeblock walls

guarded only vacant lots awaiting a tighter real estate market.

The dusty sandstorm gave the amber streetlights the gauzy glow of distant planets: visibility was almost zero. It was so bad, and growing worse, that it was like driving blind. Even the high beams were useless. I could hear flying grains of sand softly pinging against the car's metal body. I sensed a righthand turn coming and swung right into a bank of orange haze where my street should have been.

Clunk. The car slid into a ditch full of soft-drink cans beside the inevitable high wall. Like magic, which was definitely this evening's theme, a police car appeared.

"What happened here? You have to be more careful," said one of the two officers in Arabic. "License and registration, please."

"Here's the registration—I'm new in the country and don't have a local license. This is my American license." Professional expatriates would never have deigned to speak Arabic, even had they been one of the minuscule minority that spoke it, but I was too much of a show-off to miss this chance to impress with my Damascene Arabic—unaware, too, that virtually any Arabic-speaking foreigner was automatically assumed to be a spy.

"You're American?"

"Yes."

"Why do you speak Arabic? Where did you learn it?"

"I studied it in Egypt."

"Don't give me that—that's not Egyptian, that's Palestinian you're speaking."

I had forgotten the Saudis' intermittent rancor against the Levantine Arabs, whose accent I found so mellifluous and easy to copy (and which they could never tell apart). Just as we were patching up this misunderstanding he glanced at my license.

"Just wait a minute—what's this?"

"That's my American license. I don't have a Saudi one yet, but—"

"What do you mean, 'American license'? Show me where it says 'America.' "

He held it out. In the gloom only one word was large enough to read: MASSACHUSETTS. I examined it. No 'United States,' no 'America' anywhere.

"In America, licenses aren't granted by the federal government, but by the state registries of motor vehicles. So the name of the state—"

"Do you think I'm a Kurd?" he snapped. "I can read English letters, and I know Florida, Texas, California, Meetchigan. So what's this?"

"Massachusetts is a state."

He scrutinized the license again, as if preparing to back down, then found another word, which he pointed to contemptuously.

"*Commonwealth.* What are you, British? Are you Indian? Please get out of the car." He motioned for his partner. *"Ta'l ya Nawaf."*

They conferred, barely visible, by their patrol car—*for what seemed like an eternity,* I thought to myself—and then Nawaf came over and greeted me in both languages.

"Salaamu aleikum! I tell my partner you are not giving him a bullshit—I studied traffic science in Texas and I know American licenses. And I know your state, too. It's the best state!"

We chatted—he was friendly and extremely religious and demanded to know why I had not converted to Islam, since I knew Arabic and could presumably see, in the Koran, the perfect fulfillment of Judaism and Christianity. Surely I rejected the infamous sacrilege that God had a mother and a son? When I side-stepped that one he chided me for not being a better driver, since the Saudi traffic laws—"like almost everything else here"—were based on the American system. I tried to pump him about his visit to Massachusetts.

"I never visit there—I know it from history. America is full of good people but bad things—sex and crime, and some people are so backward—they worship the devil and follow the tower"—he meant *al-bourj,* the zodiac—"but Massachusetts is the only place they know how to deal with witches—by hanging them! Good night, my friend."

What really thrilled him, I think, was that Salem is an Arabic word.

Cradle of civilization, cradle of monotheism, cradle of the prophets, rocked by wars and tortured by fanaticism, and laughed at behind its back by so much of the world—a "crazy" place full of "crazy" people. For Americans who had no interest in the rest of the world, the Middle East epitomized "abroad"—ominous, backward, swarthy, extremist, anti-American, and xenophobia-inspiring. It was a symbol of the threat to world peace, the number one candidate for Cradle of World War III.

In the winter of 1980, it was a metaphor for a mess. The Shah of Iran had been overthrown, and Iran's new government had taken nearly one hundred U.S. diplomats hostage. Israel and Egypt had just signed a peace treaty, at a stratospheric cost to American taxpayers. Lebanon was a sea of blood. The Shiite leader, Imam Moussa Sadr, had vanished on an official visit to Libya, was presumed dead, and now the Shiites—whom no one had ever heard of—were raising hell. The region throbbed with malevolent tension. Donkey ladies were first sighted in Riyadh.

Perspective was a plague. Everywhere there were tragedies, nowhere were there clean hands. American whim seemed to rule a region that craved, but rarely obtained, American understanding, partly because the chasm between Arab peoples and their governments seemed undiscovered by us. As a reporter, I watched an American senator ask a Saudi official where on earth the Palestinians had come from "to begin with," and what did they have against the Israelis? Daniel Patrick Moynihan had a delightful visit with Prince Abdullah bin Turki, but shook his finger at him with a stagey frown the instant photographers appeared. Other U.S. politicians told the Arabs that they were running for office on a "pro-Arab ticket," which confounded even the Arabs in its illogical anti-Israeli fervor, calculating that it was worth losing a minor election to gain potential business friends in Riyadh. The gold medalist, though, was the lobbyist who conveyed earnestly to a Saudi plutocrat his profound hopes that the "railroaded" Sirhan Sirhan would be paroled. "Show this man Dira Square," the Saudi murmured to me—Dira was where killers and rapists were beheaded on Fridays. The cliché of the rich Arab (no more or less accurate than the cliché of the rich American) was already decades old when I got there, but had lost none of its potency. Explaining anything about the Middle East at home, I was at square one. In New York, my story about the Riyadh cop and my license elicited the laughter I was expecting, followed by, "An *Arab* driving a *car?!*" and this from a graduate of Princeton. We were a great mercantile empire, but at times only slightly less parochial than Arabia.

Religion, though, was what bound us to this other, sandy planet, and kept us apart. I was fascinated by the almost soap-operatic interconnections of the warring faiths of the Middle East—my own narrowly Catholic and narrowly secular culture had not prepared me. The Muslims acknowledged the divine origin of the Torah and the Gospels, and regarded Jesus as greater than Muhammad, because he performed miracles. Modern Egypt was on the side of Moses, not Pharaoh. They even accepted the dogma of the virgin birth! Jews and Muslims shared dietary taboos and a rejection—written into their law—of Christian missionaries. Many Jews and *all* Arabs were Semites. Muslims, too, were a chosen people—the Koran called them "the best of all nations raised up for mankind."

The fact that we were their spiritual children made me think. Judeo-Christianity had given rise to Islam (in my mind I had always cast Muhammad as an Arabian Joseph Smith, Jr., though I never dared say so), and in turn the mostly Jewish and Christian world in the West had a spiritual stake in the perilous feuds between Islam and its rivals.

Lovers of sausages and the law should never watch either one being made, and I began to think that this caveat should apply to believers, Jewish, Christian, or Muslim. Their globe-spanning religions took on an eerie dimension in the "back room" of their origins: Arabia and Israel, and the tribal, racial, linguistic caldron that had produced the Abrahamic faiths. You didn't find it in synoptic scriptures or buried cities, but in the inherited imagination of Jerusalem and Riyadh. To this extent, I decided, it was not their oil sheikhs but their prophets who were the true captors of the West.

This powerful emotional allure gave nearly every visiting alien a strong bias of some kind. No one walked away unscathed. It seemed that everyone who had ever lived in any of the "war-torn," "bloody," "oil-rich," "embattled," "encircled," "fratri-cidal" Middle Eastern countries became a lobbyist at some level—for larcenous Arab governments, for Jewish thugs, for American meddlers. I felt ideally impartial, since fortunately neither religious supremacy nor money was my weak point, yet they both fascinated me, as did the truly awesome scale of the feuds here. As an alien, I had to try to see how these pieces fit.

Religion was, like oil, a valuable and exploitable resource whose most recent "boom" here followed oil's only by a few years. Unlike oil, it was not unrenewable, but infinite, and versatile—only the cutouts of Moses, Jesus, and Muhammad were necessary as a cover for any political direction. Like oil, it was a means more than an end, and its earthly end seemed to be fighting aliens: Jews, Arabs, Persians, Americans. I had a strong notion it was just ethnocentrism in drag.

That is what all the wars were about. And it was not only among rival chosen peoples! We Americans were the focus of most of it. For the Saudis, we had brought the terrible news that the twentieth century had arrived. Nearly every country in the region, but foremost Saudi Arabia, had a dependent and cynical relationship with the rulers of the United States. We were useful aliens, and blessedly far away—wasn't this why the first Saudi king, Abdelaziz, had selected American rather than British companies to extract his oil in the first place?

We were lucky—so much of the income of the rich Arabs and the aid we gave to the poor Arabs ended up back in the U.S. as bank or Pentagon assets. This, coupled with an odd assortment of factors every Arab knew—Eisenhower booting the Israelis out of the Sinai in 1956, the 1969 moon landing, the pervasiveness of American culture—persuaded this apparent race of conspiracy theorists that we were invincible, on their side, and only waiting for a heavenly sign before solving all their tragic problems for them. Israelis, ironically, seemed to think the same thing. Why was the responsibility ours? Whenever I saw American ambassadors or envoys or secretaries of state trying to talk to an Arab or Israeli leader, I saw the answer in the darker man's eyes: *Because this is all your fault.*

As a reporter in Riyadh, I wrote about business, oil, official visits, and other subjects whose implied importance was that they affected the future of Saudi Arabia, or of the United States, or both; and that the information I reported would increase mutual understanding. It took me three or four years to realize that the vital story was the unwritten one: how do we look at one another? What are the implications of our policies and pretensions? These big issues were usually only confronted by major journalists, but they were the ones who made the shortest visits: usually five days at the most, not nearly enough time for their eyes to focus. Also, Arabs were almost never frank with foreign reporters.

I had begun my exploration of the Middle East a few years before, in Egypt, and thought that I was learning my way around Arabs; I did not realize that my real curiosity was about how they viewed "us"—everyone else. We always omit our presence, forgetting how drastically it affects what we are recording. Once in particular, though, thanks to smuggled booze, I caught a glimpse of what I really wanted. At a small palace in Riyadh, where I'd been invited for supper and a screening of *The Prince and the Showgirl.* After picking at the traditional mounds of lamb and rice, the guests began smoking hashish and swilling scotch. It was a remarkable cross-section of Riyadh (i.e. male) society—several young princes and Saudi commoners, including my friend Hamdan, three Lebanese businessmen, a Palestinian accountant, a Syrian carpet dealer, and me.

At one point in the old movie, Elsie Marina (Marilyn Monroe) overhears, during a German telephone conversation, the conspiracy the adolescent Balkan king (Jeremy Spenser) has been plotting against his father, the regent (Laurence Olivier). The Balkan king is unaware that Elsie, a Milwaukeean, understands German perfectly. Exposed, the patent leather-haired Nicholas VIII snarls, "It is most unfortunate that you should have heard that. It might prove exceedingly dangerous for you!"

"Dangerous?" scoffs the luscious and courageous Elsie. "Oh, don't give me that. I'm an American citizen. Nobody can do anything to me!"

"Eiri fik, ya gahba!" ("Fuck you, bitch!") shouted every Arab in the room in unison.

This astonishing outburst was my first great thrill in Riyadh—it was a promise of how much there was to know about how we looked at one another. I felt that "Iran" (the very word had become shorthand for "the debacle in Iran" or, among real patriots, "the loss of Iran") was only an omen. We misunderstood and hated one another. Something was going to happen here. What? Fortunately, I had the time to snoop around.

I was alone. Running a one-man office, I had Riyadh all to myself. I woke up with my shortwave radio—the Nejdi heat, even at 6 A.M., is enough to wake you up—methodically listening to the news from London, Cairo, Baghdad, Beirut, Mecca, and *Kol Israel* from Ur-Shalim-Al-Quds. Thus pepped up, I thanked St. Francis de Sales, patron saint of journalists ("I hate a lie more than I hate the Devil") for my luck—since real reporting was officially discouraged, I had only to write effortless articles about trade embargoes, visiting luminaries, and new hospitals, made easier by my ability to plunder the morning newspapers and radio news for leads.

Within six months of landing in central Arabia I had perfected the inoffensive five hundred–word business piece, full of color and quotes, and could generally knock it out before lunch, avoiding the telephone for the rest of the day, free to try to discover a good Arabic novel or new neighborhood, find a dissident, nap, or prowl around with my camera. I had begun to compile a photograph album of architectural atrocities: a populuxe Schiaparelli-pink monstrosity with stucco champagne bubbles riveted in place up the outer wall; a full-scale replica of the White House; a mosque with tail fins. Luckily, the suspicious policemen whose job it was to enforce the ban on public photography (a security risk) were delighted to see someone immortalizing these proud new structures rather than the traditional, crumbly mud-brick houses in the older neighborhoods (cool, thick-walled masterpieces with inner courtyards and gardens), and I proudly added the Festival Palace to my collection.

2

The Spoken Word

*M*uhammad Alwan was a veteran Near Eastern Languages teacher: he never asked us, his eight-week summer class, why we were studying Arabic. I understood why when we sat around drinking coffee one morning and got onto the subject ourselves. Alwan was fifteen minutes late, and it was a hot, dewy

July morning. We wanted to persuade him to hold the class outdoors, on the shady quadrangle in front of the Harvard Law School Library.

"Samira, you convince him. Wellesley women are supposed to have a way with Harvard men," said Mumtaz, a Pakistani girl from New York.

"Only in bed," said Samira. This was mildly shocking coming from a Saudi Arabian, even one who wore tight jeans and Lacoste shirts with no bra. Most of us knew so little about the Middle East that we did not pause to wonder what a Saudi was doing taking this introductory course in her mother tongue.

"In Tel Aviv, we have classes outside during the whole spring." This was Deborah talking; until she uttered this sentence we had not known she was Israeli. Now we knew she was Israeli because she added, "I'm Israeli." It was suddenly clear that she had been eager to tell us this for weeks. Her nationality wasn't obvious because she, like me, had been born in Boston. Only a few minutes ago she had, in the Boston way, described this perfect weather as "pissa."

"You're from Israel?" said Raymond, a reedy blond whose father worked in the Middle East. (As CIA station chief in Saudi Arabia, I found out four years later; the Saudis expelled him for revealing the royal family's secrets to the White House. He resigned from the CIA and was immediately hired by the royal family as a "consultant." They had obviously been deeply impressed by his abilities.) "Why are you studying Arabic here?"

For only a moment she seemed unsure which word he was stressing in that question.

"So I can give orders in the West Bank!"

Since Deborah had a wrestler's build, we had no trouble believing she could keep Palestinian villagers cowed; a few days later Samira suggested, well out of Deborah's hearing, that she should become a female wrestler under the name Mount Zion. When Alwan revealed the mysteries of Arabic script to the class by writing simple words on the board, I listened closely to Deborah as she instinctively murmured the Hebrew equivalents, almost as if correcting him. When he taught *bait,* house, she muttered, *"bayit." Ras,* for head, provoked *"rosh."* Many were virtually identical: *Jamal* and *gamal* for camel, *yad* and *yad* for hand, *dahab* and *thahab* for gold.

"I'm studying Arabic so I can use it back in Jeddah," said Raymond, whose father must still have been, in the summer of 1978, a thriving and respected spook. "Even though most of the waiters there don't speak Arabic—they're all Indians and Pakistanis!"

"In Pakistan we normally study it to read the Koran," said Mumtaz. "Of course, that is normally the case with men. We call it the language of the angels. I'm loving to learn it. But you know," she added, to Raymond, "those waiters and office boys and what-have-you from Pakistan don't get the slightest respect in Saudia Arabia. The Arabs make such a to-do about solidarity with all Moslems, you know, but they really exploit those poor people. It is a kind of a slave trade, between the Arabs and the people who traffic in the supply of imported labor."

Samira asked Deborah, "What political party do you belong to in Israel?"

"Gush." Religious fanatics who sought to recreate the ancient Israelite and Judean kingdoms in the modern Middle East. It was a group especially popular with American transplants in Israel.

"Gush Emunim? Deborah, they're awful!"

"Yeah, right. The other parties think we should bow down to the Arabs, who might recognize our existence if we hand over half the country. Recognize my existence? Thanks a lot. Uh-uh."

The only person here not recognizing her existence was Juma, the Black Muslim, who wore a red, green, and black crocheted skullcap. He was the best student in the class, and young, barely twenty. The Egyptian teaching aide had upset him deeply once by alluding to crime in Egypt: "Egypt is very nonviolent but there's a lot of, you, know, petty fraud and cheating." "But not Muslims cheating Muslims!" said Juma severely. "Juma, of course Muslims cheating Muslims. Would you think more highly of them if they cheated only Christians?" she replied. "If you want to understand the region when you go there"—he was always talking about going to Mecca—"you will have to be realistic." Now Juma kept his gaze trained on his notebook as he practiced his right-to-left Arabic signature over and over again. Everyone else awaited their turns to explain what they were doing here, except for Mumtaz.

"And you know, before the oil discoveries, in my father and grandfather's time, the Arabs were very poor, and the Indians and Pakistanis who made the pilgrimage to Mecca brought money and humanitarian gifts to the native Muslims there, 'for our brother Arabs,' you know. And you see who is now the servants of those Arabs."

"I got this job with TWA?" explained Bucky, a brand-new graduate of Boston University and the handsomest man in this class—Samira had once brought him coffee, with her own, unasked. "We have a training and maintenance contract with Saudi Arabian Airlines. You don't have to know Arabic, but I figured it will give me a leg up. God, I didn't think it would be this hard. I'm reading about Islam, too."

"Everyone's going to get plenty of money from the Muslims," observed Juma placidly.

"You can be one of the servants of the Arabs!" Samira told Bucky brightly.

"They've sort of been taking our money in at the gas pumps with no problem," said Raymond to Juma.

"America's going to go over to the Arabs, just watch," said Deborah to no one. She looked at her watch and yawned, and flipped open Peter Abboud's *Elementary Modern Standard Arabic*.

"It's a great religion, but Saudi Arabia is so strict," Samira was saying to Bucky. "Women aren't allowed to drive cars. The princes have all the money. And it's very hot." Then she explained that she had grown up in Boston, a surgeon's daughter, and while she spoke perfect Arabic she had never learned to write it. She often argued volubly with Alwan when he called her to the blackboard to make her connect letters to form script. I had wondered whether this was some third language—Alwan was from Iraq and I thought it might be Persian or some Mesopotamian dialect she knew by chance. "The language is a bitch! Because written Arabic is completely different from any of the spoken dialects. In a way it's harder for me than for you guys. Why are you learning it?" This was directed at me.

"I have a fellowship to study in Cairo. I'll have to teach to earn a stipend. I'll study the language there but I need a head start."

"Why Cairo?" asked Deborah, looking up from her book, as if I were a Nazi war criminal. This was before the publicity-crazed Anwar Sadat had made peace with Israel.

"I visited there once, and I liked it. I'd be at the American University."

"But why the Middle East?" asked Bucky. "Are you going to look for a job there?"

"How on earth did you get interested in it?" asked Deborah.

If you were not actually Jewish or Arab and had no clear profit motive, you were regarded with the greatest suspicion for having any interest in that part of the world.

"Well, if you got interested in Israel," said Juma to Deborah, but did not finish his sentence.

"Look, I didn't *get interested* in Israel, it's my home. I'm Jewish. It's not like I just decided to join a cult or something."

Well, Islam isn't a cult, I wanted to reply on his behalf; was that what she was implying? Perhaps Deborah was cross at leaving 150 million Arabs behind her in the Middle East, only to come to her hometown and find a Muslim giving her lip. Juma was certainly put out to hear an apostate American getting hissy about someone besides herself wanting to live in the Middle East. In a minute one of them was going to say, Well, why don't you go back there?

"Well, why don't you go back there?" asked Juma.

"Don't worry," said Deborah with great emphasis, but not too aggressively.

Alwan now swept into the room, straightened his narrow tie and immediately overruled our now halfhearted bid to have class outdoors. It occurred to me that at some point four or five of us would be in the Middle East at the same time, without knowing it; none of us really belonged there, and surely the region would be better off without us. I did not have a chance to answer Deborah's question about how I had become interested in the Middle East—not that my answer, in 1978, would have been worth listening to—but at least I had been given a taste of the touchy partiality of the region.

Ten years later, the question had me searching my conscience for my true motives in spending what was, at the time, a third of my life as an alien in the Middle East. Anyone writing about that part of the world should. Books—particularly ones with academic pretensions—generally have big axes to grind. In an ideal world, I often thought, every book with an inscrutable title like *101 Questions and Answers about the Middle East* or *The Arab-Israeli Conundrum* or (an actual, notorious example) *Islam in History: Ideas, Men and Events in the Middle East* should have a mandatory one-page preface explicitly setting out the author's relevant religious and political sympathies and/or any other direct or indirect vested interests he or she has in the Middle East. The stereotype of the region was wild-eyed, fanatical, and violent, but much of the American damage done to it, I had come to see through the news media, was done through nuance. Readers would certainly benefit from knowing whether an author was a fanatical Zionist or pro-Arab profiteer, a bigot who thought fanatical Zionists (or Arabs) were conspiring to rule the world, or a professor whose ruminations on fanatical Zionists and Arabs were crucial to his attaining tenure or securing his next visit visa to Iraq or Saudi Arabia, or his being a regular on National Public Radio.

It is easier, but a little more involved, for a mere adventurer to come clean. I traveled to the Middle East because I was mesmerized by Egypt's ancient history and by the desert I had seen unshaven fugitives stagger through in uncounted hypnotizing movies like *Beau Geste, Tobruk,* and *The Lost Patrol.* These were the same deserts of Cain, Gilgamesh, and Moses—and of *Tintin au pays de l'or noir.* I had a passive sympathy with Israel, but had read Sami Hadawi's *Palestine: Loss of a Heritage* and thought: if all that is true, then I am an Arab-Israeli agnostic; but let's see. The fabulous wealth of the Arab countries was a draw, but not a major one, since I grew up before the Arab oil boycott. For the same reason, terrorism—which, with the oil wealth, made the 1970s and 1980s, according to J. G. Shaheen, "the era of the Arab joke"—was not a major deterrent. I was an outsider, with no wish to convert, to make converts, or to settle down anywhere and no need to toe any party line, so I would never feel compelled to stay once I had had enough or to be less than frank praising or criticizing any party.

I wanted to learn a new language, too. I had no marketable skill, and one of my older brothers had urged me to learn another language ("a hard one"). Yet another brother had a single resonant word of advice: "China." But China was too far and too foreign, the language much too difficult, and I did not find the Chinese sexy. I mean this in the most literal way; it was one of my distinct criteria. Does anyone with a nonprofit interest in a foreign land not owe it largely to the sexual pull of the culture and people? Even if not, I don't think I'm overly prurient for having thought so. This assumption of mine was often confirmed by the long procession of Egyptologists, Arabists, Iranologists, kibbutzniks, missionaries, and anthropologists I saw, whose fixation on the bible lands was notoriously carnal. Perhaps they, too, were motivated by *Beau Geste* or *Lawrence of Arabia,* not to mention *Scheherazade, The Dance of the Seven Veils, The 7th Voyage of Sinbad* ("In Dynamation—The New Miracle of the Screen"), *Sins of Jezebel, Samson and Delilah, Solomon and Sheba,* and *The Ten Commandments*—the apotheosis of what Gore Vidal's Wise Hack called "tits and sand."

(To the West, of course, fleshpots had preceded oil wells as the Orient's seductive staple.

Emma Bovary and Frederic Moreau pine for what in their drab (or harried) bourgeois lives they do not have, and what they realize they want comes easily to their daydreams packed inside Oriental clichés: harems, princesses, princes, slaves, veils, dancing girls and boys, sherbets, ointments, and so on.

In short, Edward Said goes on to explain in *Orientalism,* nineteenth-century Europeans sought in the Middle East sexual thrills unobtainable in Europe. The twentieth century was a very different story. Now Middle Easterners of all persuasions could satisfy their fetishes most easily in Europe or America. This was largely due to the popularity of Western pornography, including the American prime-time TV variety—one of the major influences on Arab and Israeli perceptions of us. A generation of volatile Arab love-hatred of the United States—potentially decisive in dictating the course of our economy for the next one hundred years—was predestined the day the first VCR was sold in the Arabian Peninsula.)

Among the other primal draws were the inherited Middle Eastern images littering the collective imagination of the West: Jesus's stable, the pyramids, Sindbad's ship, Aladdin's lamp, Crusader castles, the Rosetta Stone, Hammurabi's Code, the sewers of Baghdad, the howling deserts and aromatic cities that produced *Casablanca, Algiers, The Thief of Baghdad, Ten Graves to Cairo, Khartoum*—it is hard to think of an Arab capital that doesn't occur in a movie title, or shouldn't (Muscat and Damascus have not had their turns). Even defunct cities like Sodom and Masada lived on, in metaphors. For Christians and Jews, some regional associations need no qualifiers: the Law, the Star, the Wall, the Cross, the Crescent, the Temple, the Serpent, the Lamb, the Rock, and the Book all carry the MADE IN THE MIDDLE EAST sticker.

The attraction of the region's different personalities is reflected in its many aliases: *Near East* is scholarly, evoking archaeological digs, winged lions, ancient languages, and date palms. It smacks of colonialism too, and, like "Far East," geo-ethnocentrism. *Middle East* (Mideast in headlines) covers much broader territory—sand, oil, terrorism, food (olives, figs, lamb, rice, sherbets—just what were sherbets?), belly dancing to that hokey snake-charmer music, and above all wars. (In TV shows, swarthy white-slavers in Rolls-Royces are always from made-up kingdoms in the Middle East—the Near East would never inspire terror, or self-righteous racism, or whatever TV writers try to inspire.) "The Holy Land" means tour packages and pilgrimages, and doubles as a neat, nonaligned euphemism for "Israel" and "Palestine," especially when referring to the occupied West Bank. "Bible Lands" smacks of missionary memoirs, Sunday school slide shows, and of course, tits and sand. All these images were suffused with gorgeous, blinding sunlight and the shimmer of mirages.

But at the age of twenty-one, I had an additional motive for drastic change, the sense of there being no other alternative; a daring choice might tempt an unusual twist of fate. My first gambit failed: as a Harvard senior, I had been admitted to New College, Oxford, to study Jacobean drama and was desperately applying for every fellowship that could have paid my tuition there: the Marshall, the Mellon, the Knox, the Rhodes, and a dozen other Anglo-Ivy meal tickets whose names have got blurry with the years. Not only did I get turned down for all of them, the one I wanted the most—the Fiske-DeJersey—acknowledged receiving my application but apparently lost it, since I never heard from them again. Luckily, I had applied to the American University in Cairo's English Language Institute to study for a master's degree in teaching English as a foreign language, only because on a visit to Cairo in 1977 I had trespassed on the university's mid-city campus and decided on the spot to try and spend a year or two there. It had an immediate, overt appeal as academia in a city much bigger and better than Oxford or Boston (or any other city, for that matter), and being Middle Eastern, it appealed to all of my inarticulate Bible Lands preconceptions. Across from the walled oasis of the university was the Mugamm'a, a colossal Stalinesque-pharaonic government office, built in the 1950s, and covered with an inch of dust, that seemed to speak volumes about modern Egypt's dormant power. Two palace-lengths away flowed the olive-green Nile. When the university offered me a place in their master's program, to start in the fall, I grabbed it with both hands, as the Israelis say.

In the last week of the summer Arabic course, Sanaa, the Egyptian teaching aide, told me how much I would love Cairo. "It is so full of vitality—theaters, concerts, new books, all sorts of fun. And Egyptians are very friendly and gentle people." Best of all, she pointed out, I could practice reading Arabic every day with the city newspapers.

"Egyptian newspapers are the best in the Arab world, and the Arabs have excellent newspapers, you know. American newspapers are so provincial by comparison."

"How do you mean?"

"Well, the Boston *Globe* is all local, all about Boston and New England and America. It really amazes me. An Egyptian newspaper gives you all the news of the world in much more detail. America is very isolated by not paying attention to the world, don't you think?"

I puzzled over that. My first thought was to point out that the *Globe* was twenty times the size of any *al-Ahram* I'd ever seen at Out-of-Town News—that the bulk of local reporting was deceptive; then I remembered that, as with any major U.S. paper, seventy-five percent of the *Globe* was advertising. It occurred to me that there was much more to report on in the United States: more local government, for example. And the U.S., with a far higher literacy rate and living standard than Egypt, would have more people interested in reading a much greater variety of local writing. And surely greater freedom of the press was another factor. Did any of this make sense? Or perhaps we did, after all, de-emphasize international news.

"I'll let you know once I've become a regular reader of *al-Ahram*," I said diplomatically.

"Of course, there's so much to write about at the local level in America," said Sanaa.

She did not allude to the popular Arab belief that the U.S. news media were all controlled by Jews and thus hostile to the Arabs. This welcome omission reminded me how, a few months previous, I had given a close reading to a newsmagazine article at a friend's insistence. When Israel had invaded Lebanon in March 1978, a Palestinian classmate of mine handed me a copy of *Time* magazine.

"When you've read the way they report on us, and then see the reality, you'll be ready to carry a gun," she predicted. I read it and disagreed, but now, in August, I dug it out and reread the article.

There was really nothing bigoted in its typically coy, cautious report of the invasion and the killing of 2,000 civilians by the Israeli army. The Israelis, of course, needed no introduction; but "strictly speaking," according to *Time,* "Palestinians are Arabs who live or have lived in the area now consisting of Israel, the Gaza Strip and the West Bank, all of which was once called Palestine." Did Americans of *Time*-reading caliber need this pre-school description of Palestinians? Probably.

Jerusalem, in a passing reference, was "what a majority of Palestinians regard as the heart of their lost homeland." Surely Jerusalem was, and is, the heart of old Palestine, regardless of how anyone regards it? That "regard as" was that deft editorial hand at work, carefully distancing *Time* from this regrettable notion of the Palestinians. And why insert "a majority of"? What else would any Palestinian regard as the heart of Palestine? I tried to discern whether this was only the usual tepid, "massaged" reporting, with its excruciating but shallow impartiality, or a white-wash with a subtext denying any suggestion that the invasion was an atrocity. Or did I have a bee in my bonnet about fairness to the Arabs because I was about to go live among them?

Somehow, in the article, the victims of the invasion were not there—except in a sidebar devoted to Christian villagers welcoming the invaders (who, as it turned out, would still be there twelve years later). One of the Israeli generals was described, in an unmistakably gushy context, as "grinning." Israeli soldiers were often described as "young," which is usually journalese for heroic.

The following week, *Time's* "World" and "Nation" sections were entitled, respectively, "Hard Choices for Israel" and "Difficult Days for Begin." There was nothing about the 200,000 Arab refugees, or in fact about Lebanon at all, except as it related to Begin's pain (". . . Begin slowly started massaging the pectoral muscles on the left side of his chest. It was a nervous habit that betrayed the anxiety of a former heart attack victim enduring new stress . . ."), caused not by the invasion but by Jimmy Carter's refusal to endorse it. There were no newsphotos of old Lebanese ladies surveying the rubble—so the caption would have run—of their devastated homes, or—another old standby conspicuously absent—a closeup of a child's stuffed animal in the ruins of a hovel. There are certain mandatory clichés of reporting about Arabs, and the sympathetic ones were all absent. It was common to portray Arabs as victims, especially if it were strongly hinted that they were victimized mainly by "their own." I searched in vain for the impromptu views of an Arab taxi driver ("We can only blame ourselves," he would be saying) in the closing lines, or at least a reference to the fact that for many of the Palestinians this was at least the fifth time they had become refugees. What was wrong?

I pondered *Time's* breezy assertion that "the Arab dislike of Palestinians arises largely from the fact that under the British, who ruled Palestine through a League of Nations mandate for 30 years after World War I, they became the best educated people in the region." This was "the height of *something,*" as my father would say. It palmed off a purely imaginary prejudice, perhaps to comfort its readers, whom it assumed also disliked Palestinians, on the Arabs; this bigotry ricocheted twice against the Arabs themselves, who were not only bigots but "disliked" the Palestinians for a stupid reason (their good education); strongly implied that the Arabs were not educated themselves; and gave the credit for Palestinian successes to the British, whose clumsy malevolence toward Palestine had removed it from the map.

On the whole, the article did not convince me to carry a gun. And after all, my Palestinian friend who thought it should was studying business administration here in the U.S., not defending the refugee camps.

It made me wonder what Arab newspapers were like. What would you discover reading them? I had no idea; the mere thought that I had no idea struck me as a stirring reason to go exploring. What did Arabs think about? Did they have advice columns, a comics page, or book reviews? Did they only print propaganda? You could see *al-Ahram* and *Akhbar El-Yom* at some of Boston's more exotic newsstands, carefully catalogued like precious commodities in the racks of overpriced Hebrew, Polish, Russian, and French newspapers, but detached from their native land and readers they could answer none of my questions.

I was fascinated by the region without knowing anything about it, and it was a little startling to realize that almost all the Middle Eastern influences at work on my imagination were Made in the USA. It was proof that I was not alone in being fascinated by that region, but it flopped at helping me know what made Middle Eastern imaginations work. Were their images of us any truer than ours of them? My own moves were dictated by bogus nostalgia, real curiosity, aimless libido, some moral purpose, and to a certain extent failure; which of these motives were wrong-headed? Which would be rewarded? Of course, none of these questions actually surfaced in my Nilotic dreams as I made travel plans for Cairo.

3

Mother of the World

$\mathcal{I}$ was in my little cubicle four stories above the baking pavement of Falaki (Stargazer) Street in Cairo when Nohad, the dormitory attendant, told me that I had a visitor. At that particular moment I felt I deserved a break, since I was suffering from a sinus infection aggravated by the blast-furnace heat of the city, and had just located, in the semi-alphabetic labyrinth of an Arabic dictionary, a hard word *(jalaouza)* from a scurrilous article. It meant gang, as in "Zionist-imperialist-American gang." Egypt was now making peace with Israel at Camp David, and the other Arabs were beside themselves with rage and betrayal. In the brief period before Lebanese, Syrian, and Saudi Arabian newspapers were banned from Egyptian newsstands, they denounced Sadat, America, and Israel all together with rhetoric that enthralled me for hours, making my own prized glossary of abuse: *qazam,* dwarf; *kha'in,* traitor; *afa'i,* snakes; *tamasih,* crocodiles; *sarasir,* cockroaches; *murtazaq,* mercenary. Egypt's ally King Hussein, ruler of Jordan—*'Ahil El-Urdun*—took sides against Egypt and thus became, in Sadat's words, *'Ahir El-Urdun,* the whoremonger of Jordan.

It was not a visitor but a young messenger with a tiny envelope on a silver dish. Inside the envelope was an invitation to dinner that night with a business acquaintance of my oldest brother, an Egyptian named Lutfallah Nasr, whose cousin had served for several years as Egypt's ambassador to China. I had visited Nasr in his office for a cup of tea a few days after arriving in Cairo, and he had promised to invite me to his home soon; he hoped I would come "only for charity, to honor my home," and assured me that he and his wife could "find some crumbs to offer such a precious guest, whatever we have." He made his home in the top two stories of a dusty (rain was rare) Art Deco apartment building only two streets away.

I had been in Egypt for one month, and was teaching morning English classes every day except Friday and Sunday—the weekend was split to accommodate the Muslim and Christian sabbaths (ironically, in Arabic and Hebrew, the same word, *sabt* and *shabbat,* respectively, refers to sabbath and Saturday). In the afternoons I studied Arabic, linguistics, and the methodology of teaching English. Foreign students were offered Sunday bus outings to Giza, Saqqara, Memphis, and the ancient Coptic monasteries at Wadi Natroun, and with Egypt and Israel ending hostilities there was hopeful talk of camping trips to Mount Sinai. In the meantime, everyone's time was spent getting around the city.

My childhood picture of Cairo had been of a vast suburb of neat pyramids, with the sparkling aquamarine Nile purling through the middle. I imagined parks of red people picnicking among kingly statues like the serenely noble Pharaoh Men-Kau-Re my father showed me at the Museum of Fine Arts. The funerary paintings suggested a serene place of unrivaled color and cleanliness; of miraculous artistic genius. Fourth-grade geography embellished this cartoon land with turbanèd peasants using a *shadouf* to ladle Nile water into a ditch to irrigate their cotton fields. The river was not aqua but turbid green. Cairo itself, I learned, was a sprawl of dusty buildings with little black and white taxis and men on bicycles crowding the sunny streets. All the writing was illegible—chicken scratching, not hieroglyphics. None of this came as a disappointment. My love for Egypt was true love, whatever the place looked like.

Real Cairo with its strange mixture of English mansions, Art Nouveau villas, and Moorish mosques under the African sky surpassed any childhood dream I had of this city. The narrow Nile valley throbbed with seventy centuries of pent-up history, with the novelty of Moses having lived just across the river in Giza—Goshen—and Jesus having grown up in the ancient Jewish neighborhood now called Mar Girgis, four tram stops south of the American University in Cairo. Cairo was noisy, but warm and incomparably majestic, even under its layers of brown dust, even though it had become a real place where people bought vacuum cleaners, had nervous breakdowns, dreamed up advertising slogans, or made fortunes in lethal weapons, as my host did.

Egypt's inter-Arab troubles meant lean times for Lutfallah Nasr, who made his living this way, selling arms, though socially it meant only that his vast dining room echoed, that night, with American English rather than Iraqi or Saudi or Syrian Arabic. When I stepped out of the elevator—a gleaming, smoothly whirring old gated and screened contraption, all mahogany and brass trimmings, an Edwardian time machine—the first words I heard were "just like a real shit-kicker!" This was not what I expected to hear from a suave member of *le tout Caire*. I presented my invitation to a Nubian man in a white turban and blue robe and looked out the window on the landing.

This was central Cairo, just two blocks from Tahrir (Liberation) Square, and this building, at 5 Youssef El-Guindi Street, overlooked a high school and the palm trees of the American University. Beyond that lay the immense square—actually a deafening rotary—and the Nile. I could not imagine anything more beautiful than the skyline of an ancient city where one was about to be ushered into a dinner party, handed a martini, and given the opportunity to sniff out intrigue.

I was ushered in to meet, not Lutfallah Nasr but a beautiful red-haired woman with a very pale complexion whose freckled chest bore the weight of an enormous emerald necklace. This was Madame Aida—Mrs. Nasr. She took my arm, led me to a bar, and asked family questions while the barman made my drink. I was entrusted to a small table of drinkers; this was a seated cocktail hour. It seemed cozy, more civilized than standing around, getting sore feet, and waiting to desert one group for another that looked more interesting. In no time I saw this as a terrible drawback.

"If you ever come to Kinshasa, come visit me," said the plump American in the open-collar yellow shirt who was on my right. He was drunk. This was Nasr's son-in-law, a new graduate of the Foreign Language Institute, spending a week in Cairo en route to his first diplomatic posting. "It's in Zaire, as if you didn't know."

"He can stay at the Kinshasa Howard Johnson's," said another American, in a military uniform.

"Only if it's not full up from the Kinshasa Elks Club convention!"

Miles, the fledgling diplomat, said *Kinshasa* at least once in every sentence. Either he was swept up in the romance of the place, or thought it was plain funny. I decided that he thought it was funny, though there was an edge of panic in his voice. Perhaps it was bravado—he seemed determined to repeat it until he had made it familiar. Something about Miles suggested that the very idea that there were other countries in the world besides the United States was screamingly funny but a little scary. His wife did not seem embarrassed by his drinking or his nervous talk, but perhaps she, too, was apprehensive about going there. Or perhaps it was the thought of enduring a hundred more cocktail parties with Miles that made her look apprehensive.

The soldier's wife asked me about the Grateful Dead concert at the Pyramids a few days earlier, probably assuming that no shabby American would have missed it.

"It was full of people who didn't know where they were," I told her. "They were stoned. You could see the bedouin from the desert, their silhouettes, all around the horizon—in the desert air, the racket from the concert must have echoed for miles. There were hundreds of them. And the marijuana smoke!"

It had run three nights at the esplanade in front of the sphinx and pyramids. The Dead performed with Egyptian opening acts, including some spellbinding Nubian drummers, at the invitation of the Egyptian Ministry of Culture. At the American band's request, cable had been run up into the burial chamber of the Great Pyramid of Khufu. The third night's finale was "One More Saturday Night," which had chemically blissed-out Americans sobbing with emotion while Egyptians tapped their feet.

"Those would be the nomads, I guess."

"The bedouins—the nomads, yes. The Americans were the ones smoking pot. Most of the ones I talked to were from California."

"Where are you from?" asked the military man. He never did introduce himself, though his wife had volunteered that her name was Cookie. I told him. "Where did you go to college?" I told him. "You mind if I hold that against you?" he asked, and in fact did not speak to me again.

"Here I am, in Cairo, Egypt, eating Russian food with Americans," said Miles. He was helping himself to a caviar hors d'-oeuvre from a servant's platter. No one was paying attention to him. He was even drunker than before, and most of his last few sentences had begun, "Here I am, in Cairo, Egypt . . ."

Cookie's husband was talking to Miles' wife, Nagwa, about a political intrigue in Libya.

"He was cooking up a whole lot of trouble for the Shah of Iran, and it looks like the Colonel's people killed him in Libya."

"We had a border war with Libya last year," said Nagwa. "The Libyans lost. Of course, it only lasted a couple of weeks, but they took some prisoners. They captured my daddy's chauffeur"—*shoofoor*—"and tortured him. Ezz," she told Miles, to identify the chauffeur, and he nodded. "All Egyptians hate Qaddafi. For sure, Qaddafi would do it."

"Well, a lot of people would like to know what exactly happened to this Sadr," said Mr. Cookie. "It's a little bit unusual, even in Libya, for an official guest to just disappear into thin air. Him and the two people with him."

"In *al-Ahram* it says that the Lebanese man, Sadr, left Libya and went on to Rome with his friends."

"They didn't leave Libya. Not alive, anyway. And the Lebanese man was Iranian. He's been trying to work against the Shah. He has himself a deal with the Syrians, running some training camps for terrorists. My guess is, it's a plot. The Shah's staying where he is, and this guy knew too much."

"Probably a revenge from Lebanon," said Nagwa.

I could contribute nothing to this tantalizing conversation, though I knew the man they were talking about, Moussa Sadr, was a Muslim clergyman who had disappeared in Libya a few weeks before. His picture had been on the front pages of all the Cairo papers, which probably were playing up his disappearance to make Libya look bad—the Egyptians certainly did seem to resent their western neighbor and its dizzy president, Colonel Qaddafi. At the same time, Iran seemed to be exploding—there were riots against the Shah. And Lebanon was, as usual, falling to pieces—the television news had been showing noisy footage of rockets and missiles whooshing through the air and then slamming into neighborhoods on either of Beirut's two feuding halves, which then disgorged billows of black smoke and screaming citizens. The same murderous fireworks show had been on the news for nearly two weeks.

There was a creepy allure to the story of Sadr, who seemed to be at the center of each of the Middle East's tempests: the Arabs versus Israel, the civil war in Lebanon, the Iranian revolution, the rise of Libya as almost everyone's meddlesome enemy. The Imam—his preferred title—looked, to my Western eyes, like a wizard straight out of the Arabian Nights: enormously tall, bearded and with a huge arched nose, in a fat black turban and black cloak, always smiling. He had big blue-green eyes—"colored eyes," as the Arabs say. His dramatic clothes were those of a Shiite Muslim clergyman.

It seemed certain that he been kidnapped and then murdered somewhere in Tripoli, the Libyan capital, though his family and political allies, including Egyptian editorialists, were angrily demanding his release. It would make a great thriller—but even as I had this thought I realized why it would not: the Middle East was much too complicated. The fact that Sadr, an opponent of the pro-American Shah, was done in by a leftist dictator in Libya, contributed some intrigue, a puzzle to be solved, but it entailed far too much explanation. The fact that Sadr was Lebanese was lethal. Who could begin to understand a country of three million homicidal maniacs? What good was a murder mystery in a country that swam in blood? The endless complications of the Iranian revolution and the bloodbaths in Lebanon inhibited me from trying to join Nagwa and Mr. Cookie in their discussion of the Sadr disappearance.

"Or very likely the Palestinians," said Mr. Cookie. "They sure have had their problems with Sadr."

They had? Another complication. Worse and worse! "Palestinians are Arabs who live or have lived in the area now consisting . . ." I felt a little less bad about America's simpleminded loyalty to Israel—no wonder we didn't understand what on earth was happening in the Middle East, when most of the news came from places like Lebanon. I was comforted that no one could read my thoughts.

Why was this military person so engrossed in politics with Nagwa while Miles, the diplomat, just sat there drinking? Cookie sat there listening to the discussion about Lebanon, which I had ceased to follow.

"Things are a mess," I said to Cookie.

"Just this morning the radio said an American congressman was killed down in Guyana, in the jungle," she replied. "I forget his name."

"Leo Ryan," said her husband suddenly.

We became aware of servants standing and smiling welcomingly at us.

"Please," said Nagwa to everybody, and we began to look around toward the dining room. To me she said, "Is this your first visit to a Middle Eastern country?"

"I've been here before, but this is still my first country."

"Have you ever been to any black African country?"

"I plan to visit the Sudan at Thanksgiving," I told Nagwa as we moved to the dining room, which was crowded with small tables that each seated four. "I hear Khartoum is nice."

"It is very friendly, but very poor. You can see a lot of wretchedness," she smiled.

I was seated with an Egyptian lawyer, Miles, and Madame Aida, despite whose best efforts we spent most of the meal hearing about Miles' thirteen-hour plane trip to Cairo from Washington. When he went to the bathroom, I asked Madame Aida about Moussa Sadr.

"I don't know politics," she smiled. "Lutfi dealt with him a little."

That spoke volumes.

"You have to remember," said Gamal, the lawyer, "that in a place like Lebanon, it isn't the Lebanese that do most of the killing. It's a relatively open country, so all the other Arabs, and the Israelis too, use it to settle scores. The Palestinians kill an Iraqi there, the Syrians maybe kill a Saudi Arabian, the Saudis pay some Lebanese to kill somebody. The Palestinians are there in the first place because the Jordanians tried to kill them all. The Libyans maybe killed Moussa Sadr. Do you know about a man named Khomeini?"

"No. But Moussa Sadr disappeared in Libya, not Beirut."

"It was an accident, I'm sure. Whatever led up to it took place in Lebanon. Moussa Sadr was an agent for the Libyans, you know. The Lebanese are quite shameless."

"I thought he was Iranian."

"He was born in Iran. The Shah sent him to Lebanon to preach to the Muslims there, but he got involved in politics. He has very devious dealings with the PLO, the Syrians, and us of course—he visits Cairo often. The Israelis hate him as well. I have a strong feeling that the Israelis helped to get rid of him."

"Working with the Libyans?"

"Why not? The Israelis are all over. Secretly, of course. They are what the Lebanese dream of becoming—tough, very smart commercially, real manipulators. Unfortunately the Lebanese would rather kill one another."

But he had just said that it wasn't the Lebanese who did the killing. Why was feeling against the Lebanese running so high?

"Of course, they are angels next to the Syrians," he said.

"Are you Cassolic or Orsodox?" Madame Aida asked me.

Dessert was served. I asked Gamal about Sadat's negotiations with the Israelis—would they come to anything? It seemed as though all the other Arabs were determined to isolate Egypt completely if there were a separate peace.

"All the Arabs are willing to fight Israel to the death—of the last Egyptian," he smiled a little angrily. "Actually, none of the Arabs are fighting Israel, but they are pretending to. In Egypt we can no longer pretend. It is bankrupting us.

"President Abdul-Nasser cared a lot about the other Arabs, but they have done nothing for us. Egypt can stand alone if she has to. Most of those governments that are threatening us barely qualify as governments. Libya is a bunch of thugs. What is Syria? A coincidence of geography. Look at Iraq—it was made by a British tailor."

The borders of modern Iraq were, in other words, the creation of the British Empire. You were never allowed to forget that Egypt was both a nation and a state—its borders had not changed in 7,000 years. Other countries were former colonies, with invented names, formed by expansion, foreign mapmakers, with fragmented identities and huge, wounded egos. Not Egypt, which had always been Egypt. Many Arab countries seemed to define themselves by the lone political dogma of their opposition to Israel; Egypt's identity was vast and complete enough to alter this detail in its modern political ideology without a major dislocation.

This special Egyptianness was also evident in what was not being said at this meal. Although most of the guests were newcomers to Cairo, none of the Egyptians present made the city a topic of conversation. Cairenes have a majestic habit of assuming that their city is the center of the world. In their colloquial Arabic, the word for Cairo, *Misr,* is identical with the word for Egypt itself. Unlike New Yorkers or people in Los Angeles, who can kill hours chatting about "the city" and "this town," they rarely talk at length about their identity as Cairenes or the specific glamour of Cairo. They are short on "attitude" and long on poise; perhaps it was the sheer ancientness of their society. It made them tolerant and uncompetitive—they certainly had nothing to prove to anyone. They thought they were hot stuff, but the fact that they were not talkative about it made it easy to take. Or at least this was my impression at the time.

Lutfallah was moving from table to table, shaking some hands and smiling. He had a particular business smile that animated his whole face—when he was not wearing it, he looked barely tolerant of his guests. He came to our table and squeezed his wife's hand as I was remarking to Gamal that I had never seen an Egyptian clergyman dressed in the cloak and turban Sadr wore.

"Egyptians are Sunni Muslims," Lutfallah interjected with smiling impatience. "I think that Ayatollah Sadr you are talking about is a Shia Muslim, which is something different." He seemed deeply annoyed to hear people talking about religion. Still, I was surprised that he answered my question, and not only because it was not directed at him. Egyptian Christians usually went out of their way to affect ignorance of Islam—his concession to this convention was to call a Sadr an ayatollah erroneously. "I don't think Americans need to worry about the theology in this part of the world!"

The theology of this part of the world, as obscure as the seventh century itself, would soon be the subject of newspaper editorials in Chicago and Cheyenne. Ninety percent of all Muslims were Sunni and had no hierarchical clergy; most of the remainder were Shia, who revered a familial chain of saintly "imams" beginning with Muhammad's son-in-law Ali and continuing through Hassan, Hussein, and so on until the twelfth, al-Mahdi, whose second coming would herald the Last Day. Sunnis regarded Shiites as gaudy, priest-ridden, and relic-mad. Shiites were, by slight margins, the majority sect in Iraq, Lebanon, and little Bahrain in the Persian Gulf; only in non-Arab Iran were they the vast majority.

After dessert came Turkish coffee in tiny cups. Madame Aida pointed out that this coffee was like a perfect husband—"hot, sweet, and black." This hardly described Lutfallah Nasr, who looked like Alfred Hitchcock. "This is the way we tell our fortunes, too," she said.

Nagwa visited our table and told mine. When Miles rejoined us, she left her table, where she had been helping her father describe President Sadat's sterling qualities to an American diplomat and his wife, and came over. She kissed her mother and turned my empty cup over, then picked it up to study the pattern of the muddy sediment around its eggshell-thin sides, and frowned. "It's very interesting," she said solemnly. "I see a trip—definitely, a journey—very soon. Perhaps sooner than you think. You are going to a place where everyone is black."

I never did go to the Sudan. Instead, I had a Thanksgiving dinner at the house of the president of the American University that made me rethink my secret desire to be a U.S. diplomat. I had been considering a diplomatic career. After all, part of the reason I was in Egypt was to decide on a career, and President Richard Pedersen had been an ambassador.

The Pedersens lived in a large apartment on the riverside Corniche El-Nil in central Cairo, just upstairs from one of Sadat's daughters. I lived nearby, having moved from Falaki Street to rent an apartment in Tolumbat Street, a block from the Corniche. At least a dozen guests partook of the immense turkey two Egyptian chefs had lugged from the kitchen. In addition to a friend of mine, there were two AUC professors, a visiting American student on his way to work on an irrigation project near Khartoum, and a populous family singing group, the Farrow Family Band, on a U.S. government-sponsored tour of the Middle East. They did not mind that no one had heard of them—their wholesome act was mainly for export, and they had performed at U.S. Information Service expense in forty countries they could not pronounce. The Farrow paterfamilias said a graceful prayer over the meal, and we all began gabbing. Mrs. Pedersen told me about her son, who was away in the United States. Mr. Farrow described a surprise party his wife had thrown from him in Kay Tar (Qatar): "I was feelin' my way into the hotel suite and when I opened the light there was the most *blessed* whoopin' and a-hollerin'! I was so taken aback you could have bought me for a penny! LaCheryl had cooked up the whole scheme with the young'uns without me suspicioning a thing!" I talked at what must have been unendurable length about my students. Dessert was served to even higher crescendoes of gabbing. In addition to the plentiful food, they had an enormous bar. There was no telling when they would be rid of us.

"It must be difficult, hosting so many people on a family holiday like this," I said.

"This is what I love more than anything else," she smiled, and her face shone with sincerity. She had to be joking. She wasn't. This was the high point of being a big noise in Egypt's social scene? I wanted to say, *you poor thing*—words no one needs to hear from a twenty-one year old. I thought of her when President

Carter visited Cairo a few months later. Sadat had achieved peace with Israel and was determined to parade his superpower guest in triumph all through Egypt. The exhausted Carters eventually did consent to a whistle-stop train trip from Cairo to Alexandria, to wave to peasants along the route. For weeks before the visit, the embassy staff looked like death. They had to arrange the expulsion of all the guests from the deluxe Nile Hilton to make way for American journalists and White House staffers, wore themselves out in meetings with Egyptian reporters and officials, and had to keep other diplomats informed. Were the other embassies envious of all the fuss, I wondered, or secretly smirking? Sadat was shameless. "Do the Americans want someone who can talk sense to the Arabs?" he asked a visiting California congressman. "*I* can talk sense to the Arabs. Do the Americans want someone to get the Cubans out of Ethiopia? Let me do it."

Eventually I began to appreciate Sadat as a courageous "eat your broccoli" president—he fought religious fundamentalism and the strident nationalism that demanded he equip a gigantic army for a war against Israel that would never be fought. He was vain and corrupt, but farsighted and not a demagogue. Like the Shah, he was overly concerned with how he impressed powerful foreigners. By the time he was assassinated, Cairenes were joking about a new stamp, bearing Sadat's portrait, that "didn't work." A postal customer complained, and was reprimanded with, "It's a beautiful stamp, our president's image on one side and glue on the other. You wet the back and it sticks to the letter—what doesn't work?" "Ah!" clucks the man, "We've all been spitting on the wrong side."

As his peace with Israel became real, it slowly became clear that much of the Egyptians' disdain for the other Arabs' opinions was posturing. One by one the Arab embassies closed; Iraq and Algeria closed their airline offices too. A little airline was founded solely to fly between Cairo and Israel so that Egypt Air would not be banned from Arab airspace. The Palestine Liberation Organization office in Tewfiqiya Street closed, and at AUC Palestinian students, whose refugee papers were processed there, looked worried. When Saudi Arabia broke off relations, a student of mine with dual Saudi-Egyptian citizenship only shook her head despairingly when anyone talked politics. On the radio, Sadat sneered that "half the Saudis can't even read and write!" Banners appeared everywhere proclaiming Sadat "WAR HERO—PEACE HERO," and as Americans were buttonholed on the street to hear the common citizens' flattery and great expectations—usually the common citizen was also selling "parfooms and essences"—it dawned on many Americans that whatever was happening in Egypt, we were going to be held responsible for it, for better or worse.

Carter's arrival in Cairo woke me up. The trees that crowded the entrance to my building at 12 Tulumbat Street thrashed around noisily as Sadat's helicopter flew over from his presidential palace just west across the river, to the airport, due east. His motorcade was greeted euphorically, but it seemed to be the spotlight, curiosity, and a feeling of new times coming that motivated the mobs. When the president drove past AUC in an open car on his way to address the Egyptian Parliament a block away, flaks with loudspeakers had little luck whipping up shouts of *Ahlan, ahlan, ya Sadat! Ahlan, ahlan, ya Sadat!*—"Welcome, welcome Sadat!"

Many American diplomats were a little skeptical, but for some reason none of their wives were. When I suggested to an embassy wife that many Egyptians were embarrassed by their president's buttering up the Americans and telling off the Arabs, she glared at me and said, her voice cracking with emotion, "The other day, a ragged little boy—he couldn't have been more than ten— stopped me in the street to tell me *'America very good!'* "

That was it? This was her proof that critics of the new love match were too cynical?

"I wish I knew how they can pick out Americans from all the Europeans and the others," she added more composedly.

Because there were so many of us—the odds were on their side. Also, Nohad, the dormitory attendant, had told me, by our big shoes.

4

Aliens in Egypt

Every other morning I taught English to a class of teenagers at the English Language Institute, a halfway house for new Egyptian students conditionally admitted to the university until they could handle the all-English curriculum. The women, in the majority—for AUC had a very feminine aspect—were more soignée than any I had ever seen in my life. Spike heels were in, as was anything colorful, midi-length and woolen—crazy in Cairo's heat—and as much gold jewelry as possible, especially in the form of long earrings and orchestras of gold bracelets. In any given class, one devout Muslim girl might wear a sort of cloth helmet to conceal her hair, leaving her makeup-free face bare; the rest wore lots of makeup and, in case of glasses, big saucer-wide tinted lenses that beautifully set off their long Egyptian eyelashes. My co-teacher Tim Dickey commented that they probably had to get up at midnight to get looking so perfect at 8 A.M.

About half the faculty at AUC were Americans, and almost all the students were Egyptians. The non-Egyptian students tended to be wealthy Arabs or the children of African and American diplomats, who seemed always to be competitively calculating how many obscenities each knew in how many languages. Rounding out the student body that year were two dozen junior-year-abroad students from the University of California, who lived in the Falaki Street dormitory and often wandered in a pack down busy Muhammad Mahmoud Street, on opposite sidewalks, tossing a bright orange frisbee back and forth over the honking traffic, and endangering the turbaned heads of the Upper Egyptian peasants, who cackled genially. These Americans preferred informal and individual friendships with the native students, so the undergraduate Egyptian-American Freindship Society had no American members—which, I was relieved to discover, meant little. No American wanted to watch slide shows of the Appalachians or the Everglades, nor would it have been fair for them to join in the rounds of American Trivia. Besides, the Americans were largely ornamental here; the foreign aspect of AUC lent a certain cachet to a very Egyptian place.

The American University, founded in 1919, was one of the institutions exported by idealistic and sometimes missionary-minded Americans to improve the tenor of education in ancient developing countries; others were the American University in Beirut, which had been founded as the Syrian Protestant College, and Roberts College in Istanbul, which was now the Boğazaci University. Its student body, traditionally affluent, was always top-heavy with Armenians and Coptic Christians, though the numbers of poorer students and Muslims were constantly rising. AUC offered Egyptians an American-style education, in English, complete with a great library, computers, and visiting cultural attractions, often not Americans, such as the Amadeus Quartet, John Cheever, and Alexandre Lagoya. Americans attending its Center for Arabic Studies got excellent language instruction in standard Arabic and the Egyptian dialect, plus field trips to Coptic monasteries, Islamic cemeteries, and agricultural cooperatives, even to Alexandria. There were Egyptian matrons studying for degrees in teaching English as a foreign language, an adult school for poorer working Egyptians who wanted to study English, and folkloric shows, book fairs, and film festivals open to the public. During the Six-Day War—*El-Naksa,* the Setback, as the popular understatement had it—Nasser had publicly fumed at the imperialist American institution brazenly occupying this choice site in his capital city, and threatened to rename it Palestine University, but no one took him seriously. Everyone who was associated with this serious, neutral, clean-cut college was proud of it, and AUC actually seemed above reproach.

Months passed, and I began to reject the idea of staying in Egypt. I did not want to spoil my memories of the low-key life here, and loved it too much to hang on to the irresponsible life of a graduate student as some rather wan American expatriates did. This was a country for grownups. Cairo's beauty, poverty, and foreignness all reminded me that I should think of my future.

Despite my promise to Sanaa in Cambridge, I never became a regular reader of *al-Ahram,* but did clip out articles to practice translating. *The Minister of Transport today inspected the preliminary excavations of the planned rail system and confirmed that further steps toward relieving the transport crisis in accordance with the cabinet's recent decisions with regard to new initiatives would be the subject of careful study. Before leaving to inspect projects in Menoufiya Province, the minister confirmed that . . .* The drone of official Arabic was a soothing contrast to the colloquial language of Cairo, which had the same kvetching pitch and velocity of the torrents of rising and falling Yiddish I had often heard in Brookline, Massachusetts, or New York's 47th Street.

I ruled out diplomacy as a career—holding the party line looked like too humiliating an exercise even when we were popular, and I saw the scars on some of the capable Americans whose hearts were not in it. It would be all very well if you represented a tiny country with a flag and a national dish, someplace that always got the benefit of the doubt, but speaking for the manifold interests of the United States government involved a lot of stress and salesmanship. Besides, the second half of the year was full of ugly omens: the revolution in Iran, the hanging of the Pakistani prime minister by his military successor, and the immolation of Lebanon—this time, in 1979, it was mainly Lebanese against Lebanese—which sent new waves of refugees to Cairo.

These were mostly Americans, almost all teachers from the American University in Beirut fleeing the "escalating artillery duels" that now "rocked the Lebanese capital," the radio said, day and night. They gravitated toward the American University in Cairo. We—the little corps of graduate students and English teachers who staffed the English Language Institute—were unprepared for the breed of American that lived in Beirut. They had escaped from Lebanon with their lives, but shuddered when they saw Cairo. It struck them—they claimed it struck them—as dirty, ugly, and backward. The Egyptians wore polyester, they said. No one spoke French. It was so tame. Look at all the tourists! These city-mouse Americans, already homesick for the glamour of Beirut, bragged about things I would never have dreamed of bragging about.

"In Lebanon, you hear a dozen different languages when you go down the street," Ginger Gordon, an American University in Beirut faculty wife told us at lunch one day in the AUC garden. "There's so much life—it's so European. In the cafes, you see journalists, exiled politicians, spies. Hamra Street is so chic, all chrome and glass. You see the latest Paris fashions. The sea is so blue—the sky is so blue. And all the different nationalities. When you go by the airport, you see all the little private jets that belong to, you know, the Saudis and the big Europeans."

Beirut had all the appeal, in other words, of a trashy novel.

"Cairo's sort of big and cloddish by comparison. It's a desert city. In Beirut you feel glad to be alive"—that was indisputable, I thought—"you can have a morning swim at the beach, ski in the mountain at lunchtime, and be at a nightclub for dinner. There's no place like Beirut."

And this from a woman who had left because her best friend, a Lebanese woman, had been raped and her husband castrated on a night out in that fabled "mountain." All sides in the three-year-old civil war had taken to dragging their captured enemies through the streets, tied to a car bumper, until they were dead and unrecognizable. The straightforward massacre, in one case with hatchets, was still in use too. The stories were sickening. A new factor, not present in the first round of the war, was the rising anger of the Shia Muslims, enraged by the unsolved disappearance of Moussa Sadr; 300,000 of them had marched to Damascus to present demands to Colonel Qaddafi when he visited Syria. Somehow, though, Lebanon was made bearable by the fact that you could swim and ski in the same day. What would they say if they discovered New Hampshire? But Laconia probably lacked some of Beirut's pleasures. Lebanon had an Arabian Nights mystique, but with a convertible currency, which allowed expensive imports and brought these Americans all the comforts of home: German beer, Skippy peanut butter, even American condoms. In Egypt you bought local or Eastern European products—synthetic Polish jam, Bulgarian wine, canned goods from Greece, African soap. And Lebanon boasted the famed Bekaa Valley hashish. One of Ginger's younger male colleagues gave me an even better idea of the kind of fun that drew crowds to Beirut.

"If ten men are fucking one another in a line," he asked me, "which one is having the best time?"

"I give up," I answered without considering it.

"The second from the front," he smirked. "He's fucking somebody, and he's getting fucked, and he can, you know, play with the one in front of him." Then he explained how he had discovered this.

I had suspected it all came down to something like that.

After the Lebanon refugees, grousing about the scarcity of croissants and the indignity of living in an overcrowded Arab city (some of the stupider Lebanese claimed not to be Arabs, and some of the stupider Americans had believed them) came the Iran refugees. Almost none of them had anything good to say about Iran or the Iranians. These too were teachers. They never got sentimental about Tehran or Isfahan, where most had worked, though their horror stories were nothing compared to what happened in Lebanon. Most had to do with Iranian students vandalizing statues of the Shah or holding frightening political demonstrations. Regardless of how they viewed Iran, very few of the teachers did not sympathize with the Iranian revolution, though it was thoroughly anti-American. "The Iranians aren't exactly impartial," according to Tim, who had lived in Iran before coming to AUC, "but we impair their impartiality by being up in their faces the whole time. You should have seen all those teenagers from Lubbock, Texas, from Bell Helicopter families in Isfahan riding their motorbikes all in circles around the mosque. They'll miss us like a toothache over there." Even then it seemed a given that Americans would be booted out for good.

Cairo had lots of room for us Americans—but elbow room at AUC was getting very scarce with all of these migrating faculties. Most had not found jobs here, only hung around to pick up job or tutoring leads. The Iran refugees in particular were in no hurry; they had been so overpaid by the Iran's imperial government that they had lots of time to decide their next move. Few wanted to go back to the United States. None of the British teachers considered returning to Britain—a few of them talked of going to the Arab Gulf or South Africa. One, Linda Leon, went to Saudi Arabia—the Women's College of Riyadh University—but was back in Cairo a month later, severely shaken and talking of starting a tutoring service in Cairo.

I forget the exact wording of the long, fraught speech she

delivered from the comfort of her wicker chair in the big AUC garden, but the gist of it was, "I was put in jail in Amherst for protesting the Vietnam War, I got malaria in Chad in the Peace Corps, I traveled through Turkey alone and got harassed, I taught in New York and got mugged, and I spent the whole Lebanese civil war in Beirut not getting fazed by the bombs, but I won't be told to veil my head, and not be allowed to drive, and made to take taxis, and have my phone tapped, and have every taxi driver try to convert me to Islam, and then try to fuck me. No one ever tried to lock me up and bore me to death before."

Linda was a lesbian, and I wondered why she didn't find it more congenial, being restricted to the company of women in Riyadh. Saudi girls were said to be ravishing.

"Oh, they're all brainwashed. They're all taught to fall in love with King Abdelaziz al-Saud, who founded the country. Bunch of bullshit. They say their prayers all day long—almost every part of the women's college had a partitioned area for prayers. They'd be in there, bowing over and getting up and all. We used to call it 'the gym.' "

But didn't she find the girls attractive?

"Lots of them were stunning, but so pampered and, like I say, brainwashed. I don't mean to sound patronizing, but they reminded me of, you know, wonderful puppies."

We were all aliens in Cairo, but had no trouble finding a place in a city with the wisdom of Cairo's years. What was there to say about a place with dignity, civilization, a sense of identity? I wanted to write about it but could not. Egypt fit together much too well to make flashy reading. I could not caricature the Egyptians, and didn't want to. It was poor country being pushed to its limit. The Arabs in their press attacks on Egypt failed too.

None of us were prepared for the bitter cold and rain of Cairo's winter. The spattering rain turned the dusty buildings and sidewalks slimy with mud, and all the elaborate brown gates of the pillared mansions and schools turned gleaming black and reflected in the brick-framed puddles. Under the leaden skies and driving winds, Cairo suddenly looked like London. The transiting teachers fleeing Michigan and England were jolted into thinking of warmer climes.

The oil countries of the Persian Gulf, which after Nasser the Arabs called the Arabian Gulf, were a natural draw for English teachers. There were lots of jobs at high salaries, English was in demand and (conveniently for expatriate English teachers, who for some reason were almost always monolingual) widely spoken: all of those countries except Saudi Arabia had been British colonies. All were tiny and fabulously rich. Kuwait was the richest, and relatively liberal, but they hired mainly British teachers; eentsy-weentsie Bahrain was the pleasantest place to live but offered few jobs; Qatar was boring and straitlaced but lucrative; Saudi Arabia was *the worst*. It was a fundamentalist Islamic theocracy. Even our Arab colleagues told horror stories about the roving posses of the Society for the Propagation of Virtue and Prevention of Vice, who carried sticks, made citizens' arrests of people holding hands, and would demand to smell your breath for liquor.

Despite the triumph of the revolution in Iran, which had been claimed by Islamic militants, religious horror stories did not horrify us. The Gulf seemed so far from the tension and violence the Middle East was known for. Those countries had no wars, no refugee camps; no poverty or overpopulation or hysterical arguments about Arabs versus Jews versus us. The Arab Gulf was golden sand, palm trees, peace, and huge wealth: an oasis of comfort. The horror stories—all of them on a religious theme—seemed rather quaint compared to the mayhem of Israel and Lebanon. Egypt was a sane, important country with real problems. The Gulf states were living a fantasy. They seemed like toy countries.

Teachers of English as a Second Language (ESL), who looked to the Gulf for work, tried to get to know some of the Saudis, Kuwaitis, and others who lived in Egypt, to try to get a truer picture of those countries, which were all but impossible to visit. None issued tourist visas, and their consular officials were notoriously hostile.

There was a good-sized community of Gulf Arabs in Cairo—these were not the rich Arabs the newspapers wrote about, who bought buildings in London and lost millions in an evening in Monte Carlo or committed landscaping atrocities in California. Most were students at Cairo University, studying medicine and engineering, and some of them dated American University students. These were generally Saudi Arabians whose English was not good enough to get them into British or American universities, or who were studying at their own expense, so preferred colleges cheaper and nearer to home—Cairo was barely a two-hour flight from Jeddah on the Red Sea. And some simply preferred an Arab and Islamic milieu to San Diego or Boulder. These Saudis all seemed remarkably polite and religious. One, a Qatari, was deeply in love with Pam, an AUC Mennonite girl from Oregon, who once told me, "My parents would disown me if I dated a Catholic." Her tone of voice suggested that they would be doing exactly the right thing, but she made no secret of her desire to bag Ahmed, her Qatari Muslim.

My friend Hamdan was not so ready to settle down. He was one of the large contingent of Saudi Arabian premed students at Cairo University, many of whom would later drop medicine and go into business back in "the kingdom." He referred to his country as "the peninsula" (a mark of the radicals, who were uncomfortable with the fact that the royal Al Saud family had named the country after themselves) and smoked hashish. Hamdan first made AUC friends when he came up to us in a bar in Zamalek, one of Cairo's posher neighborhoods. He was five feet tall and stocky, with impressive acne scars. When he had ascertained that we were Americans, he had a question. This was the only reason he had come over; the blond American at his table was waiting for him with visible impatience.

"What does *dominant* mean?" he asked.

"It means, go for it," he was told.

The other oil Arabs, who generally came as tourists, were acutely embarrassing to Ahmed and even to Hamdan; they were like turbocharged ugly Americans. They fled to Egypt from the austere Islam of Saudi Arabia, Kuwait, or Libya only for alcohol, drugs, and sex, and threw their money around like little kings. At the Sheraton they slouched in the bar or lurched through the casino, always with a full escort of pimps, whores, and young hangers-on ready to do their bidding—buy hashish, make a phone call, find a taxi—for a huge tip. Somehow these wild tourists gave the impression of innocence: they seemed so new to debauchery, drinking tumblers of warm whiskey in the late morning, with a sour face. You often saw them praying on the sidewalks, shaky and bleary-eyed. Some were never seen at all, since they stayed in their rented apartments, rutting and drinking, day and night.

Years later, in Riyadh, whenever I heard Saudi Arabians bitterly denounce Egyptians as nothing but pimps, whores, and thieves, I felt sure that I was listening to someone who had surrounded himself, on his Egyptian holiday, only with criminal types. A good many young petro-Arabs were robbed of almost everything they had before boarding the plane back to Jeddah or Tripoli.

Most of this Gulf misbehavior was behind closed doors—nothing like the rampantly schizophrenic high jinks of "oil Arabs" in London. It was a hot topic of the 1970s. My favorite phenomenon was the shoplifting that went on at Harrod's and Marks & Spencer. No shoplifting went on in Cairo; there was a reason it only happened in Europe. While London seemed staid to Americans, even at its raunchiest, it was Dodge City to Arabs: all forbidden things were legal or at least common. A young Arab could skip his prayers, stay drunk around the clock, eat pork, smoke hashish, have unlimited sex with blondes and fondle them in public, shout obscenities, and ogle half-naked women in the street. In this lawless atmosphere, no wonder some of the more innocent ones thought they could get away with boosting a pair of socks.

It was common, in Saudi Arabia, to look down on Europeans and Americans for selling sacrilegious pleasures, then making illogical laws against drugs, drunk driving, and roughing up women. They could not keep track of that pesky line between what was licit and what was not. They often thought that the Manichean, if hypocritical situation imposed by Islamic law, which they so often violated, was saner than the West's compromise with vices, regulating and tolerating them within limits. Saudis seemed to have no desire for their vices to be legal at home, and were boastful about the iron force of their Koranic laws. They wholeheartedly despised their Egyptian pimps, drug suppliers, and catamites for being lax Muslims.

They were cousins; most Egyptians were descended from the Arabs who captured Egypt in A.D. 640. Egypt had been invaded and ruled by foreigners from Cleopatra until King Farouq, and they valued their Arab ties. Once I was joking with one of my students about the different kinds of tourists that passed through Cairo. I ran down the full audit of nationalities: American, French, Dutch, Indian, and so on, and she answered "good" or "no good." When I came to "Saudi" she laughed out loud. "There are good and bad." "But they all act like apes [sa'adeen—a weak pun]," I joked. Her smile vanished. "They are *Arabs,*" she said loftily.

We were not. What were we, how did we look to them? How did we look to Egyptians who had never set foot in AUC? I could only imagine how a feature writer for *al-Ahram* might see us: pale invaders with no language skills, shabby compared to the moneyed Egyptians we taught, looking like children in the open-air museum of Cairo. How easy it would be for a biased reporter to draw false conclusions about the Christian angle of the school's history and the disproportionate number of Christians there, about Jewish Junior Year Abroad students padding along behind Menachem Begin when he came to Egypt and prayed at the Adly Street Synagogue. A deft touch could make sinister the proximity of the U.S. Embassy at 5 Latin America Street, particularly if he were to describe it as "the sprawling, thickly antennaed American mission." Only the lightest touch would be needed to suggest the likelihood of CIA informers among us, or the certainty that the Center for Arabic Studies students would all end up as spies. And what about the wealth of AUC (he might mention "an elegant marble library housing all the latest American novels") contrasted with poverty ("a stark contrast to the crippled beggars reclining on the fractured sidewalks, bleating for coins")? Or "the wall-eyed beggaress with the mottled baby craned her neck at the cheers issuing from the immaculate tennis court shielded by the high wall, upon which flapped a torn poster of the Egyptian president."

And, Good Lord, what would he make of the quotes he could garner from some of the American students?

"We're the most civilized country in the world," according to Kirk Pettie, the freckled, blue-eyed son of an American lieutenant colonel attached to the U.S. Embassy. "Believe me, man, if they offered U.S. visas to all the Gyppos, ain't nobody'd be left here but the mummies!" Kirk, an avid churchgoer, is an anthropology major at the American University. (Though surely Kirk would sound more articulate in translation, especially into journalistic Arabic.)

Or: *"I feel that I'm being valuable here," smiles Judy Osherow, a graduate student in sociology. "I'm working on a birth control project here in Fayoum Province, and really enjoy getting away from Cairo and helping the peasant women see the importance of a small family and liberating them from male-dominated religion based on fear." As she speaks, four peasant women raise their hands in claws behind her back.*

Or: *"I'll never go back to America," declares fashionable, chain-smoking Sam Cox. "I couldn't wait to leave! When I talk to some of these students who want to emigrate and get an American passport, I tell them, 'Take mine!' Let's see how long they can live without culture." Egyptian students listen somberly to the embittered native of Binghamton, New York.*

Actually, it was unlikely or impossible that my imagined feature would ever be written. It was not the Egyptian style, and their thin newspapers did concentrate, as Sanaa had said, on national and international news; most local color was left to television. Cairo editors were not attracted to the kind of features Americans liked: old pubs, forgotten neighborhoods, endearing traditions, ordinary people doing extraordinary things. *Al-Ahram* printed no cozy descriptions of al-Batiniya, the City of the Dead, El-Fustat, the Parisian mansions of Garden City; the Muslim ladies who prayed on the steps of the Catholic cathedral to have children; the poor pajama-clad children who sold gum on the sidewalk at night, doing their homework by the light of the streetlamps; the Saudis; all Cairo's exiled royalty—including King Idris of Libya—the splendid, Cecil B. DeMille–Babylonian Jewish temple on Adly Street. Besides, when we were criticised with real bitterness it was generally for the wrong reasons: for poisoning political enemies, serving an international Jewish conspiracy, or encouraging Muslims to apostasize.

By late spring, I had learned a great deal, but felt let down by my discovery that Egyptians were warm, witty people very secure with their self-image, and largely comfortable in the world, seeing so little of it as alien to them. I began to feel the necessity of going deeper into the real Arab lands to look for the cultural clashes that detonated all the trouble. Clearly my efforts to probe the mutually antagonistic East and West were misdirected in the old and subtle culture of Egypt.

Aliens just did not faze Cairo; not the frisbee-throwers, the coeds in halter tops, the embassy wives, or the huge mobs of braying tourists. It was hard to try and pose as an observer in a place where, increasingly, I felt observed by the city they called *Umm El-Dunya,* Mother of the World. And by late summer, there were Israeli tourists. After thirty years of cruel and humiliating military, psychological, religious, political wars, there would have been nothing as ominous and deflating as a band of Israelis walking openly down the street, but when it happened, the Egyptians hollered "Shalom!" and tried to sell them perfumes.

There was only one place in the Arab world where the fault lines of religion, culture, wealth, and modernity intersected: in the shimmering mirage of Saudi Arabia. Arabia was, in the space of a few decades, experiencing the shocks that had come to the West and the Church over centuries in a series of smaller shocks: the reformation, the French Revolution, the world wars. Additionally, as home to Mecca and Medina, it was the Islamic holy land.

It was not hard to gain entry to the insular kingdom. The *Saudi Gazette,* the first Saudi newspaper I wrote to, hired me as a reporter, without naming a salary or asking me for qualifications, and I put my master's degree on hold. An attempted coup d'état in Mecca made the Saudi government temporarily wary of granting visas to journalists, but when it came through I bought a plane ticket and braced myself for *real* Arabia.

5

A Pimp with Prayer Beads

*T*he fellow with the prayer beads sitting beside me on the flight to Saudi Arabia did not want to speak Arabic; he preferred English, though he did not speak it all that well. This was often the sign of a student, Arab or otherwise foreign (he was about the right age) or an intensely religious Muslim who finds it profane that non-Muslims should kibbitz in the holy tongue. I doubted this was the case with him, because he blandly informed me that he was a "hustler." His name was Faisal, and he lived in Holland; visiting Saudi Arabia on business.

"What country are you from?" I asked him.

"I'm Arab."

"But what country?"

He would not say. Would a European tell you he was European and not tell what country he was from? He did not look Arab to my philosemitic eye, which slowly considered his profile, shiny hair and accent, and turned in a verdict of Pakistani or possibly Indonesian. But why lie?

The airliner was cruising over the Syrian desert, where patches of snow clung to black hills amidst the reddish wasteland. Moments before, passengers had craned their necks when the captain said we were passing over Beirut. I was reading Nizar Qabbani's *Diary of a City Once Called Beirut,* a little fifty-four-chapter prose poem published shortly after the Lebanese civil war.

I am Beirut . . .
A city once known as Beirut . . .
I keep this diary to send you before I commit suicide . . .

Factional poison purls through the sea around me, killing
the big and the small fish, sinking ships and deflowering
the bays. It swallows the paddling children, one by one . . .

I am Beirut . . .
Archaeologists and guidebooks will remember me as they
remember Sodom and Gomorrah, Pompeii, Agadir, Hiroshima
    and
other cities to which God sent owls of doom, and threw down
without a stone left upon a stone . . .

Did you ever see my other face? . . .

Look for me under "B" in the encyclopedia. You'll find a
picture from my girlhood—before they slashed me and
   threw
acid in my face. The picture you see was taken in the '40's,
when my sea was as pure as the Magdalene's tears and my
orchards bulged with fruit, my mountaintops were
   blanketed
with snow . . . you could scent my orange blossoms all the
   way
from Cyprus . . .

Faisal was holding his newspaper wide open, so that it lapped
over my arm. He was reading an article with huge headlines,
about Iranian threats to execute the American diplomatic hostages. It was January of 1980; no one guessed they had another
year of captivity to endure. Faisal flashed a jailer's smile and
turned to me.

"You think Khomeini is fuck?"

"Excuse me? Do I think Khomeini is a fuck?"

"You think?"

"I don't know very much about him at all. What do you
think?"

"Strong man."

Faisal supplied Dutch prostitutes to tourists in Amsterdam, but
generally limited his own tricks to men; he had actually boasted
about this while the plane was taking on passengers, meals, and
luggage at Heathrow. He would have been executed for this in
Iran. I felt obliged to point this out.

"It's not like that. It's dignity. America and Europe make shit
all over people. Muslim people aren't able to be allowed to know

anything about one another. Khomeini is changing everything. Doing something for Muslim feelings." He offered me a cigarette. I could think of nothing to say, so said nothing.

"I deal with Americans more than any other people. I deal with English, German, French, Arab, Persian, everybody, even Jew. Americans have no culture. English say it, French, Arab, everybody. You're only rich."

The aircraft rocked slightly and dipped, turning south into Jordan in a wide slow arc. The *ping-ping-ping* buttons sounded as passengers summoned stewardesses for their last drinks before approaching Saudi airspace, when the drinks carts would be secured. Faisal, whose mood was deteriorating rapidly for some reason, drained the gin from his clear plastic cup, munched the olive, and announced contemptuously, "I always fuck American girl."

"That doesn't mean anything, that your European customers say Americans have no culture. They would always agree with a hustler—they'd agree with whatever you said, because what do they care what you think?"

"I don't like Saudian people, too," said Faisal. "There are too many in Amsterdam. I used to work in Beirut, and they like it. Saudians like London, Paris, Amsterdam. You know why?"

"I can imagine."

"Because they don't like Moslem people. In Beirut they go to the Casino du Liban, they have party with Christian girls. They don't want to see a Moslem."

"Why are you going to Saudi Arabia?"

"To make business with my friend. Antiques."

"You could buy antiques in Iran. Wouldn't you prefer that?"

"Not now. No *licence d'exportations.*" This rolled off his tongue. "After."

"After what? After Khomeini?"

"When everything is ready! I can go to Iran whenever I want."

I could not get back into the diary of Beirut ("My first love was Europe . . ."), and wished that I had *Without Marx or Jesus* to read instead; there would be something in that odd book—a Frenchman praising America—to fling back at Faisal.

"I may visit America—I can have American visa. New York," said Faisal. "But my friends telling, 'Be careful. It's the most violent place anywhere.' "

"Full of hustlers," I said.

This conversation was not the omen I wanted for my first-ever arrival in Saudi Arabia; I had not even told Faisal I was a reporter lest he hex my career by sneering at the press or regretting he had blabbed so much. Below us, Jeddah was an ocean of looping and crisscrossing amber lights against black, bordering the pitch blackness of the sea at night.

6

Whispers in Jeddah

$\mathcal{E}$nglish-language newspapers in Saudi Arabia and the Gulf needed reporters who wrote English fluently, but were years away from being able to hire Saudi Arabians, so most of the journalists brought in were American or British. Americans had an edge because the British were thought to be arrogant. Some editors had pangs of conscience, hiring Westerners at all, when their own Third World was desperate for employment. It was out of the question to hire other Arabs; English was the second language in Iraq and in Egypt, but Iraq was socialist and Egypt was out of favor because of the treaty with Israel, so neither nationality was practical. In fact, editors preferred to steer clear altogether of Arabs, who might stir up political trouble. Pakistanis were good English speakers and, as Muslims, had a sensitive understanding of the society they were reporting on; since Pakistan was so poor, they could be underpaid. After the troubles in Mecca, however, the government became wary of importing more Muslims, so Indians slowly replaced the Pakistanis. One progressive editor at a rival newspaper who got annoyed at the Indians' archaic brand of English vowed to get rid of them in favor of more Americans—black Americans. "They speak English," reasoned Walid al-Abyad, "they are mistreated in America—they'd love to come here. They see themselves as part of the Third World—as our brothers. I'm placing some advertisements in Atlanta." Walid had previously considered Sudanese reporters, since English was a strong second language in Sudan, but the Sudanese were not only Muslims but black. "An Arab executive will be much happier talking to a black *American,*" he decided, and hired three well-educated and experienced Georgians.

The kinship (it certainly existed) between African-Americans and Arabs was nearly Walid's ruin, since the common denominator of color subtracted from his black reporters the sense of foreignness that made his white reporters so timid and respectful. When John Mark, one of the Atlantans, discovered that no churches were permitted in Saudi Arabia, he got into an argument with Walid in which the word "bullshit raghead" was used;

another of the group, Matthew from Marietta, told Walid to "get fucked." Their contracts were not renewed. Only Julius stayed, became Abdulmajid, and quit the newspaper to enroll in the Islamic University of Medina. For the next few years, most reporters were, like me, Christian, American, and pasty-complexioned.

Our newspaper's head office was in the trading port of Jeddah, in a rat-infested stucco ruin (once a fine specimen of nautical moderne) on a side street near the docks, full of feuding bureau-crats and the grating roar of old air conditioners. The alleys were strewn with massive spools of newsprint turning a filthy yellow in the sun. I was one of the newest staffers, and immediately assigned the job of Riyadh bureau chief because none of the other reporters—they were Indian, Somali, British, and American—spoke Arabic. Riyadh was an insular capital: the embassies were not located there, but in Jeddah. Until a few years before, it had even been something of a forbidden city, and a special permit was required to visit. The royal government assumed that the Riyad-his, whose xenophobia was proverbial, would need time to adjust to infidels on their soil. The royal capital had the worst infrastruc-ture, the fieriest clergymen, the most intense heat, the meanest police, and the most paralyzing sense of insecurity. I recalled a European writer's opinion that "the city that receives is always the strongest one"—Jeddah was strong, Riyadh weak.

Since most of the 7,000-strong royal family lived there, it also boasted the wildest parties: whole bands with hundreds of guests were flown into Riyadh in the afternoon, and all exported again two or three days later. It radiated sexuality and sexual repression: thousands of men prowled the streets while the women, banned from driving, entertained themselves indoors or watched the city from the back seats of roomy American sedans. Arabic was a necessity. No one else wanted the job, and I was assured—warned—that no one would visit me there.

I was delighted. Not only was Riyadh an intriguing one-man show, it was the center of political power—that is to say, financial power, the financial power of the Al Saud family. Saudi Arabia boasted ancient cities like Mecca and Medina, the green mountainous retreat of Abha, and the American-developed oil town of Dhahran on the Persian Gulf, but everything was ruled from that unlovable baked-mud metropolis with its science-fictional new atmosphere of overscale modern architecture and quaint old Arabian ways.

A number of key Saudi personalities were associated with Riyadh, though they all shared some form of exile from the place. Naser Saeed was there—a Saudi dissident who had organized the first strikes against the oil companies in 1956, demanded an end to the U.S. military presence, an end to slavery, and free elections. He was sent into exile in Beirut and Cairo, always dodging harassment and, he claimed, assassination attempts provoked by his ever more wrathful denunciations of the royal family. Finally, in December 1979, he was kidnapped by Saudi agents in Beirut and shipped to Riyadh in a crate. I looked forward to walking the scorching streets of Riyadh, wondering in which prison he was slowly going blind. The Kingdom of Saudi Arabia claimed to hold no political prisoners, and this was a story I longed to break.

During Saeed's incarceration, his socialist movement was co-opted by religious fanatics who renamed it the Islamic Front for the Liberation of the Arabian Peninsula (they refused to pronounce the words "Saudi Arabia"). The operative word was "front"—it had become a subsidiary of the new Islamic government in Iran—but its aims were basically the same: the overthrow of the Al Saud family, the establishment of an Islamic republic, the expulsion of Americans from the country, and a more anti-Israeli policy. The front's manifesto otherwise contained almost no social reform. Despite its foreign sponsor, Saeed's movement was said to have its basis of popular support in Riyadh, a city whose intrigues otherwise involved only bootleg whiskey, British stewardesses, and a few cross-dressing princes.

Riyadh was also the hometown of Abdullah Tureiki, the founder of OPEC. Like Saeed, he was a malcontent, a socialist, not currently allowed to live in Riyadh. His was one of the greatest revenge stories of all time: this dark-skinned Arab, whose anti-Americanism was legend, had actually studied engineering in the United States, in Texas, in the 1950s. Eight years of being called a "nigger" in the Jim Crow south whetted his appetite for humiliating this parvenu superpower, and he succeeded brilliantly. Unfortunately, his own country, an equally crude and actual slave-trading monarchy, did not share his views and so he divided his time in banishment between the U.S. and a few other Arab countries.

And there was one of the Arab world's greatest novelists, Abdelrahman Munif, whose socialist views had cost him his citizenship; now he lived in Baghdad. His novel *Sharq al-Mutawassit* (East of the Mediterranean) was the first Arab novel to describe the use of torture by Arab governments to control and destroy their people. There was a story waiting to be written about him from his own city, which had cast him out.

Munif's books were avidly read, though like most black market items (whiskey, bacon, pornography) they were prohibitively expensive, even the skinny *When We Left the Bridge.* It was common for Saudi students to pool their resources to buy a Munif novel on the black market, then take turns reading it. In the Eastern Province, I was told, young Saudis traveled to the little island state of Bahrain, visible from the Arabian mainland, to buy his books and have a dirty weekend reading them; the Saudi government was said to be pressuring Bahrain, too, to ban the books.

A weekend visit to Riyadh left me with the impression of a hundred-mile-square De Chirico painting. But until my residence permit was granted, I stayed in Jeddah, getting to know the newspaper.

Jeddah was blue skies, the blue sea, and suffocating humidity. The heat made my feet a full size larger. And the city went on for miles. You could not walk here. Its staggering surface area, its newness, and its sense of never having been touched by war, gave it an American feel. My apartment was at Kilo 4 of the Mecca Road—as measured from a rotary in front of the Meridien Hotel, which marked the beginning of the road to Mecca, sixty miles away. The building was just off Muhammad Feda Street, between the Old Airport and the Al-Thaghr Elementary School, where little Saudi boys played tag in navy blue trousers, white shirts, and blue ties—a snob school, I was told. Elsewhere schoolboys wore their traditional ankle-length white thobes and round caps, ranging in size from yarmulke to pillbox. And these boys' hair was fairly long, in spite of a media campaign condemning *khunfusa*—"beetle"—hairstyles, a mistranslated reference to the Fab Four.

I spent my first week at a gray metal desk sticky with the rings of thousands of glasses of sweet tea, reading clip files. What a cruel trap Saudi Arabia was for short-term visitors intending to write about it. The government did not allow foreign news services to open bureaus, and only allowed reporters to make the briefest of visits. With rare exceptions, the result, in these articles from American and British dailies, consisted of predictable drivel: A Land of Ancient and Modern Side by Side; Camels Compete with Cadillacs in Oil Kingdom; Old Ways Survive in Mecca/ Mecca Enters the 20th Century; the progress/benightedness of women, the blessing/curse of oil wealth, the iron hand/direct democracy of desert-style *majlis* rule, and other quick 'n easy features.

This was precisely what the Saudis sought in their royal ban on foreign news bureaus. The beneficiaries were the royal image-makers and local reporters—even the laziest local hacks were sought after as stringers with foreign newspapers hungry for scoops. This was, of course, illegal, according to the law of the land and the terms of my contract, and at the beginning I lost sleep over my own surreptitious telexes to Beirut and Bahrain. I realized only with time that the Ministry of Information was delighted with this arrangement: they were assured that *Time, Newsweek,* the *New York Times,* and the wire services got their coverage, and anyone who filed anything too touchy would be deported.

"Do your homework for Riyadh," I was told. Instead of having a reporting beat in Jeddah, I read up on the ministries and the royal family. Both subjects overlapped in the cabinet, where half the positions belonged to princes and half to commoners; the latter were mainly talented Hejazis (Hejaz being the western region on the Red Sea, where Jeddah and Mecca were located), while the princes were, by definition, from Riyadh. Senior princes were the king's brothers, with a second tier of princely nephews. There were thousands of princes, because the Al Saud family had used multiple marriages as a form of diplomacy with the hundreds of Arabian tribes and other families. Certain prominent families, such as the Al Sheikh and Sudeiri, had virtually become part of the royal class.

The Al Saud were a clan of tough, devout warriors; the first king, Abdulaziz, united the Hejaz, central Arabia, and al-Hasa— the Eastern Province—to form the Kingdom of Saudi Arabia in the 1930s. By the 1980s the family had grown nearly beyond control, and now even required a secret government department, headed by an anonymous senior prince, solely to gather intelligence on the royal family itself. There were white and black princes, scholarly princes, incredibly devout princes and decadent princes; some, through intermarriage, had more Armenian than Arab blood, though the majority married only within their own vast family. All were rich; all were Sunni Muslims.

One prince I met (the size of the family defeats the use of pseudonyms) had a lifestyle that intrigued me. He lived in Riyadh and had a farm for his horses outside the city. On his frequent vacations he flew straight to New York, checked into the Pierre, and immediately abandoned his suite for a series of Greenwich Village bars where he could have sex with twenty men in an evening, lounge in a bathtub with a dozen men urinating on him, sniff cocaine, be bound, whipped, and washed off in time to be back at the Pierre by dawn, nap, and then lunch with his investment consultants. The prince's fun spoke volumes, to me, about his social access, his good upbringing and credit rating, and his perfect understanding of Arabian and American rules. He was someone who truly knew both worlds and should have held much more power than he did; unlike any number of Saudi kings, he would never be fooled by America.

On the whole, the royal family was chiefly important for its king, Khaled, who also served as prime minister; the powerful crown prince, Fahd, and his full brothers who held the portfolios of defense, interior, and the emirate—princedom—of Riyadh. There was room, in the tangle of this family tree, for an impressive bureaucratic class.

I made friends with Omar, an Egyptian reporter on our Arabic sister paper, *Okaz*. He read American novels and had already dubbed the Saudi press corps "the Stepford Journalists." Omar wanted to write a book about the *intifadet-el-haram,* which gave away his political leanings. This "uprising of the holy place" was more properly known, here, as the "blasphemy of the age."

A few months previous, in November 1979, more than 4,000 people had died in an attempted coup d'état—the battle had taken place in the holiest shrine in Islam, the gigantic mosque in Mecca. Dozens of revolutionaries disguised as pilgrims—it was the height of the Haj season—took hostages, holed up in the ancient labyrinth under the acres of marble flooring, and fought a bloody battle there and from the towering minarets. It was the ghastliest event in Saudi Arabian history, and a notably black moment for Islam. Omar, though a Sunni Muslim, had been encouraged by a sign of political life from the Saudi population. We discussed it on my little prefab balcony overlooking the empty playground.

"It was supposed to be a revolution. They say it was just a group of maniacs, but it's a lie. The king was supposed to be there, and they were going to kill him."

"Wasn't it a group of religious extremists?"

"Yes, why else do you think the government has got so religious now? No more women on television. No more music in restaurants. Tomorrow they'll ban music completely. They don't know how far to go—how far is enough. In America, in Egypt, the government knows what people want because everyone is always saying so. Here, with an absolute monarchy, they have to wonder what on earth their people really feel. No wonder they just gab about their old traditions and being the holy land and blessed with oil. If they mention anything else they might have another uprising on their hands. And then what will America think?"

The leader of the revolt, Juhaiman al-Otaibi, was a rural religious fanatic. He was not really the monster they made him out to be, only the kind of loony xenophobic zealot the Middle East is so kind to. Born Jewish, he would have made *aliya* and lived out his years happily lynching Palestinians on a West Bank settlement. Born Christian, he might have been the scourge of the infidels on Pat Robertson's southern Lebanon radio station, or joined the Church of Christ, Christian. But he was born Muslim, a son of the desert who grew up increasingly disturbed at the seeming occupation of his country by licentious, thieving foreigners, and inflamed at the rampage of *bid'a*—"innovation." One of the sayings of the Prophet asserted that "In *bid'a* is Hellfire." Usury, televisions, the monarchy, the U.S. military presence—relations with the infidels and the use of their technologies, not to mention being servants of their multinational interests, were all *bid'a,* and Juhaiman went to war.

He began by handing out tracts—very literate ones, which he had written and had printed in nearby Kuwait, denouncing the monarchy and its sacrilegious practices. His followers, recognizable by their short mustaches, long beards, and midi-thobes, formed cells throughout the kingdom, and then, in mid-1978, began preparing to overthrow the government by killing the king on a visit to Mecca. Omar claimed to have seen it coming.

"A Saudi friend of mine came to see me a week before the uprising—he used to be a medical student in Cairo and he used to drink and gamble and fuck girls. Then he turned religious when he moved back here. So he came to see me, very changed—a beard, sandals, and a short thobe—you know it's considered arrogant to wear one that drags on the ground, so theirs were quite short. He wanted to repay me twenty riyals he owed me—about six dollars. I told him, Forget it! But he insisted! He forced me to take the twenty, and said, 'This is between me and God.' You see, he was clearing his accounts before martyrdom. And sure enough, he died in the uprising in the mosque."

Omar had a copy of a telex the U.S. Embassy in Jeddah had sent to Washington after meeting with the Saudi defense minister, Prince Sultan, to discuss the revolt. The immensely fat prince had been defense minister for two dozen years, and was one of the world's richest men. He was corrupt in the gaudy but typically nonviolent Saudi way. I had learned that he took commissions on several important defense contracts and it seemed to be a habit. The kingdom dealt with such cataracts of money that his deals were more like casino skimming than actual robbery. Sultan's pictures were all over the place, and he was always smiling, seeming to say, ". . . and nobody gets hurt." He was very pro-American, and was selected to meet with anxious American officials, to soothe them with the government version of events: a group of fanatics, no conspiracy, no social unrest.

It was a bizarre performance. On the surface, it was full of businesslike bonhomie, and the diplomats and intelligence officers were a respectful audience for Prince Sultan's explanation of the attempted coup: who Juhaiman was, what he wanted, who sided with him, and how the battle against him was won. But the transcript and summary of the meeting which the U.S. Embassy telexed to Washington told a second story: despite his power and wealth, Sultan's speeches were not only totally mendacious but apologetic. The prince's transparent lies and empty bravado were standard Saudi boilerplate, scarcely expected to be believed. The Americans' questions and comments gave away—but possibly not to the prince—that they did not believe a word he was saying. Or rather they saw it as an ingenious alloy of fact and fiction which their intelligence capabilities were, at this early stage, unequipped to analyze; but they knew that the government had been far more surprised, and far more frightened, than it let on.

Not that it made any difference. As friends and allies, they had to accept Sultan's explanation. As chief Saudi arms procurer, he was one of America's most prized golden geese. But why had Prince Sultan felt obliged to go through this humiliating charade? Despite the elevated rhetoric, there was a thread of childish slyness, as if telling his parents a naughty fib about how stable his government really was. These skeptical, avuncular Americans knew better, but, after all, most of them didn't know any more about this country than its government did. They told Washington that there were some serious inconsistencies in his generally reliable story.

Despite this artificial and mendacious exercise, which must have diminished their mutual respect, they all felt very much on the same wavelength. I was mystified. The Saudi king's reluctance to admit a revolt, and his silence over mischievous Iranian rumors (that the U.S. and Israel had occupied Mecca) had given rise to anti-American riots, and in Pakistan an American marine had been killed when the embassy was sacked. Wasn't President Carter peeved? And yet why were the Saudis so compliant with the intrusive American investigation?

"Because," I was told by Bob Palmeri, an American diplomat, "the Saudi Arabians have a quarter to a third of the world's known oil reserves, and all the world's big economies stand or fall by the availability of that oil. And those oil fields are all but undefended. So you see how much we and the Saudis mean to one another." He laughed loudly—he almost never ended a sentence without laughing loudly.

Omar and I discussed it with our Saudi friend Khalil one night at al-Hamra, a semi-developed wilderness of beachfront and flyovers north of the king's al-Hamra palace and the American embassy. This giant concrete park was dotted with several tones of Islamically correct abstract sculpture—I marveled for the sixtieth time at this puritan sect's forced enthusiasm for the most hideous and banal statuary, safe only because it never attempted a human image. We bought paper cups of delicious *bileila,* a snack made of chickpeas, from a cart and sat facing the Red Sea, which even at night projected an aqua glow through the humid black air and amber lights. Large Saudi families gathered within the range of the waves' steady hiss every night to eat local delicacies and drink Pepsi as they sat on the blankets they spread over the broad sidewalks. Packs of teenage boys crouched on the sidewalks watching televisions plugged into their car's cigarette lighter and eating fried chicken.

We came around to the subject of the *intifadat-al-haram* indirectly, since Saudis tended to be closemouthed about it, by wondering out loud whether or not the international press had been fair in reporting it.

"Of course," said Omar, "the government wasn't much help in clarifying what was happening." To say the least—they had imposed a total news blackout by cutting off all telephone and telex lines to the outside world.

"It was a terrible thing," said Khalil. "It's hard to believe America didn't stop it from happening."

"How were the Americans to know that it was happening at all?" I asked.

"They know what people think before they think it!" said Khalil, and took a swallow from his thermos of *siddiqi*, the local homemade gin. The name meant "my friend." American teenagers in Jeddah's marketplaces wore T-shirts that proclaimed SID DEEKY IS MY FRIEND.

"Juhaiman's group were underground," said Omar. "Almost nobody knew about them."

"Everybody knew about them," said Khalil crossly. "But hardly anyone complained about them because you can't complain about anything religious here. They were protégés of Sheikh Bin Baz." Bin Baz was an old, blind, pockmarked preacher who represented the religious right and had the ear of the king. "The cripple is afraid of him." He meant King Khaled, who walked with a cane and rarely spoke in public. "Their leaflets were all over the place. I read them." Khalil drank more *siddiqi* and eyed the broad street shrouded in floating skeins of fog. A Nile green Rolls-Royce glided to a stop several yards a way and a wobbling driver stepped out to chat with some teenage boys watching American wrestling on their sidewalk television. Khalil's eyes narrowed.

"A prince," said Omar.

"Some stupid prince," said Khalil. "Juhaiman could have rid us of the whole clan of thieves. But America and Israel stepped in to save them, and France, and Britain."

This wasn't an unusual point of view. It was Khomeini's: he condemned the *intifada* as an Israeli-American plot, but within a year was describing Juhaiman as a great Islamic, anti-American martyr and even had a postage stamp created to commemorate the *intifadat-al-haram*.

It galled me that the U.S. played whipping boy for the Saud family. The Saudi government, which guided the editorial line of the kingdom's seven dailies, encouraged vigorous criticism of the United States, to fit into the Arab mainstream and to deflect criticism from itself. Because the government was, in fact, in some ways a virtual colony of the U.S., this tradeoff allowed them to look evenhanded. Uncomfortably for us Americans, it made us look ridiculous. Ultimately, I was sure, their ploy would backfire on them, when the people began to wonder why the government was such a pliant ally of such an objectionable superpower. In the meantime, though, it complicated the mythology surrounding Americans. Listening to Khalil made me thankful for the hundredth time that I was not an American diplomat; and not only because the Iranians were holding so many of them prisoner.

"The only good thing to come out of it is that we'll get a parliament," Khalil pointed out. "The king has promised to form a *majlis al-shura,* a sort of advisory council or congress. The people will have some role in the government for the first time."

"When will it start up?"

"It's being studied by a committee under Prince Naif, the minister of the interior," smirked Omar, meaning *never.* Arab ministries of the interior did not deal in gas and oil leases; they were the security and intelligence departments. Prince Naif was a Saudi Arabian version of J. Edgar Hoover, minus the broad-mindedess.

"It may take time," conceded Khalil, "but the cripple was very frightened. I think it will happen soon."

"There's already a *majlis* system, isn't there?" The majlis was such a staple of reporting on the oil countries that the word hardly merited italics any more. Princes, governors, even the king held their own majlises, group meetings, where citizens came to speak directly to their rulers and make demands. "This is a form of direct democracy too revolutionary for even America or Russia!" I had been told by Massoud, my editor. It was traditional. Arabian rulers had held majlises for a thousand years.

"To complain about noisy neighbors. To say dowries are too high. And especially to get money. That's all they're for. Majlises are quaint. Go to one in Riyadh! You'll meet some bedouin." This was sarcastic; after all, he was a cosmopolitan Jeddawi and often boasted that on his first visit to Riyadh he had cried at the very sight of the city, and never gone back.

"What do you know about Naser Saeed?" I asked Khalil. I asked everyone this and rarely got an answer. Khalil sipped more *siddiqi*.

"He wrote a book called *Tarikh Al-Saud*, The History of the Saud Family. He tells a lot about their secrets. If you manage to catch that book, they will kill you," he added confidently.

"Have you seen it? Have you ever read any of it?"

"I have only heard about it. It's a thousand pages long—like an encyclopedia, published in Beirut or Cairo, or maybe Baghdad." He cackled. "For whoever needs a thousand pages to tell us this family is rotten! And if they find you with it, *khalas!*" I had never heard of this book—it had been published only one year previous, after Saeed's abduction—but now had much more of a mission for Riyadh, with visions of tracking down the Arabian equivalent of Emmanuel Goldstein's *Theory and Practice of Oligarchical Collectives* in *1984*.

"Peter, how much do you earn?" Khalil asked abruptly.

"How much do I earn?" What a question! I told him and he meditated for a moment.

"That's not a lot. You'll never be rich with a salary like that. And your family background is not Arab?" My nickname here, as in Egypt, was Boutros—Arabic for Peter—and I could read and write the language. I was often taken to be an uppity second-generation Palestinian or Lebanese who had ceased to identify with the Arabs; Khalil knew that was not the case, even though his grandmother thought me a total fraud. "The light-skinned ones are the worst," she assured him, "and the Christians—God forbid! They learn five words of English and forget who they are." She always greeted me with a mocking, "Welcome, Boutros! How are things in America?" and a screech of laughter.

"You know it isn't."

"So"—he looked at me warily—"why are you here? Why did you leave America to come to this place?"

"I was implicated in the Watergate break-in," I told him. "This is part of my sentence."

He laughed—even the remotest bedouin knew that "Watergate" was funny.

I had not forgotten about Moussa Sadr, who had still not turned up. The disappearance that seemed, when I first heard of it, like a freak international incident, a magic trick still trying to work itself out after going tragically awry, now more resembled the middle chapters of an Agatha Christie mystery. Sadr never reappeared after the afternoon of August 31, 1978, when an official Libyan car had picked him up at his hotel in Tripoli for a meeting with the Libyan leader, Colonel Qaddafi. He was reportedly sighted in Baghdad, Damascus, and Tehran—false leads, unless, like the Blessed Fr. Pio Forgione, the Imam possessed the gift of bilocation.

Libya had claimed that Imam Sadr and his two traveling companions had flown to Rome on August 31, 1978. The Imam's family poured scorn on this, asking why on earth Sadr would have gone to Rome, of all places, when he had pressing business in Beirut and his wife was very ill.

The Italians investigated and found that neither Moussa Sadr nor his assistant, Sheikh Yaacoub, nor their journalist companion, Abbas Badreddine, had ever entered Italy. The Vatican concurred, saying that Sadr—with whom they were on good terms—could not have entered Rome without their knowledge. Enter Agatha Christie: the missing men's suitcases were discovered in the Rome Holiday Inn a few weeks later; they had been left there on September 1, 1978, the day after the men had disappeared in Libya. Mrs. Sadr and Mrs. Yaacoub flew from Beirut to Rome and identified the suitcases as their husbands'. Colonel Qaddafi insisted that Sadr had been kidnapped in Europe, and provided many uproarious but unhelpful statements alleging that "the Israeli, Iranian and U.S. intelligence agencies, plus the Red Brigades and extremist German organizations, were behind his disappearance."

Events had conspired to uncover Sadr's importance after his

disappearance, which had come at a low point in his political fortunes. Imam Sadr had been a relative, in-law, and close ally of Ayatollah Khomeini. It was with Khomeini's blessing (and that of Savak, the Shah's intelligence agency) that Sadr left Iran for Lebanon in 1959 to lead Lebanon's one million Shiites. He was the architect of the Shiite awakening that would hand the Israeli army its first decisive defeat and inflict on the United States its worst casualties since Vietnam. The Islamic revolutionary government of Khomeini did not accept Libya's explanations of the disappearance, and demanded that Sadr be released from his Libyan captivity. The Saudi Arabians took the same position. They were not Shiites, in fact they hated them, but they hated Libya more.

Oddly enough, Jeddah was a logical place to start investigating the mystery, because this commercial entrepôt was the gateway to Mecca, and every important Muslim had to pass through sometime or another. And the newspaper had a file on Imam Sadr. He was born in Qom, Iran, on the ides of March, 1928, into a family of distinguished religious scholars from southern Lebanon. He was appointed leader of Lebanon's Shiite Muslims by the consensus of the Shah's government and the senior ayatollahs of Iran and Iraq, including Sadr's distant relative Ruhollah Khomeini.

In Lebanon, Sadr formed lasting friendships with Christian as well as Muslim leaders and founded orphanages, vocational schools, and religious societies for the miserably poor Shiite communities of Beirut, Baalbek, and southern Lebanon. When things began to go wrong for Lebanon (Palestinian refugees and the rise of the PLO, the civil war, Syrian intervention, Israeli raids), he moved to improve the Shiites' social position with boycotts and massive political actions. He protested the violence that was slowly destroying the country, and went on a dramatic hunger strike at a mosque in Beirut to demand peace. It was in the middle of this protest that a land-mine explosion killed thirty young Shiites at a militia training camp near Baalbek, and the Imam was forced to announce that he was secretly building a powerful military organization known as Amal.

At the time, the many factors of irony in this were unavailable to me. Little Amal would fight impressively against Israel, though not before almost dying out. What revived Amal was the Imam's disappearance. It would fracture into new groups—Islamic Amal, Islamic Jihad, Hezbollah—that would terrorize Lebanon and the rest of the world for years, and be co-opted by Syria as a wholly owned client. Worst of all, it may have contributed to Sadr's untimely disappearance. Sadr received financial aid from a great variety of individuals and countries, including Libya, and was known to differ acrimoniously with Colonel Qaddafi over how Libya's money was spent and how Amal was used. Qaddafi wanted Amal to attack Israel; Sadr used Amal to prevent even the PLO from attacking Israel, to avoid Israel's pitiless retaliatory strikes against the Lebanese.

Most interestingly, our Sadr file contained clippings from Egyptian newspapers reporting that Imam Sadr foresaw the fall of the Shah and the establishment of a republican theocracy in Iran; he saw himself as a likely candidate for president of Iran. No wonder he kept such a high profile in Lebanon, and distanced himself so carefully from the Shah's regime, and retained his Iranian citizenship despite acquiring a Lebanese passport in the 1960s.

The diplomats were here, not in Riyadh. The former Imperial Iranian Embassy had become the Embassy of the Islamic Republic of Iran and now bristled with revolutionary spirit. The inevitable break, between Saudi Arabia and aggressively anti-monarchist Iran, had not yet come. Saudi newspapers still duly reported the courteous telegrams that the royal court exchanged with "Sheikh Khomeini"—they rejected the title "Imam"—but already there was tension between this militant mission and Saudi officialdom, and any visitor to the building was harassed by its Saudi security guards.

I often went to chat about the case with the Iranian chargé d'affaires, Ali Asghar Nahavandian (who later embezzled diplomatic funds and fled to Europe), and when I was detained by the guard, who made me fill out detailed forms, Nahavandian appeared on the building's stucco porch to demand I be allowed in. The embassy staff and guards often got into shouting matches.

"You have no right to capture the guests of Islamic Iran's embassy!" was Nahavandian's shout, in heavily Persianized Arabic. The guard replied with a sort of grumble amplified to a shout to dismiss this shrill foreigner, and they would often keep at it after I had slipped into the reception alcove, where an Ethiopian receptionist presided. His Persian seemed rudimentary, and Ethiopians were among the most poorly paid imported workers—could Iran afford only him? Or did the Saudis strictly limit the number of Iranian staff? One day I asked him.

"I have a hard job to fill," he answered readily, and in perfect English. "There can be only so many Iranians posted here, and other Persian speakers would tend to be from Iraq, Bahrain, or Kuwait, and they would be Shiites and thus unacceptable to the Saudis. Others who speak Persian would be Americans or Westerners and thus unacceptable to the Iranians. I was previously employed as a chauffeur by the ambassador of the Imperial

Iranian Embassy, His Excellency Jaafar Raed, so I was kept on by the representative of the Imam, as a secretary."

The interior of the chancery was a bizarre study in gore and chic, and would have seemed perfectly in place as the set for a John Waters movie; *Desperate Living* comes to mind. There were actually three components: the garish, overstuffed, and gilded Louis XV armchairs known derisively in Egypt as Louis Farouq, presumably left over from the Shah's day; beautiful Persian carpets, woodwork, glasswork, and marble; and the monstrous atrocity photographs demonstrating the Shah's brutality. These huge posters and glossy blow-ups of severed heads, splayed corpses, gouged-out eyes, and stark documentary shots of torture victims (nailless hands, seared backs, bullet-riddled torsos) loomed everywhere; there was no way to avoid looking at them. The commonest motif was the shoe containing a severed foot—a very close shot. In later years, when the Iraqis and Lebanese began showcasing the atrocities committed against them, they made widespread use of the shoe with the severed foot, but it started as an Iranian concept. At some point it ceased being a mere news-photo and was introduced as a concept in decor that swept all their embassies. High along the walls there were banners proclaiming CLERGY AGAINST CORRUPTION AND NOT CIVILIZATION, DEATH TO AMERICA, and CHINA, RUSSIA, AMERICA, AND ISRAEL ARE ENEMIES OF OUR NATION. It was obviously the embassy's wish that any point of view expressed by its diplomats should be considered with this twenty-minute course in their suffering fresh in mind; they generally kept you waiting about that long.

Here I drank tea with Nahavandian and his consul, who seemed to have nothing better to do in this hostile city.

"It vos hoped," Nahavandian told me, "zat Moussa Sadr could

have been the president for Iran of Islam. Until now Imam Khomeini is doing everything to find him." He supplied detailed information about Iran's assistance to the Muslims in Lebanon, and gave me armloads of propaganda, which drew baleful stares from the guards when I signed out.

Despite my steady output of business articles, the editor got edgy about my visits to the despised Shiite lair. "Why would an American reporter want to listen to anything they have to say?" he grouched. One day the Ministry of Information asked him the same question, and I was sent to Riyadh.

7

The View from Maazar Street

I lived for one year in room 103 of the deluxe Riyadh Inter-Continental Hotel in the Saudi capital. No hotel is sumptuous for that long: living in one room is living in one room, no matter how cozy the easy chairs or how speedy the dry cleaning service. Most grating as the months wore on was the in-house video program, which was rebroadcast every three days with only the slightest changes. Two unvarying offerings were *Gambit* (1966) with Shirley MacLaine and Michael Caine, which I knew by heart within four months (the best line was Mac-Laine's, as a bar girl posing as a millionaire's wife: "A most impressive art collection, Mr. Shahbandar. It must be worth hundreds of dollars!") and an episode of *Charlie's Angels* entitled "Angels in Chains," in which the sexy detectives infiltrated a redneck women's prison to find a missing inmate. The jailers were running a prostitution ring, which the Angels aimed to crack by playing the game in skimpy party dresses, always dodging the hostility of a grouchy lesbian "screw" played by Mary Woronov. "Angels in Chains" was a masterpiece of soft-core erotica, and its concessions to its American prime-time audience neatly fit the decency code for Saudi closed-circuit programming.

I was based in the hotel because my editor, Massoud Madani, had made an ads-for-accommodation deal with Raymond Khalifé, general manager of the Inter-Continental and doyen of the city's hoteliers. The sprawling beige hotel, faced with sandstone and marble, sat behind curving drives and profuse gardens in Maazar Street, opposite the boxy palace of Prince Muhammad "Abu Shirreyn," whose execution of his granddaughter for adultery touched off the "Death of a Princess" scandal. It was not the severely alcoholic old prince's intrigues that worried me at the time, though—it was my own. Shortly after moving into room 103, I watched a succession of workmen fix recessed ceiling lights that didn't need fixing and carry out other unnecessary maintenance on the room. So I assumed that my privacy was being permanently compromised by the Interior Ministry. My suspicions were routinely confirmed for years after I moved out of the hotel: I impressed every major journalist who registered in the Inter-Continental—columnist Georgie Ann Geyer, David Ignatius of the *Wall Street Journal,* David Ottaway of the *Washington Post,* Bob Reinhold of the *New York Times,* Joseph Fitchett of the *International Herald Tribune,* and a dozen others—by guessing their room number before they told me.

Massoud visited Riyadh once a month for meetings at the Ministry of Information, where the minister and the kingdom's seven editors-in-chief settled a loose information policy—the papers were privately owned but beholden to their largest subscriber. The government dumped hundreds of copies of each paper at the ministries and universities each day, which amounted to a biggish subsidy. Only rarely did the minister actually issue orders to the editors; in one case, when the Syrian government massacred 15,000 of its citizens following an uprising in the city of Hamah in 1982. Most of the newspapers wanted to print bold editorials lambasting President Hafez al-Asad. "We hate his government," the minister conceded to the editors, "but what can we do? Syria is a brother." "So," sighed Massoud that afternoon, "we'll just bash Begin again."

It was on one of these trips (they were short—he was a Jeddawi and found Riyadh hideous and claustrophobic) that Massoud took me around to the ministries to meet some of the officials. He wanted me to cover business, but most business was generated by the government, so I had to be familiar with the ministry budgets, new projects, and contacts. And the presence of the king in Riyadh drew prominent official visitors: Margaret Thatcher, Helmut Schmidt, Indira Gandhi, and—always secretly—Egyptian and Iraqi officials, especially in the summer of 1980, as Iraq prepared for war with Iran.

I looked up Hamdan, my Saudi friend from Cairo, who had moved back to his family's house in Riyadh. One afternoon, as we were playing backgammon at his house, the telephone rang. Hamdan answered, said, "One moment, please," and handed me the receiver. "Hello!" I said, but heard only a girl's laugh and a click. "Crank calls," explained Hamdan. "Girls just call around until they find another girl to talk to, or a foreigner. They won't talk to a Saudi man. My sisters do it all the time."

I looked up Donna, one of the friends Linda Leon had made here before fleeing back to Egypt. We had little in common, but made plans to start fermenting grape juice into wine; she was looking for good recipes, and I promised to deliver all the ingredients. Donna lived west of the city in an isolated desert suburb consisting of ten high-rise blocks for university faculty, which made a far more suitable premises for winemaking than my hotel room.

Crime was not reported in the Saudi newspapers, only punishments, and while the amputation of hands (for stealing) and flogging (for drunkenness) were carried out in hospitals and prisons, respectively, beheadings were public. Executions took place in front of the downtown mosque after noon prayers on Friday perhaps ten times a year, and reported the next day; they were not announced in advance. Expatriate workers, American and British especially, were fond of the spectacle and were often politely pushed to the front of the crowd for the best view. Dira Square was closed to traffic on execution days. Between the khaki-hued mosque on the west side of the square and the tall clock tower in the middle, the plaza was strewn six inches deep with sand and cordoned off. Soldiers in green berets stood around the sandy perimeter, hands locked behind their backs, facing the crowd, gazing at the foreigners with what seemed to be intent curiosity.

Subsequently I decided that I had been dragged to witness the beheading, though at the time I knew inevitably I would see one. To hear my friend Al Peyton talk—he was a cost controller at Northrop Corporation's Riyadh office—you would have thought he had left Los Angeles for his job in Riyadh solely in the hope of seeing an execution, and when he phoned me an hour before Friday prayers with news of an imminent beheading I went along. Al had been cultivating a translator in the Ministry of Justice, who finally notified him of a decision to implement a decade-old death sentence. The criminal, one Awad al-Qahtani, had robbed and murdered a widower with two young sons ten years before. Since the next of kin were too young to make a mature decision on whether to accept blood money from the murderer's family or to demand his head, Qahtani was sentenced to prison until the elder turned eighteen. That had just happened; the boy wanted Qahtani dead, and the judge scheduled the beheading for the same week.

When we reached Dira, the balconies of the six-story apartment buildings opposite the mosque were full, and young Saudi boys were perched all over the pedestal of the clock tower. Spectators crowded the tops of the huge Mercedes trucks blocking the side streets, and there were the soldiers, their sunglasses flashing in the sun, looking serenely at the throngs beyond the ropes.

A trussed, headless body with bloody shoulders lay prone on the sand at the edge of wide splashes of blood. A severed head, blindfolded and with tousled hair, sat sideways at least five feet away. The crowd showed no signs of dispersing.

"Damn it," said Al.

Two soldiers led a second blindfolded man out of the mosque.

The loudspeakers on the mosque crackled and split the air with a shrill verse from the Koran, then identified this unfortunate as Qahtani and recited his sentence as his hands were bound behind his back. He was made to kneel in the sand very near the first victim, and I tried to put the word "doubleheader" out of my mind as the executioner, a very courteous black man in ordinary Arab street clothes, patiently positioned Qahtani with his neck stretched out as far as possible. He was probably sedated.

I had not noticed his sword, but now it glittered and swung in a bright arc. *"Kalil,"* commented a nearby Yemeni, clicking his tongue—the sword was dull, probably blunted by the first beheading. I looked away at this Yemeni, at his beautiful kohl-rimmed eyes, while the executioner grunted three more times and the crowd murmured feelingly as though in slight pain. "Man," said Al. The head had still not been severed from the slumping body; when it had lain in the scorching sun for half an hour and the mosque's altar boys—as I thought of them—rolled their thobes up to their knees and waded in to lift it on to a stretcher, the head abruptly flopped down, dragging by—*ugh!*—a sinew? A thread? A third boy hopped after them on his skinny brown legs and huge feet, and re-flopped the blood-soaked, lifeless head on to the chest. Qahtani was slid into the back of an ambulance—*an ambulance?* yes, it had a red crescent on the side—which raced away with its siren whooping.

"That was nothing," was Hamdan's response to my story. *"I saw King Faisal's murderer executed. He deserved it! There were thousands of people crowded into Dira and filling all the side streets. It was Faisal's nephew, Faisal bin Musa'ed. He was only in his twenties, and I don't think they drugged him. It was just a few days after the king's assassination. Everyone cried when his head fell—not for him, stupid, but because it couldn't bring back King Faisal. Because it wasn't enough. That was a historic day. But I'm glad you saw something," he added loftily.

The U.S.–Saudi Businessmen's Association held its sumptuous breakfasts in the banqueting hall of the Inter-Continental. The business breakfasts were a godsend—I had no car yet, so I was having a hard time learning my beat. "Just hang around the lobby and you'll get news and interviews," urged Massoud, who was determined to turn our thin daily into the kingdom's indispensable business paper. He had changed the banner motto from "Jeddah's Quality Newspaper" to the only slightly less ludicrous "Saudi Arabia's Business Daily"; the staff had proposed "Yesterday's News Tomorrow." It was an uphill battle—our competition, the *Arab News*, was said by Naser Saeed's group to be CIA-funded, and was certainly a much slicker product. Although we used a British format and spellings, many Americans read it loyally to protest the *News*'s militant editorial cartoons. In any case, I did successfully cruise the lobby for stories. It was the regular haunt of David Rockefeller, John Connally, Spiro Agnew, Afghan mullahs, and other luminaries with only a lust for petrodollars in common, but nothing beat the breakfasts for gathering newsworthy businessmen and diplomats in one place.

The Saudi and American sponsors of the organization often emphasized that it was the role, the duty, the sacred mission of the business community to foster communication and mutual understanding. The guest speakers were usually cabinet-level officials from either country—Caspar Weinberger and Minister of Petroleum and Mineral Resources Ahmed Zaki Yamani were especially effective—who spent their time at the podium earnestly pleading the special interests of their government. This gave the audience, always overwhelmingly Western and American except for the Arab waiters and doormen, a selective peek over the high walls separating the two communities. A few Saudi merchants attended, but on the whole they did not need this little window on their own country. It gave me a queer thrill, interviewing Saudi and American businessmen after these breakfasts, to listen to their cross grumbling against the other. Only profit kept them together. The Saudis had the immense cultural advantage of knowing America, sometimes intimately, and speaking English perfectly. The Americans were the provincials: eager, a little tentative, strangers to everything around them, careful not to offend.

"Recently I was waiting for a flight at LAX with my wife and daughters," Saudi Minister of Planning Sheikh Hisham Nazer told a group of nearly 200 breakfasters. (This was in the early 1980s. He would later be ordered by the king to stop calling himself sheikh—only the royal family and clergy were allowed to use titles. Still later, he became minister of petroleum, replacing the similarly de-sheikh'd Ahmed Zaki Yamani.) The sea of Americans murmured appreciatively at his homey reference to Los Angeles Airport, and there was a ripple of applause from the aerospace clique—all southern Californians. Some breakfasters had notebooks out between the little cream jugs and plates of scrambled eggs and beef-ham—staffers of the U.S. Embassy commercial section.

"There was an American lady sitting near us, and she heard us speaking in Arabic. Being a typical friendly American"—I rolled my eyes—"she moved closer to us and asked us where we were from. 'From the Kingdom of Saudi Arabia,' I told her. 'Oh my God, how can you stand to live in such a awful place!' she exclaimed.

"Well, she didn't mean to be offensive, and my whole family chuckled"—*Oh, I'll bet*—"but we had quite a nice conversation. She had some idea that women in Saudi Arabia were cooped up indoors and forced to feed the camels or something."

This led into the usual anodyne homily about mutual understanding through business. I took no notes. Luckily the speeches were off the record, to assure an atmosphere of frankness—it was an unnecessary concession to privacy, since so little said was ever newsworthy, though the policy was doubtless kept in order to help conceal the existence of the association. Officially, no foreign clubs were allowed. Nazer moved on from the clout of the business community in changing public attitudes to an anthem to free trade, a plea for energy conservation in America, and the obligatory mock-stern homily about supporting the Palestinian cause. By closing on this note, however, he gave it greater than usual emphasis. Only a few days earlier, the Israeli Air Force had violated Saudi airspace near Tabuk and dropped two huge bales of toilet paper out of their American-built planes—or so rumor had it.

After his speech, Nazer swept out of the room; Saudi grandees really knew how to sweep out of a room. There was a touch of Superman and Darth Vader in these tall, handsome men shrouded in the black, gold-trimmed capes skimming over the acres of soft carpeting in their supple Italian loafers. The rest of us clomped out. As two or three official Saudis stood in a brief huddle by the gleaming limousines, like vulturous superheroes, the ocean of pale Americans crowded out of the banqueting hall like extras in some Wall Street disaster epic. Not one in a hundred understood a word of the language the Saudis were now speaking among themselves—it might have been a superhero code. With its admixture of the medieval and the futuristic, somehow the whole mode of science fiction applied to Riyadh. Nazer was not a prince, but he was part of the constellation of tribal brothers with twenty-word titles who deployed all the world's most awesome technology to enforce royal decrees based on ancient tradition and nepotism. Superpower Americans, perhaps the most secure and self-centered guest community in Saudi Arabia, were delighted to be hired hands on Planet Riyadh.

Our aura was fading fast, however. The awe that America commanded, with its skyscrapers, freeways, magnificent telephone system, and raw riches, was diminishing as Saudi Arabia casually acquired all of these things with great rapidity. Soon their superb industrial and military infrastructures would be complete; already they were our equals in their standard of living. Our emphasis on material well-being backfired when these Arabs had everything we had, with much less trouble. The Saudis saw themselves as our absolute superiors. The secular chaos of America's elections, boisterous press, and above all the public sex culture, seemed, except in small doses, to disgust them.

I had ten minutes to circulate and bother the merchants for reactions to Nazer's speech before leaving for an urgent rendezvous downtown. The Americans filed into the lobby of the Inter-Continental's ballroom complex, accompanied by a dull roar of shop talk. Since the city had no bars, theaters, cinemas, or real clubs, this was the month's best opportunity to mingle and discuss business, royal corruption, the Shiites in the Eastern Province, the ban on foreigners owning land, shoplifting Arabs in London, the hypocrisy of it all. They all would like to have seen London's Arab and Iranian shoplifters get their hands cut off. Most of all, there was grumbling about the Shiites. Mutual respect and understanding through business had brought little understanding of those dwellers over the world's most coveted oil reserves. The Shiites were not in a position to do much business, and their oil reserves were government property. The Shiites were the poorest and most oppressed citizens in the country, only because of the government's sectarian bigotry—most of the population, and all of the money, was Sunni Muslim. As the least privileged segment of society, the Shiites had had to work for a living; the only native blue collar workforce, they worked in the oil industry. A few months earlier, in November 1979, the Saudi National Guard had killed 17 unarmed Shiites whose religious procession suddenly turned political. Troops also arrested at least 200 young Shiites in their homes. Shiite boys got upset and bashed in the windows of Saudi-British Bank branches in Qatif and Safwa. Americans had no sympathy for them—the Shiite ayatollahs in Iran were holding more than fifty Americans hostage—so their attitudes matched the Saudi government's. The business community had no contacts outside the ruling class, so that despite their excellent royal contacts and shrewd deals they were always the first to be taken by surprise when any political thing went rancorously wrong—they were always the last to understand, the angriest and most betrayed.

"In 1973," an American businessman, Preston Brooks, confided to me one Fourth of July, as he gloatingly watched his Saudi guests drink beer on his lawn in Suleimaniya, "one of my Saudi business friends said, 'I'll never think of you or America in the same way again.' Fucking bastard!"

The U.S. had, in that year, arranged the largest military airlift in history to help Israel defeat the Arabs in the Yom Kippur War; Brooks knew that, of course, but was furious that an Arab would mix politics with business.

Carter was president. At the Inter-Continental this morning there was a lot of talk about the impending presidential election and Ronald Reagan, the clear favorite of the heavily Republican American contingent here. The Saudis needed convincing: not only did Reagan have a history of brainless anti-Arab remarks, he was an actor. There was an Arab insult, "son of a dancer," which would probably have been "son of an actor," had acting existed as a profession in Saudi Arabia.

". . . And we can't own a single grain of sand in this country," Preston Brooks was muttering to Craig Hoover. They had been discussing Saudi real estate coups in Beverly Hills, and this topic never made it farther than the acreage and price before turning into a bitter review of the Saudi law that banned landownership by foreigners.

"I hear Yamani has himself a new place in Virginia," offered Hoover.

"Don't even mention Zaki to me, because he's my landlord, and I'm paying 50,000 riyals a month for something I don't wanna describe," said Brooks. "I've told him, 'Zaki, when the Jews were being kicked outta the Holy Land, your people must have got into the wrong line.' Because he's a Jew like the rest of them. They're all cousins! They say the Jews and the Palestinians better never make friends, because the rest of us will be in for it. They're the Jews of the Arab world."

Every sect and nationality in the Arab world was known as "the Jews of the Arab world." It was a boast. In Saudi Arabia's agricultural province, Gassim, a wealthy farmer proudly told me that his tribe were "the Jews of the Arab world." I heard it from Druze, Palestinians, Copts, even from an ethnic Persian in Iraq; from everyone, naturally, except Arab Jews. It implied wily, moneyed machismo and had no overtones of religion, suffering, or dispersal.

"The Arabs are pretty smart—in a thousand years they never even invented a *chair!*"

"Well, it would have been a little impractical for nomads to drag chairs around in the desert. They had cushions," I offered.

"You've got a point there," said Brooks, no doubt thinking, *another journalist gone bush.* Any defense of the Arabs, like any sign of familiarity with their history, religion, or culture, was highly suspect here, not only for its obvious effeteness, or the threat it posed toward commerce as the sole legitimate means of achieving mutual respect, but because of its innate poor taste. American businessmen here tended to regard themselves as martyrs, the footstools of ignorant tyrants. They could not own land, build a church, or drink liquor openly. It was commonly assumed that this discrimination against foreigners and Christianity were the gravest injustices in the country and portended the fall of the Saudi state. They would pay for this! The longer Americans stayed here and the richer they got, the more bitterly they resented their hosts. Preston had lived in Riyadh for fifteen years, and his wife had worked at the U.S. diplomatic mission here for all that time—they had more highly placed Saudi friends than anyone else, owned crates of royally imported *Iohanna Mashi* (literally, "Johnny Walker"), and hated the country with a passion. In five years I never heard them talk of moving back to Arizona, and even their vacations were spent in Europe.

Actually, the government's maddening restrictions against foreigners were genuinely popular among the Saudis—to the king, we were suppliers of weapons, technology, and security, and represented a temporary irritant to their rather closed society, but had no importance beyond that. Brooks did not realize that ordinary Saudis assumed what *he* assumed, that our presence was colonial. Many of my Saudi friends who liked America were filled with lighthearted pride at their government's ban on churches. It wasn't just nationalism: for one thing, the ban reminded foreigners not to put down roots here, and it wasn't appropriate in the Islamic Holy Land. Islam was the most advanced, the "latest" religion, and permission for any church (let alone synagogue) to teach its primitive and corrupted religion would seem like a throwback.

"Nazer was fabulous," said Hoover. Abdelaziz al-Ghamdi had just joined the little circle of men drinking juice.

"He's a very impressive man," said al-Ghamdi. "But these days we are thinking about the Zionist lobby."

"Reagan is going to get set straight," said Al Calabrese, who taught English at Riyadh (later King Saud) University, but never missed a businessmen's breakfast. Four years of teaching censored classics here had enabled him and his wife to buy an apartment in Paris.

"The American media, which I am often ashamed of, portrays him as some kind of a dope," conceded Brooks. "But the guy was the governor of California for two terms."

"You knows who owns the media," said Hoover.

"We hope for a good relationship, and we'll give him a chance," said al-Ghamdi's friend Omar al-Bakr, a dead ringer for William Frawley, gathering in his black cloak at the front.

"He used to dress up as a cowboy," murmured al-Ghamdi to al-Bakr in Arabic. He said *ra'iy al-baqr* lest anyone understand the common loan-word *cowboy*.

"Do you think he will put pressure on the Israelis to help solve the Palestinian question?" al-Bakr asked the Americans. "As Sheikh Nazer said, it is critical for us."

"And to us, too—listen, like the president's brother said, there's a heck of a lot more Arabians than Jews," said Hoover.

"Quite apart from that, sooner or later the U.S. government has to see the light. Israel wields great power in America, and at a cost to all of us," Calabrese said.

"Those poor people, in the refugee camps, still have the keys to their houses around their necks, waiting to go home, but the Zionists confiscated everything," al-Ghamdi sighed.

"We don't like to see the Palestinian people become radical— if they don't achieve their legitimate rights, they can"—Al-Bakr, having failed to locate the right expression in English, settled for Englished Arabic. "They can smash the world and scream in our faces!"

"They started doing that already!" said Brooks grimly. He was put out by this outrageously political discussion. It was bad enough that a minister of planning, addressing a friendly business audience, should mention that most inconvenient of all topics, the Palestinian question, but now, even in small talk? With a couple of nobodies who wouldn't even hire Palestinians? Brooks was bitter about American support for Israel but thought that the Arabs should help "their own" and not look to American business. He liked Saudis when they'd had a few drinks and talked about what a burden it was, having to spout all this piety about Palestine. And now al-Ghamdi, having performed his duty, obliged him.

"I myself don't like to deal with the Palestinians, because they are ungrateful. And they swear a lot—they have dirty tongues, even the educated ones."

The Palestinians and Lebanese dialects had a staggering fund of obscene expressions, almost all explicitly sexual, though the word for fuck was rarely used, only the body parts—"My-prick-in-you!" "Damned-sister's-cunt!" These Saudis rarely swore—I had often marveled at the variety of harmless, plaintive religious interjections they used instead. The younger generation, though, was something else.

Al-Bakr nodded, and Brooks, Hoover, and Calabrese all nodded—with Brooks, it was a sort of diagonal *and how!* nod. This kind of casual bigotry led Americans to believe that tactful Arabs, anxious not to embarrass them, really hated and distrusted the Palestinians—and some Saudis (notably the tough interior minister, Prince Naif) did feel that way. They also welcomed it as an absolution of guilt and took great comfort in then telling others, "Listen, these people *hate* the Palestinians!"

"Many of them are very Westernized," said Brooks. The two Saudis smiled icily at this unintentional poison compliment. Brooks saw it as the highest encomium, reserved for princes who played tennis, Arabs with blond wives, anyone with no political opinions that would offend him. Brooks had no Arab friend close enough to tell him how offensive it was; his Saudi business associates indulgently let it pass—a striking example of how mutual profit helped to perpetuate antagonism.

I realized that Brooks and Hoover were looking at me. How could they talk with a reporter around? I left to go and see Hussein.

My story for the day, about an industrial trade show at the Atallah House hotel, would be sent from the telex room a little later in the morning. Ironically, that little piece ("Trade Fair Heavy Duty Success"), which featured a cameo appearance by an

American sand importer—it was a special fine sand used for industrial filtration—was picked up by the Saudi opposition and reprinted in their monthly organ, *Al-Thawrah al-Islamiya* (The Islamic Revolution) as an example of the profligate stupidity of the Saudi government ("Regime Buys Sand from Its American Masters!").

I collected my mail, which consisted of the new *Economist*, three days late because of the censor. I checked the damages. Four pages of text missing, splotches of black ink over several advertisements, and the contents page messily glued to the front cover to conceal a Remy Martin ad. That always irked me, because with a ruined contents page I would not be able to discover what was on the excised pages in the International section, though I could guess (Israeli jets and toilet paper—*The Economist* had excellent spies in the British community for that kind of gossip).

Speeding down Maazar Street to the tree-lined boulevards of Naseriya, the royal neighborhood (it used to be a walled enclave—one of the gates still stood, as a monument, but in this neighborhood there was not a prayer of getting a picture of it), I tried to prepare myself to meet Hussein. He was the most religious person I knew, and as yet fit nowhere in the life I had begun to build for myself in Riyadh. I was making contacts, getting myself known, establishing sources in all of the ministries and anonymous-looking (because, strictly speaking, illegal) diplomatic missions, and was cultivating him because he claimed to know about the strange disappearance of Imam Moussa Sadr in Libya.

Hussein was a poor Shiite peasant from southern Lebanon who had known the Imam. He made the *hajj* to Mecca every year because it was his only chance to see his wife and daughters, who came from Lebanon by bus and, like the rest of the pilgrims, were not permitted to come to Riyadh lest they seek employment. In Riyadh he spent much of his time praying for strength: he was so good-looking that women in the King Faisal Specialist Hospital, where he worked as an orderly, did not leave him alone. And like me, he got crank calls from lonely Saudi women, though his were probably not random. I had met him while giving blood at that hospital—when noon prayer was called, the hospital sheikh hesitated before barking *"Salat!"* at Hussein. He took in his long black beard and cat's eye silver ring—a badge of Shiism—and asked a little disdainfully, "Are you one of them?" Hussein turned away, but glanced at me and sighed, "They are all Israelis."

The King Faisal Hospital was a Saudis-only referral facility mainly serving the royal family. Non-Saudis got through its doors only to do a day's work or give blood, though once I went to visit a patient. On that memorable day I stood in the blazing heat outside the guard house flipping through the computer register of admittees to find my invalid, and was stunned at the revelation of its maternity ward: the printout was an unending cataract of BABY BOY AL-SAUD, BABY BOY AL-SAUD, BABY GIRL AL-SAUD—at least forty additions to the royal payroll in one week. The regal maternity ward must have taken up half the hospital. Was this an unusual week, or was the royal family growing at the rate of a thousand princes each year? The sheer number of princes seemed to belittle the common man, the more so since no duties, only privileges accrued to the royals.

There was Naseriya Gate, surrounded on its traffic island by playing fountains, its white gingerbread, green and pink bricks shining in the sun. It led back into palace-choked Naseriya. I took a left to Bridges Street, another left on Television Street, and straight to Water Tower Park, across from the low palace where King Faisal had been shot dead by his nephew in March 1975. This was downtown, where enormous new houses gave way to skyscrapers, broken mud-brick hovels, and huge sweet-smelling bazaars. King Faisal Hospital housed its European and American staff in a splendid compound in Naseriya, its Egyptians in an apartment building in Suleimaniya, and its Lebanese in a former hotel surrounded by slaughterhouses on the edge of downtown.

There was trouble at the cross-streets below Faisal's palace. A white Toyota truck was edging slowly out into the intersection, trying to penetrate the roaring two-way traffic. The driver had a red light but—this sometimes happened—obviously did not know or care about the color of the lights on the poles the foreigners had put up on these corners. Other drivers were bellowing and honking their horns. The old man at the wheel was clearly nearsighted, too—his nose was almost flat against the windshield. When the traffic stopped he swerved through the intersection, making a left, causing the black-veiled woman in the back of his truck, and the goat, on the seat beside him, to sway and bleat at the same instant.

The shabby Riyadh Hotel housed about 200 Lebanese, mostly Muslims; and most of those Shia Muslims from the south, and they rarely left this building except to work or shop, or to visit other Lebanese. Hussein and his friends seemed to dread equally the Saudi, American, British, Egyptian, Yemeni, and other inhabitants of this city, which they unapologetically detested. Emigration, they felt—citing Imam Sadr—was an honorable alternative to presiding over starving families in Nabatiya or Tyre or Sarafand—their southern villages—but they felt too persecuted here to want to mix.

Hussein's friend Ali was especially fond of quoting Moussa Sadr. He explained to me at unnecessary length that he liked me despite the fact that I was American, not because of it; not that he had anything against Americans. This was his preface to giving me an untitled pamphlet of the vanished Imam's sayings, including remarks to "a group of Beirut intellectuals" in 1970.

> If we honor a white man we honor his race, not the man.
> The problem of racial discrimination in the United States is well known. And the attitude of the U.S. toward the weak or developing countries is tellingly reflected in Viet Nam, the Middle East, Israel, Africa and Latin America. Glorification of the American springs from glorification of the race, not the man— exactly as with the pre-Islamic Arabian tribes of whom it was said that they were magnanimous hosts. Actually their magnanimity was motivated by egoism; it was not true hospitality, since a guest enjoyed honor in this man's house; but when he left the house its owners might pounce on him, rob and kill him. Such magnanimity does no honor to man, only to itself.

This was the translation I made, at Ali's request, for him to show to the Americans he worked with at the hospital. He wanted to work on them slowly to convert to Islam, and had to do it on the job since the hospital guards gave him a hard time when he tried to visit the American residential compound. Here at the Riyadh Hotel there were no guards other than a sad-eyed concierge, also named Hussein, who sat under a poster of snowy mountains looming over red-roofed mansions and a turquoise sea, proclaiming LIBAN, drumming his fingers on the empty guest register. I earned a cigarette every time I signed it in Arabic.

8

Among the Believers

*T*hat year there were more than a million imported Arab workers in Arabia, and most were like Hussein and his friends: young, poor, separated from their families, and almost all Muslim. It was not long before the government saw the folly in this, or imagined that it saw folly. The people posing the greatest political risk were these cousins of theirs, they reasoned, these Lebanese, Syrians, Egyptians, Palestinians, and Yemenis, not the gentlemanly, money-drugged Americans, British, French, and Germans, who could not be spared anyway. As a result, sometime around 1984, the kingdom's policy on importing labor shifted in favor of Koreans, Indians, Pakistanis, Filipinos, and Sri Lankans. These "working hands," in the Arab phrase, were blessedly non-political, non-Arab, non-Muslim, and dirt cheap, and they would supply the secretaries, nurses, chauffeurs, construction workers, and accountants that the country needed, while the Arab guest workers, especially Lebanese, were sent home. By the time 1985 rolled around, it was hard to believe that an apartment like Hussein's could have existed just three or four years earlier.

His immaculate room was furnished only with a television, a coffee table, and cloth-covered foam mats around the walls; this Arab sitting room was called a *majlis*. On the television was propped a picture of his beautiful young kerchiefed wife, Amna, holding an infant. With those big dark eyes and aquiline nose she could have been an Italian peasant girl, one of Tevye's modest daughters, even a Gypsy, but the village behind her—a mosque and tall pines amid terraced hills—could only have been Lebanese. Another snapshot showed the baby (a girl, Zeinab) in someone's lap, holding in her tiny dimpled hands a framed picture of Ayatollah Khomeini. The third picture showed an imposing black-turbaned mullah flanked by three bearded young men in a town square; a yellow Kodak sign was visible above a shuttered shop. All but one of the younger men were smiling.

"Sayyid Moussa," Hussein said reverently, pointing to the clergyman. "Sayyid" meant "descendant of Muhammad," as Sadr was. "Me, my brother Hassan, and my brother Hadi." The scowler. "This was in Nabatiya. Hadi was a Marxist and didn't like religion. Now, *al-hamdulillah*, he is one of the faithful. Sayyid Moussa visited us in this period, but Hadi was drinking whiskey, *astaghfur Allah*, out in the back. We told Sayyid Moussa that Hadi did not want to be seen that way. 'Let him drink it in front of me,' said the imam. 'Why add the sin of hypocrisy to the sin of drunkenness?' "

Hussein smiled at this memory, then added sternly, "I told Hadi, if you continue drinking and playing cards, you are not my brother and I don't know you! God softened his heart."

Hussein's room was a meeting place for his Shiite friends; they were all orderlies or male nurses at King Faisal Specialist Hospital. Only one, Haj Amin, was not; he worked at the Riyadh Central Post Office, where no one knew he was a Shiite. Next door, the Imam Muhammad bin Saud Islamic University used a textbook which debated, among other questions, whether or not Shiites have tails.

"And now, tell me the news," Hussein smiled. As usual, he was not alone—Ali, Mortada, Muhammad, Haj Youssef, and another Hussein were crouched on the mats, smoking and rattling their beads. All had the same sloe eyes, black beards, and bare feet.

I began to describe the businessmen's breakfast.

"The news," grinned Hussein.

He meant news of the Iran–Iraq war, the only subject, apart from Lebanon and Islam, that he would consent to discuss with me. I commented that it was going badly, that the Iraqis were occupying Khorramshahr—Mohammerah, as the Arabs called it.

"Has America decided to help Iran yet?"

"Do you think she will, with her diplomats held prisoner in Tehran?"

"You have to," said Hussein. "You have to tell people."

"Hussein, let's get going," said Haj Youssef.

Hussein looked at his watch and then at me. "Are you coming?"

"Will we be back by evening?"

"God willing. I need your keys." He took my car keys and tossed them to Ali. "Have Youssef take his car, and you drive Peter's car to his house, then come back together. Get gas."

The informal *husseiniyas,* the religious meetings that these Muslims held weekly to exchange news from Lebanon, read the Koran, listen to Radio Tehran, and collect money for the Islamic resistance in southern Lebanon, were never held in the same place twice. Five or six cars were sent all around town picking up members from their apartments or from supermarkets, then drove with vigilant aimlessness around the city before converging on someone's house or someone's friend's house; even at my own house on one occasion, which came as a surprise to me.

My friendship with Hussein and his group, which was a secret from all my other friends, was partially a rebellion against the kingdom. Riyadh rammed religion down your throat—the sole television channel, in particular, seemed inhabited solely by glaring preachers—but forbade you to worship as you chose. My response was to attend Shiite Islamic gatherings and make wine, at which Donna and I had begun to excel. My personal fascination with the ambiguous Imam and my desire to solve the mystery were bolstered by the Iran–Iraq war, because Saudi Arabia supported Iraq, and propagandized shamelessly against Iran and all Shiites. The ugliness of the Arab world's hostility toward its own Shiites was remarkable, and I felt that Saudi Arabia was abusing its prestige as guardian of Mecca and Medina by hinting that the Shia were "deviants" and ridiculing their clergy. I had to take my stand, and I took it by being part of this friendly Shiite underground.

The first item on the agenda was always an argument over smoking. Almost all thirty of the men chain-smoked, but opening a window was a security risk. Their discussions were largely harmless, but Saudi laws against forming clubs or organizations were strict—the U.S.-Saudi Businessmen's Association was the only one tolerated in Riyadh. When the police or the religious enforcers broke up Christian fellowship gatherings, usually held in the private homes of Americans, Ethiopians, or Filipinos, the charge against them was forming an illegal organization. Even the Catholic masses, celebrated on the Muslim sabbath of Friday, were held in extreme secrecy within the grounds of the enormous U.S. Military Mission on Airport Street. What did the Saudi guards there make of the neat families and little girls in frilly dresses pouring into the base every week? They would certainly know what to make of thirty bearded Shiite men.

"Sayyid Moussa used to smoke!" Muhammad was protesting to the antismoking group, which had the upper hand as we were in an unusually small room; six men sat on a short couch with everyone else cross-legged on the floor. A large shortwave radio was enthroned on a coffee table in the center, surrounded by tiny glasses of tea and a tall suction-type tea urn. This was As'ad's apartment in al-Kharj, a town eighty miles southeast of Riyadh, famous for a dairy farm and three huge abandoned, interconnecting palaces that had belonged to King Abdelaziz. I had often visited al-Kharj on picnics, and strolled through the dusty palaces whose corridors were full of snarling cats and heaps of Pepsi cans. As'ad's little place was on a side street on the opposite side of town from the Riyadh highway, shaded by dense beige clumps of dead palm trees: this part of the oasis had gone dry. We had never come so far for a meeting, and I wondered if the group had used up all the available places in Riyadh.

It was put to a vote: no smoking. Discussion then started in earnest about the recently completed *hajj* to Mecca, where Iranian pilgrims had rioted and been beaten up by the Saudi police. Hussein, Mortada, and Haj Amin had seen it all.

"The Iranian women were marching with portraits of Imam Khomeini!" Hussein declaimed. "Their faces shone with faith! They were in formation like an army on parade—like *teeth!*" His smile was beatific. He went on describing them for so long that I felt as if I were at a medieval court where a poet or jester was providing the kind of epic storytelling entertainment that television would ultimately supplant. He moved on to an Iranian rally in which many Lebanese joined, the loud prayers in unison, the soul-stirring cries of "Death to Israel," "Death to America," and *"Allahu akbar, Khomeini rahbar!"* This meant "God is most great" (in Arabic) and "Khomeini is leader" (in Persian). "I am sorry to say that some of our brothers, from Egypt and Africa in particular, did not hear this correctly, and reported to the police that mobs of pilgrims were chanting *'Allahu akbar, Khomeini akbar!'* "

"God forgive them!" everyone muttered hastily at the sacrilegious implication.

"Then the security forces made trouble for us, and it was only with God's protection that we were not injured. Some posters of the Imam, may God lengthen his life, were torn up. That was only a prelude to the troubles in Medina."

People had died in the riots in Medina, the second holiest city, where many pilgrims paid homage to the Prophet Muhammad's tomb after making the pilgrimage to Mecca. Medina was especially holy to Shiites because many of the Prophet's family, whom they held in special regard, were buried there: Hassan, Ali Zain al-Abidin, Muhammad al-Baqir and others. Medina itself had a small community of native Saudi Shiites, who went out of their way to welcome their foreign coreligionists. Even in the Shah's day, the Shiites among Medina's taxi drivers flew little Iranian flags from their radio aerials to attract business from Persian pilgrims.

"We went to the Baqii Cemetery to pray for the intercession of the Prophet's daughter and the sinless imams, his grandchildren," intoned Hussein. "Imagine our pain, when, to reach out to the glorious martyrs from our oppression, we saw how broken and uncared for their graves were. Garbage was strewn throughout the cemetery. The walls were falling down, and it became clear to us that the royal regime has no respect for the faithful"— *al-mu'mineen,* as he always referred to the Shiites—"and none for the blessed family of the Prophet, peace be upon him. We stood by the walls and wept and prayed, and police cars in several corners of the street watched us."

His voice was tearful now, and several of his listeners sniffled and blew their noses. How would I feel if I saw Jesus's grave all broken and full of crushed cigarette cartons? I remembered the Ascension. These analogies were never easy.

While each of the Muslims present took five minutes to say what the pilgrimage meant to him, As'ad began quietly tuning in the Voice of the Islamic Republic from Radio Tehran, which had a daily Arabic transmission to the countries bordering the Persian Gulf. The Saudis jammed the signal, and I always dreaded trying to hear the faint whisper of Iranian propaganda within the ear-splitting tone used to block it out.

I was ignored in a friendly enough way, since I had nothing to contribute to the meeting. Occasionally Hussein or Mortada would lean over to ask, "Are you following everything?" and serve me more tea. My interest was in learning more about Moussa Sadr, the religious life of the Shiites in Lebanon, and in doing something vaguely risky in this monotonous city, but I was getting an education I had not counted on. Before meeting Hussein, my picture of Lebanon had consisted of slobs in fezzes playing backgammon and making shady "import-export" deals; ersatz "beautiful people" planning their skiing/swimming day trips; and mobs of angry young men randomly massacring busloads of people. It was hard to think of Beirutis, in particular, as anything but vain, since they seemed to lack the Egyptian sense of poise and self-identity. The Lebanese could not say two sentences without rhapsodizing about Beirut, and it was hard to imagine that they ever told the truth. There was a honking false note in the descriptions of Beirut before the war, the same note of ludicrous pathos sounded when *Gone with the Wind* opens with "There was a Land of Cavaliers and Cotton Fields called the Old South. Here in this pretty world Gallantry took its last bow. Here was the last ever to be seen of Knights and their Ladies. . . ."

Hussein and his friends were so articulate and had such exquisite manners that I was appalled at my misconceptions and vowed to learn more. With the exception of my parents, there were no more devout or gracious people I had ever seen. And these were considered to be the dregs of Lebanon!

And in my research on Moussa Sadr, the good Imam had come across as a manipulator, sent by the Shah as nuncio to Lebanon, who had treacherously gone over to the cause of his fellow mullah, his cousin Khomeini—until I met Hussein. Who could see such people impoverished and maltreated and not rebel? I began to appreciate Sadr's bold abandonment of the Shah. In knowing Hussein, I had walked into an Arabian sandstorm which had, like the desert tempests in the open Nejd, obliterated all my old landmarks and created an entirely new landscape.

Hussein was frank about his interest in me. He needed to preach to someone as yet unconverted, though he had announced his intention to change that; and he thought it a good idea to have an American friend, since he talked sometimes of moving to the United States. Mainly, he wanted me to convert to Islam, though he claimed he would exert no pressure; I would succumb through seeing the example of him and his friends, and then they would have an even more valuable ally in me. And he was refreshed by being with an American. He had renewed his Islam after several years as an ardent Marxist, and now felt wonderfully free of secular rancor. He wanted America to be friendly and pro-Muslim. Once he bellowed at me, as I walked through his door, *"Ta'al ila hayth an-nak'ha! Ta'al ila Marlbooro!"* ("Come to where the flavor is! Come to Marlboro country!").

". . . and now we will listen to the words of Imam Khomeini, the humbler of tyrants and smasher of idols!" Hussein was saying.

"Idol smasher," repeated Mortada slowly, so that I would understand.

"Baal breaker," I joked, and Hussein laughed loudly.

My curiosity about Moussa Sadr was finally indulged, when the barely audible news from Tehran had ended and everyone felt free to open the windows and smoke.

"The Lebanese have had everyone screwing them," was Ali's un-Islamic opening to my questions, as Hussein and the others stretched and poured tea and generally unwound from two hours of praise and glory. "The Syrians, to keep us from fighting Israel.

The Palestinians, who were forced on us because no one wants them and they cannot go home to Palestine. Israel itself, to fight the PLO. Don't forget that the Palestinians are right in their cause, but they are not good people."

"Tell him about what goes on at Rashidiya. At Arqoub," said Haj Youssef.

Ali waved his hand dismissively, explaining only, "They commit a lot of crimes against us, because they don't respect us," but Haj Youssef would not be deterred.

"They have training camps where they bring communist guerrillas and slutty women, very skinny, from Yugoslavia, Germany, Czechoslovakia. And Cubans. They have sex and act like cowboys. And laugh at us. Liberators of Palestine!"

"This is what Imam Sadr was trying to stop," Ali resumed. "He wanted to get respect for us. In Lebanon you have to get respect from outside. You need the Arab countries, like some of the Muslims, or the French, which the Christians cling to for prestige. You need allies. For us we have no one but Iran, which helps Muslims everywhere, but especially the faithful."

Ali went on to describe what life had been like before Moussa Sadr came to Lebanon: illiteracy, malnutrition, and humiliation, "even though the faithful comprised the largest community in the country." The feudal landlords of southern Lebanon fought even lukewarm attempts to improve living conditions and education there; the PLO was like a military dictatorship, and when the Israelis struck at the South to repay PLO operations in Israel, only the Shiites suffered. The big Israeli invasions sent hundreds of thousands of them north, and many, including Mortada, now slurping tea, were reduced to living in automobiles on the shoulder of the Beirut–Sidon highway for weeks.

Moussa Sadr founded Amal, the first Shiite militia, to defend the community, and used both the PLO and Iranians exiles opposed to the Shah to train young men in using weapons. No, none of the present group had joined; they had all either been too busy working, or Marxist to sympathize. I recalled that Omar the Egyptian in Jeddah had once bemoaned Sadr's effect on the political left in Lebanon: the Imam had virtually erased the Lebanese communist party's base of peasant support by getting the Shia Muslims interested in religious revival. The worker's party was left, he said, with a thin membership of angry Christian intellectuals and Syrian informers.

Politics in Lebanon were filthy. There was no point in Shiites working within a system that placed no value on them. Only God could save them, and His first step was to place a saintly religious scholar—Khomeini—in the place of the world's richest and strongest emperor, thus putting all Iran's strategic, financial, and military power at the disposal of Islam. Did I appreciate that miracle from the hand of God?

The enemies of Islam could not ignore the unconquerable force of absolute Good, especially since the power of truth had become so clear to the whole world, notably through the humiliation of the Great Satan, the United States, which was utterly paralyzed by the Imam; and here Ali digressed.

Did I have any conception, he asked politely, of the beautiful wholeness of Islam, of how it contained Judaism and Christianity? Was I aware that any really true Jew or Christian had to embrace Islam to fulfil his faith? There was doubt in the imperfect creeds passing for Judaism and Christianity, but none in Islam: one Scripture to supersede all previous scriptures; one Prophet to set the record straight on his predecessors; one way of life, encompassing all facets of life. Ali painted at great length all of the tempting beauties of Islam before returning to the threats encircling it.

"Qaddafi kidnapped Moussa Sadr because Qaddafi stands for Arabism and socialism, for secularism and Americanism, and he was afraid of Islam."

"But Qaddafi is friendly to Iran. Why doesn't Iran force him to release Sadr?"

"They are trying. They always send officials to Libya to investigate, and they reject any diplomatic relations with Libya until Imam Moussa Sadr is back in Lebanon."

I did not tell Ali that Iran had established relations with Libya more than one year before. To placate the Lebanese and Sadr's strong following in Iran, Khomeini announced, simultaneously, a special Iranian commission to investigate Sadr's fate for once and for all. The commission was not actually appointed until five months later, on April 13, 1980; Khomeini canceled it on April 14, and never revived it. A month after that, he received Sadr's family in Qom and told them that "[Sadr's] detention in Libya is a trial borne for the sake of Islam." Hussein and his friends did not know this, and I did not want to tell them; how would I explain knowing so much? They would not believe that I had learned most of it from Egyptian and Iranian newspapers. Already they may have suspected I was a spy, and their openness with me only strengthened my suspicion. They thought they were demonstrating for the ultimate authority, the CIA, how pious and harmless they were, and possibly assumed that they were thus assuring themselves of protection. Hussein had once told me that they would never have included any Saudi in their meetings for fear of being betrayed, but they expected better sense from an American, even, I presumed, an American spy. Implied in their candor was their assumption that the CIA, not the Saudi government, had the ultimate say-so over their safety in this country. No wonder they thought it would be a coup to convert me; and I took their drive to do so as a compliment on my good sense.

"Moussa Sadr is a good example to lead you to Islam," put in Haj Youssef, "but first you must know the Koran. We can read it to you."

"My interest in Moussa Sadr isn't totally religious," I equivocated. "It's also curiosity."

"To know the truth," said Hussein.

I groped for a word meaning *recreational* to describe my curiosity; the closest I could come was *istijmami,* which implied rest and relaxation. "As a reporter."

They all winced, and I guessed why. For them Islamic truth was the goal, not an aid to secular research. Islam stood outside comparative religion: it was the last, best word, making everything else redundant. Research done for the record, rather than as a step toward my conversion, was base, almost simoniac, as if I were playing leapfrog over great Muslim scholars to reach some goal of my own.

We drove back to Riyadh in near silence, past the walled residential compounds put up by foreign companies for their employees and their dependents. They were known by the company names: Alfa-Laval, Vinnell, Lockheed, Northrop. Each had a huge pool and a little row of shops, a rec center and tiny streets. Ironically, these American or British or Swedish enclaves had come to resemble medieval Arab towns, down to the tiny market square, guarded city gate, and deep sense of community, as the Arab city encircling them had demolished all its indigenous features to become a gigantic American-scale metropolis.

Hussein drove me back to my house in Suleimaniya and asked

if he could come up to borrow my copy of the Koran. When I opened the door, he quickly walked through it ahead of me and slid it off the bookshelf.

"We can read this to you, but you shouldn't touch it yet because you are unclean." This word, *najis,* meant ritually impure, as in pork or alcohol; like *traif* in Hebrew. It was why they could not drink tea that I prepared unless they had not actually seen me prepare it. He smiled, tucked the book under his arm, and walked down the dark stairwell—it was nearly eleven at night— and I smiled at his "yet."

Muslims were relentless evangelists. At any given time I was being chased by two or three different spreaders of the word, and all were well-meaning, except for Mahdi, the National Guard correspondent for *Okaz.* The National Guard was the country's second army, classified into tribes and commanded by the king's brother, Crown Prince Abdullah. Mahdi was hugely fat—his Guard duties were limited to composing odes to read at National Guard fêtes, and for us he edited "Odes Corner," a weekly feature. He generally printed his own poems, with eleven or twelve "private answers"—"Dear Brother Misfer bin Rashed bin Khattab in Medina: Thank you for your ode, which was unsuitable for publication. Let us hear from you again."

Mahdi generally harangued me for twenty minutes or so about Islam—"Accept Islam! Why would you refuse salvation? There was a religious conference in Europe with priests and Muslims— all the priests ended up converting! How can you say God is three? How can you say God has children?" But his sermon was only a prelude—after assuring himself that I was damned, he pestered me for whiskey, women, or boys. "You must know

American women. I want to fuck! Any Asian girls? I would be in your debt. Do you know any boys who dance?"

Islam is a tempting faith—in its logic, simplicity, finality, its syncretic inclusion of Judaism and Christianity, even its relative youth—but in Saudi Arabia it was too identified with money and puritanism. When *60 Minutes* filmed a segment in Jeddah, its reporter asked a girls' school headmistress, Cecile Rouchdy, about the restrictions Islam placed upon women—they were not allowed to drive, for example. "Why should we drive! We can hire other people to do it!" she laughed. And she was not even Saudi, but Egyptian, and had already converted so completely to the creed of petro-wealth that she did not see how contemptuous her answer was toward poor Muslim women.

Something else about the faith bothered me. While far more calisthenic even than a Catholic mass, Muslim prayers—repeated five times each day—had a different focus. It was wholly an act of worship, of adoration. *Islam,* of course, means submission.

Conversion was very common in Saudi Arabia and involved, in most cases—I was convinced—a cultural rather than spiritual transformation. I never knew a Christian whose values changed radically after adopting Islam, but the outward changes—especially in name and wardrobe—were always striking. Although Islam was, like Christianity, a faith of "men of every race and tongue, of every people and nation," American converts never failed to adopt, very specifically, the clothes and habits of the desert Arabs. Hameed Holloway, an urbane convert from Lutheranism who worked as a TV film critic on Saudi television, wore a breathtaking elaborate headcloth *(ghotra)* and black woolen ropes *(eqal),* and ankle-length thobe. I cringed for him as he harangued his talk-show guests in Brooklyn English while flipping back the ghotra—his elaborate nomadic chic put his Saudi Arabian guests to shame. Black Aladdin Pickett, an undoubtedly sincere Baltimorean, wore an equally fastidious Nejdi costume for his TV show on Islam. It was as if a Russian Jewish convert to Christianity in Oklahoma made it an article of faith to dress as a cowboy every day, down to the chaps, spurs, and lasso.

My horror was complete when I saw Youssef Islam, né Cat Stevens, in Riyadh: he wore a staggeringly bizarre mélange of Arab, Indian, and Afghani fashion accessories, complete with a turban and an unnatural accent. And yet he was the sincerest of Muslim converts and spoke good Arabic. This outward show was vastly important, and not only to Muslims.

It was a one-way street, of course, since apostasizing from Islam to any other faith was a capital crime, but the same rule of yearning mimicry still applied. I thought back on the churches of Egypt, and the elegant women in low-cut blouses who slipped in around the consecration, gossiped in the rear of the church for twenty minutes, and clicked out on their stiletto heels after communion, having demonstrated their differentness from the Muslims who so vastly outnumbered them. How could it be different in Beirut? I had seen an album of Christmas party photos showing Lebanese Maronites in party hats before immense Santa Claus decorations; I did not have to read their lips to know that they called him Père Noël. How bizarre, in that little biblical country, to see them frantically adopting the secular symbols of the West—Santa, a tree, a buche de Noël—to assert their alienation from their despised Muslim countrymen. Although born Christians, they were converts, but to a political and cultural creed of their own invention. It was not unknown among the Shiites: Hussein had laughingly told me that since the Iranian revolution brightened the prestige of Shiism in Lebanon, clergymen from

Beirut and Baalbek now visited Iran for a week and affected a Persian accent for months afterward, saying *Shaw* for Shah, *Ee-rawn* for Iran and denouncing everyone and everything as *Omree-kaw-ee* (American).

I saw nothing wrong with the conversion game, though I hoped that people really knew what it was they wanted, but it was rare to see a conversion that wasn't more a rejection than a revelation, and a huge display of make-believe and social climbing into the bargain. And converts to Islam at least among the Americans, tended to get along very badly with one another— you got the impression that each one wanted to be the only one and resented all the others. Each wanted to be a social lion of sorts among the Saudis—preaching to the converted being one of their specialties—and shunned other Americans, even the Muslims, so that there was no real community of American Muslims. All seemed relieved to have jettisoned the complexity of their lives back in the black slums or suburban churches, and they invariably had the simplest ideas about what was wrong with the West and what was right with the Middle East. This could not have been too difficult in this rich welfare state in the pristine desert, but the easy solutions of the Islamic state would have been much harder to apply in poorer or more complex Muslim countries—in Egypt, or Bangladesh, for example. Would they have converted there? I did not think it helpful to ask.

Needless to say, the animosity between the two groups—Middle Eastern Christians and Western converts to Islam—was the stuff of legend. American and European converts to Islam could hardly stand to be in the same room with Arab Christians, while Coptic, Catholic, and Orthodox Christians and Jews regarded the converts as mentally deficient dupes.

This contempt never jarred me: the Middle East's religious

context was so thickly mined with fussy fetishes in diet (pork, alcohol, *kashrut,* fasting), sartorial (head coverings, beards), and real estate (the war-inducing sanctity of Mecca and Eretz Israel) that the minor bitcheries of the conversion game seemed to fit right in.

9
Playing Host

$\mathcal{I}$n 1983, the world oil market gave the Saudi economy a terrible beating. Only five years before, the kingdom had been producing 11 million barrels of oil a day at $32 a barrel; now they were producing 2 million barrels a day and selling them at $28 each. Domestically consumed oil, which was heavily subsidized, cut further into their profits, perhaps as much as thirty percent. Other aspects of the nightmare were non-Arab oil discoveries, new oil-recovery technology, alternative energy sources, and some degree of worldwide conservation. The government was now approving annual budgets with huge deficits. Utility rates went up. Telephone service stopped growing because the Ministry of Post, Telephone, and Telegraph could no longer afford to buy cable, though "all our problems would be solved if the royal family would pay their phone bills," one deputy minister sighed in my presence; but the royal phone lines, which numbered in the thousands, could not be disconnected. On the black market, scotch went up to $125 a bottle, copies of Abdelrahman Munif's *Sharq al-Mutawasit* to nearly $50.

This made reporting from Riyadh much easier if less adventurous. It meant that the days of lavish summit meetings were over, so there was no danger of spending whole days on press buses or pacing palace lobbies while visiting kings or heads of state came to meet the obese and almost sycophantically pro-American new king, Fahd bin Abdelaziz. The kingdom's oil income was declining sharply, and despite the Ministry of Finance's denials of hard times coming, I could gauge the slipping economy by the nearly empty schedule of major foreign guests: there was only the same procession of Lebanese politicians and the ubiquitous Pakistani Prime Minister General Muhammad Zia ul Haq, thousands of whose troops were seconded to the kingdom to guard areas thought to be too tribally sensitive for actual Saudi troops, such as the border with Yemen.

The newspaper's emphasis on business as an evasion of politics became more difficult to maintain as the business news got so bad. Hundreds of small businesses were going bankrupt, and larger, mainly foreign firms, laid off thousands of workers as the Saudi government cut back on contracts and delayed payments. My lazy habit of poaching stories from Arabic sources was a safe course, since it never actually involved breaking any stories.

This hardly qualified as journalism. I could dress up a good local business story with quotes garnered from telephone calls to the U.S. Embassy commercial section, economists at the Gulf Cooperation Council, or government officials, though in order for them to take my calls I often had to lyingly identify myself as a reporter for the other, more popular English-language paper. Once having put that sham behind me, I could investigate the case of Imam Moussa Sadr.

Saudi Arabia was continuing to propagandize against Iran, which had begun to use the pilgrimage to Mecca—which annually drew 1–2 million hajjis from around the world—as a chance to promote Khomeini's political philosophy and personality cult. Thousands of Iranian pilgrims smuggled in portraits of their leader and organized gala demonstrations against America and Israel through the holy cities, and called King Fahd the Israeli Shah Fahd. Political cartoonists in Riyadh and Jeddah lampooned the Iranians as loony, irreligious hoodlums with ridiculously huge noses. Closet sympathy for Iran was no longer part of my motivation for following the Sadr affair; not because I had taken the Saudis' side in the propaganda war, but because Iran had abandoned Sadr so completely.

The Islamic Republic had, of course, already aborted its own investigation of the disappearance, though Khomeini occasionally spoke publicly of his affection for the imprisoned Imam. Iran did not officially acknowledge that Sadr was probably dead; if they had, there would have been no possible justification for their romance with Libya. It was the extent of Iran's new relations with Libya that shocked me. In 1982, Libya announced its wish to assist Iran in the war with Iraq, and Khomeini had a friendly meeting with Libya's Foreign Affairs Minister Abdelsalam Treiki. The two countries signed a series of exhaustive political, economic, and cultural treaties, and Libya did Iran a magnanimous favor by persuading North Korea to back Iran with arms sales. This bloc, joined by Syria, saw itself as a gallant anti-American front. Amal, a potent force in Lebanon by virtue of its actions against Israel, objected to Iran's Libyan gambit but was brought to heel by Iranian-sponsored mutinies, which resulted in the birth of such breakaway groups as Hezbollah. Khomeini was junking uncounted old loyalties in order to win his war.

I mentioned this to Hussein, but he was not helpful. America was in collusion with Israel, which was occupying his hometown in southern Lebanon, and I had still not converted. "All of Lebanon is now Moussa Sadr," he sighed, "and the world only wants us to die more quietly."

I had long since left the hotel for an office in the affluent if donkey-lady–infested Suleimaniya district and an apartment two blocks away. I was the only reporter, but had a staff of two: Jodi, the Indian office boy (he insisted on this title, though he had three grandchildren) and an Indian telex operator on secondment from the *Times of India* who grumped angrily as he punched the telex tapes for my soporific business stories and reminded me of his almost godlike status back at the U.S. consulate in Madras, where only he had been allowed to touch the telex machine. It was a rare day that passed without his recollection, Homeric in its suspense and command of detail, of the time the consular telex machine broke down and he, Subramanian Iyer, was summoned to repair it under the respectful gaze of two United States Marines. And did I know how the American consul treated him?

After passing my news story to Mr. Iyer (". . . like a *rajah*," he would be muttering) I devoted my day to transcribing my interviews with people who knew about Moussa Sadr or reading Arabic fiction, all of which I virtuously classified as a businesslike commitment to developing my language skills. Since Munif novels were expensive and hard to come by, I concentrated on the depressing novels of Fahd Ismail Fahd and the poetry of Nizar Qabbani, whose Iraqi wife was killed when the Syrians blew up the Iraqi Embassy in Beirut; Qabbani produced a very long "Ode to Bilqis" featured on the cover of the weekly *al-Dustour*. ("An ode within a week?" was Hamdan's reaction. "God, he's cheap!")

After spells of stringing for a few wire services and magazines I had quit to concentrate on writing an investigative book about the disappearance of Imam Moussa Sadr. What could be eerier and more spellbinding than the story of how the Shah's plant in Lebanon had "turned" and become Ayatollah Khomeini's man, only to be traded off for Libyan weapons? And how he had planted the seeds of the terrorist groups that would have a hand-wringing U.S. government placing concrete bunkers around the White House? And how he had vanished into thin air in Libya, victim of an unknown fate, probably murdered by the sinister Colonel Qaddafi? It was slowly dawning on me that, despite my failure to convert, my best friends were Shiites, that my project was a way of making myself worthy of their friendship, and that Lebanon was being destroyed—it needed friends.

Besides, I hated stringing. My newspaper nearly fired me for a telex to UPI's Beirut office describing the Shiite pilgrims' riots in Medina, which the government wished to remain a secret, and the best outfits—the *Wall Street Journal* and *The Economist*—had painfully high standards for reporting and painfully low ones for payment. Only the Rome-based Inter-Press Service Third World News Agency offered good pay for little work—as their representative warned, after hiring me as Riyadh correspondent: "Don't forget: no sports, no politics, no catastrophes." He wanted official press releases with my name on them, especially from the local U.N. offices. I never played by the rules and was never paid. One day, the Unicef representative called me to groan, "Do you know what they're charging us to accept your stories on us? Would you mind writing one?" I had started stringing in order to have some exposure to conventional journalism, but the risks and confusion made me abandon it.

And I had second thoughts about reporting only a few months before, in the lobby of the Riyadh Marriott, a pharaonic expanse of veined vermillion marble and burnished brass. David Ottaway, the Middle East correspondent for the *Washington Post,* was looking very worried. He had left his home base in Lebanon two days before to conduct oil interviews here, and Israel had been bombing Beirut for nearly twenty hours, killing hundreds of civilians. No Arab country was coming to Lebanon's aid. Saudis watched the bombings on televisions in store windows and cried. Now the Israeli army had invaded southern Lebanon. And there was worse to come, for everyone—Israel would devastate half of Lebanon and subsequently be forced into a humiliating retreat by the militant Shiites inspired by the now absent, but more powerful than ever Imam Moussa Sadr.

"It looks like a full-scale invasion," he said grimly. "It looks like the Israelis have made themselves a deal with the Lebanese Christians to just go in and wipe out the PLO, the government, everything."

"You're sure in the right place at the right time," I said, meaning exactly what I said. Imagine being in Beirut—at the best of times, a metaphor for hell on earth—while the Israelis were raining American cluster bombs all over the place!

"Well, I can fix that. If I can get on a flight to Beirut tonight, before they close the airport."

I thought that over. This eminent author, journalist, husband, father, was going *to* Lebanon to watch this? This was what real journalists did.

Back in my office, I sipped sweet tea and translated a shrill article by a Libyan dissident who claimed to know the fate of Moussa Sadr, clipped from *Okaz,* all the time thinking of alternative careers.

WHO DOES QADDAFI WORK FOR? "ROSITA": MOSSAD AGENT AND
QADDAFI'S FRIEND! WHO KILLED MOUSSA SADR AND ABBAS
BADREDDINE?

Imam Moussa Sadr and Abbas Badreddine came to Libya, not for the first time, and then disappeared. The Colonel claims that they left Libya for Italy, but Italian security reports demonstrate that they did not leave Libya; their names did not appear on any of the passenger manifests for the plane coming from Libya on the day Qaddafi claims they left Tripoli.

We would not be giving away a secret if we said that the issue goes back to finances between the Libyan media apparatus and the journalist Badreddine. Qaddafi had given Sadr and Badreddine $17 million one year prior to the disappearance, for the recruitment of Amal members to his service, for personal propaganda.

The funds were spent on charitable projects; revenge was inevitable.

Sadr and Badreddine were held captive in a villa in the Al-Shatti Hotel district of Tripoli. On April 8, 1981, Qaddafi issued an order to do away with them for good, and ordered Hejazi, the head of military intelligence, to execute the order. . . . Hejazi put poison in Moussa Sadr's food and in Badreddine's. Their bodies were hidden in the cemetery of a small, remote village near the border with Chad. ───────

"Of course, you have to go to Beirut to talk to Sadr's wife and sister, and his friends," Aly Mahmoud of Associated Press in Bahrain told me. Was he joking? Did he want me to get killed?

Journalists continued to come and go: the dwindling oil wealth of these countries was nearly as big a story as its accumulation had been. Ironically, now that the Saudis felt so vulnerable, they were much quicker to allow journalists to visit. They wanted the world to appreciate the dangers they faced: less money, Israel battering Lebanon, religious extremism, and above all the powerful hostility of Iran. The irony was complete as the throngs of journalists trying to get in before became a trickle. Saudi Arabia had, for the most part, been done.

I got in on the act, commissioned by the *New York Times Magazine:*

It is noon, and under the blinding sunshine, shiny red-and-white G.M. Suburbans of the mutawwa, or religious police, patrol the city's dusty but expensively landscaped streets. Their loudspeakers blare imprecations at loiterers and merchants slow to close for prayers. "Pray! Pray! Remember God!"

Bourj al-Hamam, like other elegant restaurants in Riyadh, used to discreetly ignore some of the strictures of the mutawwa, but no longer. During prayer times, the doors are locked and lights dimmed; no one may enter or leave, no food may be served, no bills settled. In the dining rooms—which have been turned into mazes of screens and partitions to separate the men's section from the family section—children cry as patrons and waiters fidget. Outside, mutawwas maintain vigil until the full 35 minutes for prayer have passed.

Religious austerity has returned to Saudi Arabia. After heady years of luxurious living, when even average wage-earners could indulge in world travel and extravagant spending sprees, the citizens of the desert kingdom are facing an uncertain economic future.

This story, about economics and diminishing political clout, was one the journalists were ready for, since it demanded only a knowledge of the past ten or so years of Middle Eastern events. It seemed long ago since the days when the Arabs were flush with money, caricatured as terrorists and evil scimitar-wielding slobs. Now they were better known to us, thanks to a string of sympathetic television documentaries.

In the old days, the occasional reporter who managed to wangle a visa out of one of the kingdom's inhospitable embassies was like a visitor to another galaxy, and had almost no idea where they were or what was going on. He wanted to get three good-sized articles out of his trip: oil ("Camels and Cadillacs"), political stability ("Saudi Arabia—The Next Iran?") and the future ("What Next for Desert Xanadu?"), plus a fourth, usually very soft piece, almost always a feature. The Saudis were extremely adept at providing colorful concepts for the feature, and the reporter generally ended up with one of a half dozen off-the-shelf stories:

Agriculture—the kingdom was miraculously self-sufficient in wheat, grown mainly in the Central Province. The miracle was brought about by paying gigantic subsidies to farmers to deplete the desert province's groundwater at a suicidal rate. This was attractive, since it involved a side trip to the beautifully spare Great Nafud, an informal course on hydroponics, and the incongruous sight of immense, defiantly green wheat and potato fields stretching into eternity under the fiery sun.

The fact was that the self-sufficiency program buried the government in huge wheat surpluses, with more than $3 billion in interest-free loans outstanding to Saudi farmers and the water tables sinking at the rate of about fifty feet per year. A visiting U.S. secretary of commerce, John Block, who called the project "crazy" and urged the Saudis to buy American surpluses, touched a patriotic nerve, causing sensible plans to cut the subsidies to be put aside, though the government fell years behind paying for the harvests. Some of the actual farming was done by Americans, who spent a profitable off-season in central Arabia.

Women: They Actually Like the Veil—many did, too. Islam protects women, through sex segregation and the veil, from the sexual exploitation of the West. This story was a switch for most visiting reporters, and combined with a little misinformation about the number of college graduates they really got behind it. The Saudis guided them toward a focus on women in business, always from old entrepreneurial families. Women reporters in particular loved doing these profiles, in patriarchal Arabia, of ass-kicking rich women.

Grads of U.S. Colleges Resettle—a favorite of reporters naive or chauvinistic enough to be amazed that young Saudis did not chuck their country, family, religion, lifestyle, and immensely lucrative professional opportunities in Saudi Arabia after experiencing the bliss of four years on a U.S. college campus: "Somehow Abdallah actually left the jeans and frisbees behind in San Diego," and "Ali married a local girl who can't speak English, chosen by his parents."

Actually, Abdallah and Ali cringed at the idea of having to raise children in America, and often wondered why Americans living in the rich, peaceful, sunny kingdom wanted to go back to the decadent, dirty, highly taxed United States.

The Disappearing Way of Life feature was rare because it was hard to find a Saudi who could talk knowledgeably about camels, horsemanship, tents, and the nomadic life. Usually the wistful elements of a panegyric to the bedouin life could be included in one of the other features.

Sports—camel races (for the lucky ones who came in April for the Royal Camel Races at Janadriya), falconry, horse racing (if an American corporate connection could supply them with an invitation to the weekly races at the Equestrian Club), and soccer. Sports had a very royal aura, with each soccer team supported by a princely patron.

The Arts—a grand celebration of subsidized painters and writers and photographers, unless a meeting could be arranged with the beautiful and talented Safiya Binzagr in Jeddah. As presented by the Ministry of Information, it totally ignored the vitality of foreign (Islamic as well as Western) artists and influences present in the kingdom. Most reporters were dragged through the halls of nightmarish abstract canvases concocted by febrile young nomads, and some reasonable calligraphic pieces, though few wrote it up and still fewer saw them printed.

Expatriate Communities—Americans musing about this hardship post. Boring, but no crime, lots of money. Often the article that grew out of the evening the reporter spent, in desperation, at the house of the U.S. press attaché or other kindly American, watching television, drinking scotch and listening to horror stories about the religious police. Some more intrepid reporters wrote about the Filipino, Egyptian, or Yemeni guest labor communities, in which case it was all labor horror stories. Typical quote (Saudi speaking): "No one invited these people here. They're earning ten times what they could earn at home. Who's keeping them here?"

Visiting reporters often saw me first, to prepare, to test their knowledge of the country before seeing higher officials; they were always given my name by another journalist who had invested a lunch in trying to learn from me what he was not learning from the U.S. ambassador or the officials he was or was not getting to meet. Since many reporters worked for newspapers which had no Middle East bureau, they knew nothing about the country they had just landed in; or, worse, knew what they had read in the *Encyclopedia Americana, Reader's Digest,* and *The Seven Pillars of Wisdom.* My nagging recitation of facts to put them in the picture—when they saw the lunch as the price for a few scandalous facts or scoop—no doubt helped me to be seen as a some kind of pedantic lobbyist for the Arabs, when all I was trying to do was to prevent the kind of stories they would have written with the knowledge they came in with. The dangers of what they wanted to write would be much too fatiguing to go into, but roughly translated into the American context, they would have paralleled something like this, written by an imaginary foreign correspondent from an Arab country desperate to understand America:

Lucy Ricardo might not recognize New York today.

America's largest and richest city, once the national capital, lies in ruins, a racially divided melting pot which refuses to yield any useful alloy.

On 42nd Street, the officially sanctioned porno district, young Americans immerse themselves in lewd activities—to the satisfaction of the city's bosses, it keeps their minds off politics. Business flourishes at the intersection with Broadway ("broad" signifying "impure woman"). This district is known as Times Square, after the Jewish-owned *New York Times* newspaper.

A few blocks away, on Fifth Avenue ("fifth" is a measure of whiskey), in buildings that loom as if constructed for a race of giants, Jews make deals, defended by an Irish police force. At least these two ingredients of the melting pot have found a way of mixing profitably.

Others are not so lucky.

The descendants of slaves who bore the brunt of fighting in Vietnam—America's "Jewish War"—lounge, penniless on the sidewalks, many freshly discharged from the dreaded "Singing" Prison, or the victims of mind-control experiments performed by the feared CIA. This Christian country, which has forgotten all of the commandments, in whose everyday speech the dollar is *al-ali al-azim,* "almighty" . . .

None of the officials interviewed for this article could recite the Constitution; like many Americans whose intellectual capacity has been diminished by a steady diet of pork and alcohol products, they were sluggish and uncurious when asked why a five-cent piece is bigger than a ten-cent piece; why no places of business here honor the $50 bill or any of the larger denominations. Nor could they convincingly explain the profound antipathies that separate the East Coast from other regions. . . .

The television references would certainly be there. Arabs thought they knew all about America because they watched *The*

Jeffersons and *Gunsmoke* and *WKRP in Cincinnati* and pornography; they did not know that we knew so little about them because of TV. They argued bitterly when I pointed out that "Slim" in *Gunsmoke* was not "Saleem," as the Arabic subtitles rendered his name; nor was the Sheriff "al-Shareef." At such times I wished that literature rather than television could be the medium that united us.

Of course, the Saudis were largely to blame. Their money, power, and high profile allowed them to hog the limelight, but they hated having journalists visit and generally kept them out. Marc Simon, a syndicated columnist, was typical. Several days of the Information Ministry's broken promises were turning him into an Arabophobe. We were cruising through the ramshackle marketplaces in the old downtown area with Ann Barzillay, a Commerce Department aide. Her boss, the secretary of commerce, was visiting Riyadh and I was occupying her on her only free morning as a favor to the American embassy, where her zealous questioning of Saudi officials had made her an unpopular guest.

"What's with the women in the black bags?" She pointed out the car window at a flock of veiled women with shopping bags.

"Those are *abayas,* the black cloaks that women wear to go out."

"Or they'll get flogged, right?"

"Well, no, I don't think so. They're traditional, like hats and gloves used to be for American women."

"I love it. It's a scream! So why are you here, anyway? You like it here?" She spoke in a very loud but friendly honk.

"Well, it's a job. I'm a reporter." We wound through the

chaotic traffic of Thumeiry Street toward cramped little Dira Square, where the executions took place, and I mentally prepared my execution story. The sidewalks were jammed with women in black cloaks and men in white robes, almost like two religious orders.

"Beautiful," said Ann, pointing at a Toyota billboard displaying the beaming likeness of the boxer the Arabs called Muhammad Ali Clay. "Ali. I love it."

Ali had actually visited Riyadh, in the 1970s, and hated it. "Doesn't anyone in this town smile?" he was supposed to have asked walking down Wazir Street. He went to Mecca for *hajj*, but the newspapers commented unkindly that he did not perform his prayers properly and could not pronounce anything in Arabic. *Al-Yamama* magazine in Riyadh criticized him for his blasphemous title, "The Greatest," but none of this prevented him from being a valued spokesman for Japanese cars.

"Look at the guy sleeping in the wheelbarrow!" crowed Ann.

A diminutive Yemeni laborer was snoozing peaceably in his wheelbarrow, cradling his pickaxe. Pedestrians crowded by, squeezing in and out of the mud-walled grocery stores and bakeries, not giving him a second glance.

Marc was being rather quiet.

"How did you make out with the oil minister?" I asked him.

"I didn't meet him. The Ministry of Information promised me interviews with five officials, and that one was supposed to be today, but they haven't delivered on any of them." He tucked his head between the two front seats to peer through the windshield. Before setting off from his hotel, the Inter-Continental (room 103) I had tried to suggest that Ann should sit in the back, as Saudi women generally did; only, I hastened to add, because we could get into trouble for driving around together. Technically, we were breaking the law, since we were neither married nor related, and the law of the land could not imagine that we had anything but coition on our minds. Foreign men and women were sometimes deported for driving around together. Any such mixing of the sexes amounted, in Islamic law, to what Catholics call a proximate occasion of sin—sin being all but absolutely inevitable. "Fuck 'em," said Ann, and climbed into the front seat. Her naive courage, blissful lack of cultural sensitivity, and mis-placed sense of security gave me a tiny thrill of homesickness. Marc was possibly resentful at sitting in the back seat; and his visit was going very badly.

"I find the Saudis very arrogant," he said. "They're a lot like some of the Israelis. You know, they answer to a higher law. Like we owe them something."

"Look at the big momma smack that kid. I love it!" Ann craned her head at an Arab woman in abaya and kerchief shaking a sticky-faced toddler who was clutching her black billows. "Just like home."

"In the sense that they resent us."

I told Marc the expression that so many other Arabs cited when sneering at the Saudis: *Ardh tahera, shaab najis,* "Sacred land, profane people." "They strike a lot of people as arrogant. For one thing, they're racially proud—they're pure Arabs, not intermar-ried with Copts or Kurds or Berbers like Levantine Arabs or North Africans."

He was hunched back in the seat, swaying with the car and scribbling on his pad, I noticed in the rearview mirror.

"Goats—beautiful," said Ann. "But no camels! What gives?"

"I'll find you camels," I promised absentmindedly, and quickly resumed my speech to the rearview mirror. "Plus, they consider themselves a religious elite. Their brand of Islam, Wahhabism, is very puritanical. They think the beliefs of most other Muslims have been adulterated. The Saudis are real fundamentalists. They have the added religious prestige of having the holy cities, Mecca and Medina, here in Saudi Arabia. And they're a political power by virtue of their oil wealth. They like to imply that God rewarded their piety with the oil. And they see themselves as Third World leaders—mediators between the poor and developed countries."

"Allah," said Ann.

"*Allah* is just the Arabic word for God. It's the same God as in the Bible. Arab Jews and Christians say *Allah,* too."

"How stable is this place politically?" asked Marc before I could bring out my "Do the French worship a different god because they say *Dieu?*" analogy. I told him that the Saudis felt badly undercut by American policies in the region. The ever-spiraling U.S.–Israel alliance estranged the Arabs, which made Israel seem comparatively loyal to us, and this self-perpetuating situation really hurt everybody.

"We actually have de facto military bases in Saudi Arabia," I told him. "The country is crawling with American military advisors. The CIA trains Arab subversives in Tabuk to foment unrest in Marxist South Yemen"—did this happen to everyone, I wondered, this talking in journalistic clichés when talking to a reporter?—"and though we don't think of the Saudis as pro-American, most of the other Arabs think they're American stooges, and criticize them for it."

"Like Iran," said Ann.

"Iran is not an Arab country," I was quick to point out; back then this was a still a subtle point. "The Iranians are Persians. Iran has a small ethnic Arab minority."

"What about the *majlis al-shura?*" Marc asked.

"Every year the king says they're nearly finished studying it. They'll probably need another shock to get it going." It was clear that this parliamentary experiment, really a large-scale advisory body, would never get going without an act of God. I had asked one of the king's brother's Talal, a former radical, whether the majlis members would be elected. "Why not?" he said boldly, and quickly backtracked with, "Elected or appointed, what's the difference, as long as they're good men? Do you think we should have elections here with 99.9 percent margins of victory?" The implication was that democracy in any form was not worth the trouble.

"So it's a crock," said Marc. "Have you been to one of the princes' open majlises? I'm supposedly going to Prince Salman's."

I had. It was grand to see the splendid prince in his black cloak receiving his plaintive or overwrought citizenry, and they treated him very much as an equal. But their complaints were petty, and most of them were in fact making requests for money, or, in the case of bedouin, Land Rovers. None were refused. It seemed to me that they gave the prince more than they went out with— all of their rights. It was, to a reporter in a critical mood, a medieval sight, a tableau of cynical patronage. It had filled me with envy.

"You should go," I said. "You'll see some bedouin." I wanted to tell him that it was a paternalistic farce and that the government would not be able to buy people off like that forever, but thought: let him figure that out for himself.

"I love it!" Ann was looking out the window at several American women in muu-muus and filmy kerchiefs. I explained that Arab women wore their abayas over their clothes—whether a silk dress or jeans; one Saudi girl had told me that she loved the abaya since she could go out "like a slob" and no one knew. They shed the veils as soon as they were indoors. Only foreign women wore such concealing clothing—few Saudi women would wear such unfashionably modest clothing all the time, and I had heard them snicker at American women.

Now we were in Dira, a narrow rotary with a looming modern clock tower in the center. This was where I had seen the beheading. I told them the story in detail as we headed away from Dira, up toward Bridges Street in the lengthening shadows. Both Ann and Marc listened raptly.

"No one here really questions the death penalty," I told them.

"I bet you it's a deterrent," said Marc.

"It's a scream," murmured Ann thoughtfully.

"It isn't the death penalty that keeps crime low," I said. "It's the fact that it's part of the religion, and the religion is shared by every citizen. In that way it's a very homogeneous country, and Islam governs every facet of life. Beheading and amputation are mandated in the Koran and so must always be part of the law here."

One of the fortunate side effects of the death penalty was that it kept Saudi prisons very tame. Since all violent criminals were killed, the jails held a pretty peaceful assembly of small-time con men and traffic scofflaws. By the standards of most countries, few had even committed a crime.

I pointed out that executions were relatively rare and were often commuted in favor of blood money payments from the guilty party to the victim's kin, at least where manslaughter was concerned. Beheading and stoning for adultery were almost unknown: in order to convict on that charge, there had to be four adult male Muslim witnesses to the act. Islamic law was often immensely practical.

It was a mark of how xenophobic the Saudis were that I often hated explaining their ways to people who would otherwise have tended toward uninformed hostility. Being a lobbyist, even an unpaid one, was against my nature and so I usually added a horror story to my spiel when I felt that people were getting too high an opinion of my hosts. There was a recent one dealing with blood money, which I considered telling. King Fahd's eldest son, Faisal, a notorious drug addict, was rumored to have shot and killed his male lover, a National Guardsman from the tribe of Shammar. The young man's family, given the choice of *diya,* blood money, or a life for a life, demanded his head. Faisal—the president of the Youth Welfare Organization—was immediately sent to Los Angeles to do advance work for the Saudi Olympic soccer team. The family was told in no uncertain terms that as long as they demanded blood the prince would remain out of their reach. They went to the king's half-brother, Crown Prince Abdullah, whose mother was of the Shammar tribe, but obviously it was assumed that the public execution of the king's son would have ruined the king.

Personally, I thought that it would have helped Fahd, who was thoroughly corrupt, to please the religious fundamentalists and other malcontents who yearned for simpler days and pitiless codes of honor. A king who would hand over his own son to be executed for murder would become a legend in his own time. Mahdi would write odes about it until he dropped from exhaustion.

"When you look at how these fucking despots go around executing people," said Marc, who was still smarting from his humiliations at the Ministry of Information, "you understand why the Israelis should just roll the hell in here and clean their clocks. Do you ever feel like that?"

Occasionally, I thought.

"No," I said, and instead of telling them about Prince Faisal I described the Imam Sadr case.

10

1984

$\mathcal{I}$ had found, in an obscure book published in Egypt, a list of the contents of Moussa Sadr's suitcase, and that of his fellow cleric Sheikh Muhammad Yaacoub. The fact that the bags turned up in Rome proved—according to Libya—that Sadr, Yaacoub, and their journalist companion Abbas Badreddine had indeed left Libya safe and sound. When the three suitcases were found in the Holiday Inn Parco dei Medici near Rome Airport on September 10, they were promptly sealed with official red wax and turned over to the Italian police. According to the book, *With Apologies to Imam Sadr,* the contents of Sadr's suitcase, and Yaacoub's, were a chaotic jumble: Lebanese, Syrian, and Czech currency; turbans, pajamas, cologne; stationery from the Al-Shatti Beach Hotel, a Persian music cassette, two tickets issued by Libyan Arab Airlines in Tripoli (Tripoli-Rome-Paris-Beirut); twelve passport photos each of Sadr, Yaacoub, and Badreddine, and Badreddine's vaccination certificate; bunches of car keys; a flow chart of the Libyan political system, reports, publications, and letters in Persian, among them an unsent letter, in Sadr's hand, to Ayatollah Khomeini in Iraq; Amal staff lists and reports; a letter from Abbas Badreddine to Colonel Qaddafi requesting payment for the Libyan Embassy in Beirut's subscription to his Lebanon News Agency; Sadr's little diary with daily notations in Persian until August 28, 1978, and blank thereafter until the end of the book; and his wristwatch, its crystal smashed, with the hands inside indicating 1:15 A.M. on the first day of the month.

The third bag was Abbas Badreddine's black Samsonite briefcase. The trouble was that Badreddine had never stayed at the Holiday Inn: the hotel's records showed that a Moussa Sadar [sic] and Mohamed Chehada (Yaacoub's name was Muhammad Shahada Yaacoub) had checked in on September 1; but Badreddine had not. A man using Badreddine's passport had arrived at Rome Airport from Libya just before midnight on August 31, produced a Rome-Malta airline ticket for a flight the following day, and was granted a forty-eight-hour transit visa. He gave as a temporary address the Satellite Hotel at Ostia. However, no one by that name checked in at the Satellite that night; nor did any Abbas Badreddine travel to Malta or anywhere else. The reservation, Interpol later said, had never been recorded, and the transit desk clerk, shown a photo of Badreddine, categorically ruled out that this was the man to whom he had issued the visa.

I had sought out Middle Eastern intrigue, but never thought that I would find such a maddening example. I read *With Apologies to Imam Sadr* carefully, but it had no answers, only some interviews with the Imam and some reprinted police reports from Italy. The author, Adel Reza, had been planning to publish a book of dialogues with Sadr on international issues, but the Imam disappeared before it was complete. So Reza filled the second half of his book with documentation on the disappearance, and chose a title reflecting his sense of an incomplete work.

I visited Cairo to see Reza, so determined to solve the Sadr mystery that I had no time to indulge my nostalgia. Most of the passengers on the Saudi Arabian Airlines flight were young Saudi rakes puking into their airsick bags and lining up in front of the restrooms, for much of the two-hour flight, to change from their thobes into jacket and trousers, much to the annoyance of the flight crew, both Egyptian (the stewards) and British (the stewardesses)—Saudi Arabia was building its male staff very slowly, and did not hire Saudi women at all.

Cairo's dusty, ramshackle charm of five years before was gone. I had completely adapted to the Xanadu-in-the-desert grandeur of the Arabian Gulf, of spacious and expensive modernity, and by comparison Cairo was a monumental hive of color, culture, and boundless energy. Cairo's antique quaintness had been supplied by my imagination, and the modernity I had taken for granted as a student now struck me differently, as something grand. From inside my taxi I watched theaters, cinemas, bookstores, bars, video shops, and cafes flash past, all set in the dusty stone motifs of Cairo Crazy architecture: mansard roofs with sphinx gargoyles, Catholic statues, Stalin gothic, and those coppery statues of befezzed heroes: Talaat Harb, Suleiman Pasha, Saad Zaghloul.

I could have saved myself the trip. Reza was planning a second book of Sadr's disappearance and failed to show up for five appointments. When I cornered him in his cubicle at *Akhbar El-Yom* in Sahafa Street, near Champollion, he provided tea, smiled sweatily, and answered every question with "I don't know," "A lot of people wonder about that," and "When this case is solved, the Lebanese will smash the world and scream in our faces." His only really frank assertion was that "Sadr is dead, brother, dead." I penciled in my notebook: *Sadr is alive.*

By pure accident, I found a much more helpful source back in Riyadh. Jaafar Raed, the Shah's last ambassador to Saudi Arabia, had become a columnist for *Okaz* and began to drop his articles off at my office to be faxed to Jeddah. One day I glanced at the signature on an article delivered by a tall Ethiopian (again!) and read Raed's name; the African said he was a chauffeur and that Raed was in the car downstairs. Within ten minutes I had brought the ambassador down some tea to sip while listening to my nagging pleas for an interview. After all, Moussa Sadr had carried an Iranian passport for almost his whole career, and made the pilgrimage to Mecca at least twice; he would have been received by his country's ambassador. What would they have talked about?

"He used to visit Saudi Arabia every year, or every other year, usually for Haj. I met him here three times," said Raed when we met in his office. Although his photographs made him look bulky and menacing, with broad shoulders and enormous eyebrows more than compensating for his baldness, Raed was just five feet tall. "The first time he came, he made a good impression—King Khaled liked him very much. And the second time I invited him over, he came and we had dinner and a long talk. The third time—that was the time things were different. He gave officials the feeling that he had really changed. And they thought he had gone over to the left."

That was 1978, Raed recalled. Sadr was very aggrieved over the Israeli invasion of southern Lebanon and the fact that none of the Arabs did anything to oppose it. Nor had Iran. The Imam's relations with the Iranian opposition to the Shah grew more intimate.

"At that time he became close to Dr. Yazdi, he was always meeting him. And Mustafa Chamran, who became chief of the revolutionary guards under Khomeini. When the revolutionary thinker Ali Shariati died, Sadr sent a cable of condolences and held a memorial service in Beirut—that infuriated the Shah. And Khomeini, too."

Ali Shariati had been a deeply religious Islamic social thinker, very much opposed to the Shah's rule; his death, in London, may even have been caused by Iranian agents. Logically the Shah would find it irritating that Sadr would honor him. The fact that it annoyed Khomeini too meant that even as early as 1977 the ayatollah was getting impatient with sharing the spotlight with other opposition figures.

Sadr's political colors changed gradually and, it seemed, conveniently. He had excellent relations with Syria and the PLO, and when they fought one another in Lebanon's civil war, he kept his friendship with both. Syria had supported the PLO until success was near; to avoid the war with Israel thought to be inevitable in the event of a PLO victory, Syria quickly switched sides and helped the Christian rightists to crush the Palestinians brutally. The Imam was convinced, early on, that the Shah was doomed, and cultivated the opposition, especially Khomeini, who was already one of his admirers. He was one of the only Lebanese to maintain his close friendship with Sadat of Egypt after the peace treaty with Israel, but discreetly.

"He was determined to strengthen the Shiites of Lebanon, and in aid of that he was ready to work with the Devil. People didn't like that. He was more of a politician than a religious leader. He was clever, and imagined he could work both sides of the street—that's how his problems started."

So what did they talk about at dinner in 1978?

"He wanted to improve his relations with the Shah."

"But he was sure the Shah was doomed. Why would he court him?"

"It was just part of a double game. He told me, and our ambassadors in Cairo and Damascus the same thing. The Iranians did not think he was sincere—they knew he was helping the Iranian opposition. I imagine he had some specific goal of his own in mind."

The "help," the "relations" Sadr had with the opposition were military: his own Shiite militia, Amal, was trained by the PLO and by the Iranian opposition, and in turn trained new Iranian guerrilla groups working against the Shah.

Raed believed that Sadr had been on a mission for Khomeini when he disappeared in Libya—trying to obtain broadcast rights for anti-Shah propaganda; he was supposed to have met up with Sadeq Ghotbzadeh in Tripoli. He pointed out that I would be killed investigating this case in Libya or Lebanon, so advised me to try Rome—or Paris. "Talk to Shahpour Bakhtiar. He can tell you a great deal." Bakhtiar had served as prime minister for thirty-two days, from the Shah's departure to Khomeini's arrival in Tehran. The little ambassador accompanied me shufflingly to his office door in his slippers and answered my last question with a laugh.

"Because they seem aristocratic to us, more so than the Arabs. And the late Shah felt a certain kinship with Emperor Haile Selassie."

All the tiny points of information about Moussa Sadr had begun to form a pointillistic portrait, in my mind, of a man who embodied more than his share of the contradictions of this part of the world. I sent an outline of an unwritten book entitled *The Strange Disappearance of Imam Moussa Sadr* to a British publisher, and turned my attention back to the local scene.

The hilly, baked-mud ruins of Diriyah had once been a bigger town than Riyadh, about ten miles away. This was the site of the 1819 siege after which Muhammad Ali's Ottoman troops destroyed the city as punishment for its defiance of the caliphate. In later years the whole site was fenced in by the Department of Antiquities, and the modern town of Diriyah was growing up in the shallow valleys around it, a high and rising tide of prefabricated apartment blocks bristling with TV aerials. Rapidly becoming a suburb of Riyadh, Diriyah was now besieged by the gigantic new campus of King Saud University—called the University City—and an even huger development: the Diplomatic Quarter.

For the embassies were finally moving to Riyadh. They would

all be built in this restricted area, along with residence compounds, embassy-brat schools, and mosques. Apparently Riyadh was now considered ready for the hundreds of diplomatically immune foreigners, though the enclosed "DQ" only had two gated points of access.

There would be no church. This was a very sore point: a group of diplomats had nominated the British ambassador, Sir James Craig, to broach the subject with the Saudi foreign minister. He politely requested permission to build a small nondenominational church, wholly at the expense of his and some other Western embassies, solely for the use of diplomats and their families; it would display no cross and engage in no proselytizing. The foreign minister, Prince Saud al-Faisal, refused the request and warned him that the matter was closed. Some diplomats said that Craig should instead have asked the king, or Prince Salman, the governor of Riyadh, both of whom were kindhearted and Saudi-educated. Prince Saud, as a graduate of Princeton, had to be scrupulously careful not to appear overly sympathetic to Western notions.

In any case, a church of any size or persuasion—even the rumor of a church, in fact—was a red flag to Riyadhis. One afternoon I asked Hamdan about it.

"Look," he said, "Riyadh is all we have. Everywhere else there are American cars, Pepsi, Christians drinking scotch whiskey all over the place—which a good Christian shouldn't even do!—Coca-Cola, and Israel and America. America owns the world! But this is one place we do have, and everything has to be our way, even if America doesn't like it."

For some reason Muslims who drank were fond of the fatuous claim that Christians, too, were prohibited from drinking, or perhaps they had met some Southern Baptists. And this idea that America was responsible for the whole world outside Arabia's borders was grating. Four years of reading Arab editorials had convinced me that America's power was vastly exaggerated in order to explain Saudi failure to influence U.S. policy.

I was not convinced by Hamdan's arguments: surely the Saudi bigotry against other religions revealed a deep insecurity in the face of other cultures and faiths and was a sop to empty nationalism and phony clerics. Even the least observant Muslim in Saudi Arabia measured power and influence in religious terms—why else did the kingdom spend vast fortunes on palatial mosques in places where there were almost no Muslims? It was a subtle and informal way of marking territory. When the city of Rome decided, in 1984, to grant a building permit for a mosque near the Holy See, the reaction of the Riyadh press was anything but uplifting: jeering articles applauded this *tanazul,* relinquishing or surrender, on the part of Rome and the Vatican. They did not rule out that tolerance or political opportunism may have played a role, as they surely must have, but that was beside the point: Europe and all Christendom were gloatingly shown to be demoralized and weak for having caved in to Islamic machismo. It was also portrayed as a crushing blow to "world Zionism." And as usual, the Pope was slightingly referred to as *Baba El-Vatikan,* the "Pope of the Vatican." I was always on guard to ask a Saudi how he would like Fahd to be called King of Nasriya Street, but the opportunity never presented itself.

"That's not true," I told Hamdan. "You have Mecca and Medina, and there are no churches there, and no Christians or Jews allowed, or anyone else but Muslims. But Riyadh has thousands of Christians, and lots of them are Arabs. Wouldn't you respect them more if they went to church, if they had a church to go to?"

"Having no churches prevents them from learning wrong things," shrugged Hamdan. "They should be grateful. It's their chance to learn something about Islam."

I tried never to react to any cultural bias; my conversations with Hamdan were always under the cover of journalistic objectivity, and I never argued a point other than hypothetically. He was too typical, too perfect a source for me to endanger our friendship. When he did become unfriendly, his resentment came from a totally unexpected quarter. It was the day of one of my last visits to Diriya.

At some point in the midst of researching the Imam Sadr case I stopped making wine. The risks were too great, when I was already wary of the authorities because of my stringing and my visits with whatever Iranian officials came to Riyadh. I had never sold my wine—the prison sentence and lashes for trafficking in liquor were more than triple those for merely owning it—but I made it in such quantities that I began to be worried.

And my winemaking partner had been indiscreet. Donna called on my office telephone ("Baroness Rothschild here!") to report on a new batch, and had gotten our code words jumbled, though perhaps we were in no danger, if our listener found our code as confusing as we often did. The jerry cans of fermenting red, white, rose, and sherry wine were our "children," known, respectively, as Scarlett, Blanche, Rose and Sherry Ann. We had an experimental batch of wine made from pineapple juice rather than grape ("Mona Loa"). Since women were not allowed to drive, my contribution to the winemaking effort was to drive around town buying the huge bags of sugar, cases of grape juice, and the special yeast we needed. I never bought all of them in a single store, because the clerks leered at you and I felt that some of them were spies. I delivered them to Donna's apartment in the Faculty Housing area of Diriya's University City, and she got busy doing the real work. We shared evenly the harvest of bottles she so lovingly labeled. And she kept me posted on the aging process, though some days some of her friends came over and "broke into the nursery," played with the "children," and called me during this boisterous playtime.

One day she called in the middle of some anti-Saudi festivities occasioned by the firing of the head of the English department at the Women's College (actually, "girls' college"—*Kolliyat al-Banat*). This Canadian woman, though not a convert to Islam, wore a black abbaya, veil, mask, even gloves—far more covering than any Saudi student wore—and gave tongue-lashings, Donna's word, to any of the American staff who showed up in tight jeans. To celebrate her departure, a crowd of women had gathered in Donna's apartment and got drunk.

"We broke into the nursery," she reported to me over deafening background music. I was at my desk, looking at Italian police reports about Moussa Sadr. "The kids are all over the place. Blanche passed out an hour ago" (We'd had twenty bottles of white!) "but we woke up Mona Loa and she's doing a nice little ladylike job entertaining everybody. We put 'Le Nozze di Figaro' on the stereo and we're having a Western culture bash to celebrate that bitch's departure. Come over!" Our pineapple wine had been a disaster, though—how could she possibly serve it? "We punched her. Punched her until she was unrecognizable. Fruit, chopped up, and some gingerale. Sort of like Hawaiian sangria. And Martha got a bottle of gin from her Australian consul sweetie."

She went on to describe their anti-Islam bacchanal (one of her friends had even decided to bring out a pound of bacon she had been saving for weeks), but the damage was done. Our secret winery was out of the closet to Saudi intelligence, who had cut off so many of my phone calls; I would now have to stop making it, and, to be on the safe side, drinking it.

And this was a bad week for tapping: the same morning, I had three phone calls in a row cut off after a matter of seconds, because the caller was an Englishwoman trying to report a "horror" her husband ran across in the Ministry of Defense. The Saudis mainly relied upon a "tripwire" phone surveillance system that alerted a live listener when certain words were recorded, but when two monitored lines were speaking to one another a live listener was a certainty. I was sure Donna and I had no live listener, but they would get around to it within a day or two, so I had to end my winemaking.

I transported my share of the last bottles from Donna's place the next day, cringing at every pothole on the muddy, meandering access road that linked Suleimaniya with the gigantic construction site Diriya had become. Being caught would be a disaster, unless I could bribe a police officer with a few bottles; while Saudi police would be completely impervious to any monetary bribe I could offer, I knew of several instances where they had gladly accepted liquor. But what about Donna's labels? I was transporting Chateau Mecca, Plonk d'Allah, and Cordon Vert Coranique—she dreamed up the most blasphemous names possible, and I tried not to imagine how many lashes they would add up to, if my hypothetical arresting officer could decipher them. Within two days I gave away all the wine.

"Why aren't you drinking?" asked Hamdan, eyeing me suspiciously. This was a few days later, and I was at his house after work, at the end of an unmerciful day, the last of Ferdinand Marcos's official visit to Riyadh. (The Philippine president had brought twenty reporters with him, of whom half were gorgeous young women. At his parting press conference, Marcos leered at them from the microphone and asked the Saudi deputy foreign minister, "How 'bout that? Do you guess that's a fine rose of a sexy lady or what?!" The Saudi stared at the floor.) Part of the reason for Hamdan's invitation was that he had taken delivery of a case of Iohanna Mashi Ahmar (Johnnie Walker Red Label) and he and his brothers were pulling at tumblers of the warm scotch in their cluttered part of the house, whose glass doors overlooked the outdoor pool, the new Buicks parked alongside it, and dusty ficus trees lining Talatin Street beyond the high wall.

I had never prepared an excuse *not* to drink.

"Just taking a break from it," I shrugged.

"You're so stupid! What's wrong with you!" Hamdan sounded upset, and it was not the liquor. His eyes were clear and full of sudden distrust. "What did you come here for then?"

"Why do I have to drink if I don't feel like it? There's all the more for you." This reasoning soured Hamdan's mood very badly and it took me a second to see why: I was not playing along. If he wanted to hear the voice of his conscience, he did not want to hear it transmitted through a Christian, an inferior; let alone a sober one. The moral high ground belongs to Muslims alone.

"Do you think you're better than I am or something?" His face had colored, and a nerve twitched in his neck. He poured more scotch into a waterglass with a daisy painted on the side. "I don't understand you."

"Play backgammon," suggested his brother Khaled. Hamdan slid the board from underneath a sofa and opened it between us on the floor. "Put on Marvin Gaye," he told Khaled. A Barbara Streisand cassette had just clicked off. News of Marvin Gaye's death had come over the radio just that morning, on the BBC, Israel Radio, Voice of Lebanon, Radio Cairo, Voice of the Masses from Baghdad, even Radio Tehran. All, in unconscious homage to American cultural imperialism, played at least a few bars of "I Heard It Through the Grapevine"—all except Radio Tehran, of course—and none failed to dwell on the exact nature of his death; now Hamdan brought it up.

"That could only have happened in America," he said.

We played backgammon until he got tired and his brother took over playing me. Hamdan made himself a fresh drink and leaned on his elbow watching the game. Their conversation, rising and falling without me, was about a new novel by Abdelrahman Munif, his best yet, supposedly set in the Eastern (oil) Province. It was published in Beirut and immediately banned in the kingdom. Copies were selling for 500 riyals—nearly $200. I wanted to ask about it, but Hamdan's mood was much too defensive to discuss his country's grudge against its greatest writer. Then they discussed the controversial Jamal Farhan, a star Saudi soccer player who had been ejected from a Saudi–Kuwaiti match for punching the referee—a Belgian. The Saudi Football Federation did not allow Arabs to referee—it could inflame inter-Arab grudges in cases such as this. All the Riyadh sports press raged at Farhan's expulsion from the game and contemptuously referred to the injured European referee as *hath'al-murtazaq,* "this mercenary."

"He should have kicked him, not hit him," declared Hamdan.

"Kuwait Radio said Farhan should be suspended," I remarked. "After all, the referee was only doing his job."

"Did you see the call?" snapped Hamdan. "God! You didn't—

you're not even a sports fan! He should have *killed* that referee!"

"Anyway, Saudi Arabia lost the game, thanks to Farhan," I pointed out maliciously. "And it was an international match, so it doesn't only reflect badly on him or his team, it's a black mark on the Kingdom."

"Isn't it a black mark on America, what you're doing in Lebanon?" Hamdan almost screamed. He snatched up his drink and added gloatingly, "Farhan has an American girlfriend, some slut from Florida."

It was late in a long and exhausting day, and daylight was failing as if it could not stay awake another minute. I drove back to my office irritated at Hamdan and his paunchy brothers, for getting drunk by midafternoon in the worst climate for hangovers anywhere on earth, and being so angry at me for not joining in. I think Hamdan was afraid I was going to humiliate him completely by converting to Islam: he had once seen some of the religious books connected to my Imam Sadr investigation, and looked disgusted. I was already under suspicion because I never touched marijuana, and spoke Arabic. Although he often harped on the superiority of Islam, he wanted me as part of his American life, the side that drank whiskey, manufactured wine, watched blue movies, and used all the newest obscenities: an unclean vessel. If I were to convert I would nose ahead of him spiritually and I was not even an Arab.

After Hussein's departure one year before, I had been working even harder on the Imam Sadr case. The King Faisal Hospital had fired most of the Shiite Muslims in the space of a month, and most headed back to the chaos of Beirut or the Israeli-held south, where Hussein's brother Hassan was in an Israeli internment camp in the border town of Khiam.

"I have transmitted the whole telex to Jeddah—*without a single mistake!*" was Mr. Iyer's cry when I got back. He shook his finger at the red-bordered copy on my desk. It was my morning story on EEC tariffs on Saudi Arabian petrochemical exports and I immediately spotted four mistakes. He was glowering up at me in front of the desk, his arms behind his back, buttoned up in his cardigan although it was nearly 120 degrees outside. Why did he do this? He slid into the chair in front of the desk and began a recitation of his day's humiliations at the hands of a taxi driver who had told him he would spend eternity in *Nar,* the Flame, for being a *Hindusi* polytheist and then overcharged him.

"They are saying there is no stealing in Saudi Arabia, they are said to be lopping off hands, yet they are charging seventy riyals to drive two kilometers!"

I gave him the rest of the day off and opened my mail while meditating on the pointless pain of my awful job in this awful place. The lack of free money, the Iran–Iraq war, and the ongoing humiliations in Lebanon and Palestine had shot the Saudis' nerves. People were unfriendlier, and their usual smugness had become a very touchy arrogance. A teenage religious vigilante had nearly succeeded in making a citizen's arrest of the American consul, Walter Pflaumer, who had kissed his British fiancée good-bye in what he considered to be the safety of the King Faisal Hospital compound. The lurking fanatic witnessed the kiss and called the police, who, afraid of siding with either party, made their escape while the consul was driven to a mosque and told to sign a confession. Such events usually bothered British expatriates more than Americans—unlike us, the British had usually worked abroad for long years, generally in Africa, and thought all natives should be cheerful and slightly in awe of them. Even the fact that my day's mail included a book—I would open that last—could not change the fact that I was in a growing snit. And then Mahdi came in.

"Shame on you! By God, shame on you! How many times have I asked you for girls, or boys, and you don't bring me anything? You must know all the foreign girls. Can you find me some this week?" He must have been uncontrollably horny; he had not even prefaced this with his pitch for me to convert.

"I found you some girls," I lied, under the influence of my ballooning bad mood. "I'll introduce you to them tomorrow."

"At last! God bless you, Boutros. Are they Americans? British? Filipinos? What will it cost me? Are they beautiful?"

"They are very beautiful—moons!" This was an eloquent, highly valued compliment. "It won't cost you anything—they just like sex. They have sex with one another, and with any man at all. They do anything."

"French women!"

"They are Saudi."

For a moment I thought he would kill me. His face was so red and angry it looked ready to burst.

"Who told you that? Shame on you!"

"They are Saudi. They like to have fun. You'll have to bring them some whiskey and some drugs."

"They must have lived in America. Are they from Jeddah?"

"From Riyadh. They've never lived in America, but they visit America and Europe to go to the opera. You can't tell anyone about this. They live in Naseryia. When can they expect you?"

Mahdi gazed at me warily and tottered slowly out of the office. He never spoke to me again.

The book, sent from a diplomat in Jeddah, was a book the

Arabic newspapers had been screaming about, *The Haj;* I had nagged everyone I knew to find me a copy. I began to read it, and, like a slowly whirling sandstorm fixing to change new landscapes for old, my snit abruptly changed directions.

11
The Written Word

*A*fter only two chapters, I leaned Leon Uris's *The Haj* against my telephone rather than hold it in my hands. This had to be the worst novel ever written. It was actually not a novel, but a fanciful memoir wound around patches of shockingly racist polemic, not Zionist but pro-Zionist polemic that did its cause no credit. I hated the word "Zionist"—other than in the context of Herzl or Jabotinsky or kibbutzes, it was pronounced exclusively by anti-Semites; the Arabs were addicted to using it to describe anything they did not like, much in the same way American children used to use the word "communist." But this was propaganda, set up as a novel solely in order to furnish an Arab narrator who could never have existed, whose sole function was to make racist and obscene remarks about his own people. It was an impossible forgery: a sort of *Protocols of the Elders of Palestine*. For that, the author's bold ingenuity had to be acknowledged. Perhaps some Soviet hack will someday follow his example with a novel narrated by an American who vapors on about why Americans stink, why we should be spat upon; how we sell our children for drugs, rape old ladies in the subway, lynch cripples for fun, how we will forever pay for our stupidity in not worshiping the KGB; how we deserve genocide, if only some selfless Soviet premier would condescend to press the button and carry it out. This was the level of *The Haj*.

Finishing its more than five hundred pages was an exhausting experience. The author spared the Arabs no indignity achievable by malice or ignorance, starting with the protagonist's name. A Palestinian Muslim, he introduces himself as Ishmael, which in its Arabic form is Ismail. Why would his father, who hates Jews, give him the Hebrew version of the name?

It is common knowledge that Arab Muslims in real life, particularly bedouin and villagers, are protective of their women, to the point of being obnoxiously male chauvinist. They rarely refer to their wives or daughters and almost never mention them by name; in Saudi Arabia, I knew of a man who once canceled his family's vacation rather than divulge his wife's name to the travel agent issuing the airline tickets. Ishmael is far more enlightened: he brags, on the first page of his memoir, that "my mother, Hagar, was a large woman with great breasts."

Ishmael lives to see the Zionist settlement of Palestine, the partition of 1947, several wars, and the ultimate destruction of his family by Arabs (including himself). He has an instinctive love of the Jews, who, as a rule, are blond and blue-eyed; when he describes the looks of his Arab brethren it is usually with revulsion. (Ishmael also comes to know David Ben Gurion—he calls him B.G. and mentions him all the time; this Arab scum is even a name dropper!) Every Arab in the book, except for his father—who comes to admire the pioneer Jews with remarkable groveling and self-hatred—feels Ishmael's lash. Little wonder: his compatriots are dirty-minded, violent monsters, all of whom, in their more articulate moments, spout propaganda that would only embarrass any self-respecting Arab hater: "We are a people living in hate, despair and darkness . . . the Jews are our bridge out of darkness . . . we are incapable of change . . . we cannot live with one another . . . we are accursed among living creatures . . . we Arabs are the worst." When the machinations of the books's throng of self-hating Arabs finally lead them to the destruction they so richly merit—as they would be the first to admit—one observes, "What we are witnessing now is the beginning of Armageddon"—a totally meaningless reference for any Arab or Muslim; would gloomy Chinese, sensing the deluge, voice fears about the coming Götterdämmerung?

Ishmael endlessly spews repulsive curses which are wholly the invention of the author who inhabits him, like a dybbuk: "May a thousand ants infest your armpits!" "I fart on your beard!" "Go fuck a dead camel!" "Your mother's cunt is an oasis for camels!"

(Ishmael is proud of the oriental flourish of this style—"Do not forget, my esteemed reader, that we Arabs are unusually gifted in matters of fantasy and magic.") And he does have camels on the brain. This animal, a patient and gentle source of food and milk, a magnificent steed and beast of burden, prized by Arabs far above the most pedigreed horse, he describes as an "ill-tempered, ugly, smelly beast." But then, he fails to be an Arab even when he really strains to: what Arab would describe classical Arabic songs as "deliciously discordant wails"?

The torrents of psychopathic self-criticism the Arab characters indulge in are not the only forms of Arab-bashing that go on. In a subtler book, one might take pleasure in noting the real author's deliberate sabotage of Arabic names to make them appear clumsy and more foreign than they are: he writes Azziz instead of Aziz, Zyyad instead of Ziad, Hashemiiya instead of Hashemia, and explains the name "al-Aqsa"—referring to the mosque in Jerusalem—as meaning "the fartherest" (it means "the farthest"), as if Arabic were such a bamboozling language that it can't even be translated properly, or boasts such imaginary constructions as the double superlative. And he defines *majnun* ("crazy") as "the spirit that makes you go crazy." These Arabs are a pretty arcane bunch.

And not notable for filial piety. In the closing pages of the book, Ishmael gleefully gives his father a heart attack by describing the rape of his mother and sister, some years earlier, by Iraqi soldiers in Jaffa: "There were eight or ten of them, and one after the other they came at the women and I saw their big wet slimy pricks coming inside them! . . . They jerked off on the naked bodies of your wives. . . . I watched Mother being fucked on the floor by a half-dozen of them! Fucked on the floor!" When his father finally succumbs *("Yahhhhhhh!")*, Ishmael wanders away and eventually blacks out—in a final ludicrous touch, he gasps his rambling last words *in writing* (". . . climb . . . climb . . . get up there to her . . . Hot . . . I am lost . . ." etc., until the words "The End").

It could only have been published in 1984.

The Haj did not deserve any real reflection for my purposes (hate literature always sheds much light on the author and none on the subject and Uris had certainly written the book, in every sense of the word, on self-hatred) but, coming at a time when I was finally asking myself what on earth I was doing in the Arab world—after years of being asked that by other people—it helped me to see why. I was here to see who we were, and who the Arabs were, and how we looked at one another. The research on my Imam Sadr book was half finished, and my outline had been bought by the British publisher I had approached. This put everything in a different light: I had a responsibility to provide answers, not just flaunt my curiosity. The thought that I would soon be an author, just as the *Haj* perpetrator was an author, reminded me of another symmetry: my project dealt with Arab crimes against Arabs and did not expose anything I held dear to any danger. Taken at any level, Colonel Qaddafi's statements that he was guilty of no crime against Sadr were preposterous. Even the research gloated, and so would the narrative. Of course, I was writing about facts, and without malice, certainly without using any innocent person, real or imaginary, as a voodoo fetish doll.

Arabia was, of course, ill served by writers of books. Burton and Doughty, Blunt and Bell had been frank, and fanatical in their life-encompassing research; like Wilfred Thesiger, in *Arabian Sands* and *The Marsh Arabs* and later in his brilliant *A Life of*

My Own, they had produced masterpieces on lost ways of life, which resembled Angie Debo's loving Creek and Cherokee history books. Far too many books about the Arabs dealt with lost ways of life—doubtless because they are still in the process of being lost. It is much harder to look at the emerging ways of life.

More recent writers, motivated by curiosity, prurience, proselytizing, profit, politics, and pure escape had also recorded their visits to this part of the world in books. But with the huge increase in Muslim oil wealth, and then the strengthening of the Islamic profile of the region, writers who had none of these motives began to come. They arrived with very little knowledge and a totally new purpose: to write a book. Without the prospect of the book, there would have been no curiosity, no journey, no little Arabic lessons, no boning up on the Koran or back issues of *Middle East Economic Digest.*

Invariably they created self-portraits. Jonathan Raban, in *Arabia: A Journey Through the Labyrinth,* described a brief Anglocentric stroll through a half-dozen marginal Arab countries. They were all former British colonies, which tend to be open to British subjects (though he does not mention this fact and may not have noticed it), and, with the exception of Egypt, not centers of power, wealth, culture, or population. With a little effort, Raban could have gone to Lebanon, to Syria, and to Iraq: who on earth could write about "Arabia" with no trace of Damascus or Baghdad—or, for that matter, Jerusalem? And this book about "Arabia" left out Saudi Arabia itself—a little planning could surely have got him there, too.

Of course, my familiarity with Arabia made me a terrible quibbler. At some point in Abu Dhabi he should have noticed that the currency was the dirham, not the dirhan. He should have noticed that the word "burnoose," which he uses, was never used by any Arab he met, because it is a North African word for the pointy-hooded cloaks found there; uninformed writers about Arabs call almost every garment a burnoose. (The plural is *baranees;* and *al-Baranees* is the Arabic word for the Pyrenees.) Why does Raban describe Arabic graffiti as "elegant"? English script is no less elegant; he is unaware that the scrawls he saw in London probably read, "Syria out of Lebanon," "Death to Saddam," and "Death to Israel."

There was something touching about his settling down to learning the Arabic alphabet a few weeks before setting off. Was there, somewhere in Morocco or Iraq, some soul brother of Raban, preparing a journey to America to explain the West to his fellow Arabs? My imagination supplied him. Was he studiously learning the ABCs so as to crack the codes of the West's over-powering civilizations? Was he congratulating himself on a sentence like,

> *The sticks, circles and half-circles of their rather repetitious letter system go through twenty-six permutations, with certain features unknown to us in Arabic—added, perhaps, by the sadistic Irish monks who codified the alphabet—such as "capital letters" (big initial letters used to distinguish proper nouns, and to let you know when a sentence is beginning, a period closing the previous sentence being insufficient for that purpose); and a novel, non-script form of writing, especially popular in books, known as* printing.

Perhaps this person would go about getting an American visa all wrong, and end up writing his book *America: Knocking at the Golden Door* based on visits to Canada, Costa Rica, Belize,

Jamaica, Mexico, and England. ("The Belizean Embassy was the nicest—they told me I could buy Belize citizenship for $50,000. I considered it, and they served me a Tab. . . .") And Raban talked too much.

Then there was *Among the Believers* by V. S. Naipaul, also banned by the Saudis. Naipaul journeyed to four Muslim countries in Asia; all of them were non-Arab. That was an interesting choice, and his writing was dazzling. But he came up against simple things he didn't know—was it possible that he did not know anything about the Bahais except the name? And there was a brief passage, when the author and his interpreter were looking at a wall of posters in Tehran, that made me pause.

> They were like posters of a people's revolution: an awakened, victorious people, a new dignity of labour. But what was the Persian legend at the top?
> Behzad translated: "Twelfth Imam, we are waiting for you."
> "What does that mean?"
> "It means they are waiting for the Twelfth Imam."

The writer is curious and arch, his Iranian host is laconic and inscrutable. But this is an illusion: the Twelfth Imam, or Mahdi, unknown to many of the book's readers, is more famous in Iran than Jesus is in Britain; his messianic arrival is expected to establish justice on earth at the end of time. A cultural translation of the passage might read:

> Even in a city so packed with stone and copper statesmen, this one stood out. My guide identified him as Jefferson. But what was that English legend behind him?
> Bucky translated: " 'We hold these truths to be self-evident.' "

"What does that mean?"
"It means we hold these truths to be self-evident."

Where do you begin? Naturally, the young guide is at a loss to explain 1,400 years of Islamic history to a casual questioner from another planet. Such details did not prevent Naipaul from writing an excellent book, but homework was not his strong suit.

Any such foreign books investigating the region were banned, dog-eared, passed around, and read by Westerners in Saudi Arabia, not only for the cachet of reading a forbidden book, but for information. Robert Lacey's *The Kingdom* and Hirst and Holden's *The House of Saud* were smash hits on the clandestine book market. Even though the VCR was a leisure-time force to be reckoned with, much reading was done by the Asians, Europeans, and Americans working in Saudi Arabia, and people were curious about the region they lived in—knowing it firsthand had gotten tricky. Before the war in Lebanon, the kingdom's moneyed guest workers flocked to Beirut to ski, swim, and gamble all in one day. When that became impossible, many made the two-hour flight to Shiraz for a week's recreation. When the revolution in Iran prevented that, they either saw more of Greece or Italy or stayed home in their walled compounds to drink *siddiqi,* but they saw less of their adopted part of the world. Raban and Naipaul were popular.

I tended to read these books with mounting resentment, because they could not help but be glib, and yet who could do a better job? Saudi Arabia in particular was a poser. A travel writer could record his thoughts about the high walls, empty streets, and pitiless heat. He would meet almost no one, certainly no Saudi, who would confide in him. Describing the difference between this alien culture and our own would be easy, but what was the point? Making people understand other people would have been to stress similarities, to see them from the inside. That meant literature, fiction specifically, and the novels about Arabs by non-Arabs—*The Haj, The Pirate, The Fifth Horseman*—were one of the writing world's most dreadful genres. Unfortunately, the Arab Middle East had little literary clout abroad to appeal to the sentimentality or imagination of Americans, as so many other cultures, even uncongenial ones, had—no *Exodus,* no *Good Earth,* no *Dr. Zhivago,* no *Cry, the Beloved Country,* no *Sea of Fertility,* no *Hundred Years of Solitude,* no *Unbearable Lightness of Being,* no *Freedom at Midnight,* no *Z,* no *Things Fall Apart.* And none of the dozens of foreign writers of history, travel, politics, journalism, polemic, or apologetics could fill that gap.

Reading what Arabs wrote about Arabs was part of my job, but little of it was fiction. The idea was to improve my everyday Arabic, and so I read newspapers, religious books—Riyadh being the religious tract capital of the world—a smuggled New Testament, magazines, especially women's magazines, and schoolbooks. Weekly newsmagazines like *al-Majalla, al-Mostaqbal* and *ad-Dastour* were too heavy on sports, politics, and business; they smothered you with the moderate party line: the Arab yearning for America to end its heartless affair with Israel.

The chatty women's magazines revealed much more. Their view of the world grew from real jealousies and real admiration, without machismo. They were unapologetic about their obsession with the British royal family, their love of consumer goods, and their interest in Western things. No one but a woman would have dared devote two pages to praising Ronald and Nancy Reagan's modest one-turkey Thanksgiving dinner. The photo showed the American first couple serving themselves from a small buffet: "Can't we Arab ladies, with our love of ostentation, learn a lesson from the world's most powerful statesman and his wife?" These magazines dealt with the tragedies and atrocities of Palestine, Lebanon, and the Gulf war through profiles of remarkable people, especially remarkable women, or as a sentimental social question. The Palestinian issue was treated somewhat as the South African one is in the U.S.—as a burning, unambiguous issue, one that outraged nearly everyone, but not one demanding fanaticism, and one that few made sacrifices for. These magazines had impressive circulation; because they printed so many glamorous pictures of women, not to mention the arousing advertisements, and scratch 'n sniff perfume ads, they were read by as many young men as women. The weak point of each was the awful fiction they printed; the sole subject seemed to be the tender girl, being married off against her will, who falls in love on her very sketchily described honeymoon.

The schoolbooks, on the other hand, were a vocabulary lesson. Hearing Arabs talk about the Big Wall of China, the Iron Veil, and even America's Greatest Recession I vowed not to make any such mistakes; for a person speaking a foreign language, the biggest blind spot is his own culture because it is the last thing he thinks of using the second language to talk about. And of course the question of interpretation was central here: Arabs speaking English often confused foreigners with talking about the Palestine War (Israel's War of Independence), the Tripartite Aggression (the Suez War), the Ramadhan War (the Yom Kippur War), the Setback War (the Six-Day War). Conversely, I saw a U.S. diplomat from Virginia make a Saudi squint in polite bewilderment by describing his state's role in the Harb Bayn al-Walayat, the "War Between the States"; but even "Harb Ahliya," "Civil War" rather than the Southern misnomer would have failed. The Arabs know it as the "Harb al-Infisal," the "War of the Secession."

Of course, this linguistic blind spot was cultural, too: of the American diplomats who could easily discuss the social and economic problems of the Arab world, how many knew the Arabic for "homelessness," "teen pregnancy," "child pornography," or "junk food"?

I had read Arab fiction in English from the days of Muhammad Alwan's summer class and my afternoons in Cairo; more recently, I had begun to move slowly through original Arabic books.

The best novelist was the Palestinian Ghassan Kanafani. His short novel *Men in the Sun,* a thinking man's *Haj,* told the stories of a small group of Palestinian refugees trying to smuggle themselves into Kuwait to find work. They suffocate in the empty tanks of the water truck transporting them through the desert, the victims not only of the lazy, empty-headed Arabs who delay the journey, but of their own silence. Kanafani, a member of the Popular Front for the Liberation of Palestine, blown up in Beirut in 1972, believed in violent solutions and wrote, like so many Arabs, with insistent political purpose; even without it, though, *Men in the Sun* was a great book.

The problem with Arab fiction was the odor of sociology emanating from all over: Sudanese novels, Saudi, Iraqi, Egyptian, Algerian, Lebanese. Even the great Egyptian, Nagib Mahfouz, was guilty of this. His stories in *God's World* were full of tricks such as using a child's perspective to show the adult world as strange, or "getting into" a murderer's head. Only within the confines of an Islamic society could such literary tactics be seen as daring or effective.

The novel was a relatively new form in Arabia. There were comparatively few publishers, and everywhere censorship, states of emergency, blasphemy laws, dictators with sensitive egos, and other enemies of free literature. The result was a typical Arab novel with typical features: Aesopian or Camusian heroes suffering alienation from society; indecision, frustration, gray bureaucracy, a chaste love affair. The symbol racket ran riot. The West was often a force of evil. The ambiguous political fable was very prevalent. Social and religious taboos forced "realistic" novels to be folksy, brooding, reverent, smothered in allegory and trite surrealism. The bizarre marriage of traditional subjects and desperately "new" forms often failed at the literary level but helped a reader to see how bad life for these writers really was.

An exception was Abdelrahman Munif—the only Saudi novel I had read was his *East of the Mediterranean*—and it was, needless to say, banned. Its luckless hero, Rajab Ismail, endures hideous tortures before going into political exile. Munif's descriptions spared nothing: beatings, fingers smashed in the hinges of doors, Rajab's body squeezed behind doors until he felt his "ribs bursting from his eye sockets," cigarettes crushed out on his neck and in his ears, and an unspeakable torture involving cats, a rope, and his genitals. These experiences conclude with Rajab's exile and death.

This novel was unique in Arabic literature: it was extremely real and harsh—no invented names, no modest silence over the methods of torture, no derivative shortcuts such as symbols or parables. While not set in a specific country, its title was a geographical indictment. The Israelis—usually the only people it is permissible to depict as torturers—had no place in the book. It was a very good story, and a very courageous book, and had earned its reputation as a groundbreaking work.

The Saudis did, of course, torture, though as a rule they used methods that left no mark on the body—this was said to be in conformity with some saying of the Prophet which reportedly condemned bloodier methods. The most famous method involved gallons of drinking water and a soft hose tightly knotted around the penis. Munif, who was now said to live in Paris or Baghdad, and whose crime, even before he wrote his first book, had been traveling to the Soviet Union for his education, was merely exiled. He had been active in the Arab Baath Socialist Party of Iraq.

Munif was the one Arab writer who had made the novel an Arab thing, giving it the strengths of journalism and folktale. Actually, he was writing history. Reading Munif was different from reading any other Arab author. He had a Tolstoyan gift for writing about people just like the ones you know. You never found yourself thinking, "Ah—the sick old lady symbolizes Egypt, the ungrateful daughter symbolizes the new middle class, the old sheikh is the comfort of Islam . . ." Even the gruesomest passages of *Sharq al-Mutawasit* made me see myself translating it and my mother reading it with pleasure.

In Tihama, al-Khazindar, al-Jarir, and all the other big Riyadh bookstores I asked for "Munif's latest," just to cover all the bases, and drew unfriendly stares. One black clerk, a Sudanese in the University Bookstore, started to say, "I know someone—" but thought better of it and turned away.

I could not do the kind of reporting that would dull the cumulative pain of putting up with Riyadh and its slim literary pickings; I could only resolve to perfect the Imam book to redeem the time and change my hired-hand status in the kingdom. I had all my friends on the lookout for new Sadr developments—movements and governments were always pledging to get him freed—and one day I received a faxed article from Beirut's respected daily *al-Nahar:*

> The Sadr Brigades Organization [formed by the Imam's sister to avenge his disappearance] has revealed the following . . .
>
> A certain Jalaleddine Farsi, who had run for president in Iran, then withdrawn his candidacy, as his great-grandfather was of Afghani origin, thus rendering him ineligible, by the terms of the Iranian constitution, and the late Muhammad Saleh Husseini, then Imam Khomeini's Mideast representative and director of Islamic liberation movements, met on August 26, 1978, with Major General Saleh Abu Shereida, chief of Libyan Intelligence and close confidant of Qaddafi at the Beirut International Hotel.
>
> Abu Shereida had entered Lebanon that same day on a forged Moroccan passport. He had a lengthy meeting with the two men and left Beirut on the morning of August 28.
>
> That afternoon, Husseini met an Amal official he knew slightly and told him, "I'm heading to Libya—is there anything I can do for you there?" "No, have a good trip and give my regards to Imam Sadr," was the reply. Husseini answered, "Whatever you say, but you might as well know your friend isn't coming back."
>
> On the evening of August 27, 1978, Husseini and Farsi flew to Libya. We have documentary evidence that proves the two were among the kidnappers of the Imam and his companions, and thought it right to share it with the masses and the officials of the Islamic Republic.

12

Inside Stories

*A*s the embassy reception was not far from my house, I planned to leave at the last minute after the long nap needed to get through the 120-degree afternoon. The *toz* whipped in orange wavelets over the enclosed prairie across the street: I lived on the perimeter of the old Riyadh Airport, now abandoned in favor of King Khaled International thirty miles west of the city, a fantasy in marble and glass with whole orchards of trees inside the terminal buildings.

Some form of manifest destiny—it was actually the unholy alliance of landowning princes and city planners—was pushing Riyadh west. The nicest neighborhoods were now those between Suleimaniya and the new airport; Suleimaniya itself, once a bumptious boondock in the distant northwest of walled Riyadh, was now midtown. As the city limits moved relentlessly in the direction of Los Angeles, successive city centers sprang up and were beaten down again by ever grander shopping malls, hotels, and villa parks to the west. My window—the half of it not occupied by a growling air conditioner—used to look out on a street bed and the naked horizon; now it was six lanes of al-Arouba (Arabism) Street, marble-clad apartment blocks, and the Sheraton one mile beyond. Just to the north, the old airport land—once an intrusion of civilization, perfectly flat behind its high chain-link fence, with the whine of landing aircraft—was a silent wilderness.

For most of 1984 and part of 1985 I had been without a valid residence permit and now bitterly resented Saudi Arabia. It was only a bureaucratic quibble (Prince Naif, the interior minister, had not yet approved a renewal of my "sponsorship"—all employment in the kingdom being a form of indentured service), but I was tense without it because a foreigner must carry his residence permit with him at all times. He may not travel from one city to another without it and the permission of his employer. And of course I had been unable to leave the country. Nine months of a foul mood compounded by 124-degree temperatures, and now, after a welcome cloudburst the day before, *toz,* which always brought me bad luck.

(I had fallen into the little superstitions that thrive in fanatically antisuperstitious places. The Islamic commandment against graven images had resulted in a fetishistic Saudi removal of heads from the black silhouettes on traffic signs, for example, and architects had to make exorbitantly costly changes in designs to avoid even the suggestion of a cross. This total abomination of anything vaguely idolatrous accorded them a certain idolatrous power they would never have had elsewhere. But my superstitions were simple: *toz* is bad luck, silence is golden, always wear a tie.)

The telephone, which had been out of order (the rain—no one had thought to make the underground phone cables waterproof in the desert), rang as I was tying my tie.

"Alloo—na'm!"

"Helloo?" It was a girl—Arab, but her best English hello.

"Nimra ghalat, ya bint."

"Don't you speak English? It isn't a wrong number."

"Who are you? Do I know you? What number are you trying to call?"

"I just want to talk. Since you can speak English, it's the right number."

"I'm in a hurry, miss."

"Don't you want to talk about anything, mister?"

One of these days I was going to bare my soul to one of these random callers, but they always chose awkward times to call. "I would love to talk to you, miss, but I'm in a hurry. I have to go out, to the American ambassador's house."

"I think it's early for a party. Are you American or British?"

"I am American."

"Do you work in your country's embassy?"

"I am a journalist, miss." I was always truthful with those

toneless voices, since my home line was monitored, too. She hung up.

Saudi children were playing soccer in the side street as the sun reclined, an intense rosy orange through the rust and gray of the dust storm. The minarets had begun to broadcast the penultimate prayer of the day. Down the street, the Panda Supermarket locked its doors—during prayer time no one could come in, go out, or buy anything, only glide through the dim aisles or curse on the sidewalk of al-Arouba Street. As usual, the boys ran at my car, screaming, "Spaghetti!" (It was a Fiat.)

There were no sidewalks in the ambassador's neighborhood, and no place to park, only towering, uneven walls running along both sides of the slightly concave street. Homeowners here parked in their front courtyards, inside the gates; for security reasons, that could not be permitted at his house. The narrow street was blocked by twenty American sedans, white vans with the markings of the new Riyadh Marriott, and men in suits streaming toward the tall gates topped by cameras. Some held their hands over their eyes: contact lens wearers.

"One of our wives wants a word with you," smiled the new American ambassador, at the door of his new official residence in Riyadh. His predecessor, Richard Murphy, had kept a small, unofficial villa near the U.S. Liaison Office, but the liaison office had bloated to two interconnected three-floor buildings, not to mention the surrounding streets, and was now officially an embassy. The unilateral seizure of the streets, with guard posts, traffic bumps, and huge concrete barricades, had enraged the governor of Riyadh, Prince Salman, who received the U.S. consul and laughingly told him that the Americans could not arbitrarily close down two public thoroughfares! They were not in Washington—heh heh! King Fahd, however, decided to let the Americans have their two streets. The big, temporary new residence was leased to go with the big, temporary new embassy. Both would soon be made obsolete by the gigantic U.S. embassy compound in the Diplomatic Quarter.

Like the liaison office, this stucco mansion behind the high wall now flew the American flag. This in spite of the high state of alert of all U.S. diplomatic missions in the Persian Gulf ever since pro-Iranian terrorists had nearly blown up the U.S. Embassy in Kuwait. The dedication of the embassy premises had been closed to the press, though it was held out in the open air, among the concrete barriers, and was the subject of a press release from the Saudi Ministry of Foreign Affairs.

This first official cocktail party in the residence, only a few blocks from my apartment, was a reception for a trade delegation, with the atmosphere of a college mixer prevailing as American industrialists wearing name tags were steered toward Saudi businessmen by grinning officers of the U.S. commercial section. The days of Americans seeking agents and distributors were gone: this was a joint-venture mixer, with foreign partners expected to commit forty percent of a new projects' equity. Cash was now short in the kingdom. Fahd had signed his second deficit budget, and Saudis hoped that forcing foreigners to hold a stake in their own ventures here would eliminate adventurous slobs who were looking for a quick buck.

Oil prices had been falling for three years, and Saudi Arabia's new austerity had changed attitudes all around. American businessmen who used to boil at their inability to buy land here would now never dream of making such a stupid investment.

"This way, Pete!"

Two Saudis in the foyer, whose job it was to introduce the ambassador to his Arab guests, smirked at me and then each other. The ambassador of the United States leading this man to an embassy wife! It wasn't only that it looked absurd to them—it was that the particular wife, known as "Call-me-Libby" even among Saudis, was a little bit of a joke. She was said to give handicraft shows at her house, for no discernable charitable purpose, and made embassy personnel come; they felt compelled to buy some of the overpriced giftware, mainly Tunisian ceramics and bird-cages (she and her husband had last served in Tunisia). She had sent the vice-consul out to buy flowers for her table. Saudis read about her when the women's supplement of the daily *al-Jazira* asked several diplomatic wives what they would ask for if they had three wishes. Unlike the others, who named "world peace," or "grandchildren," Call-me-Libby said she would "keep wishing for three more wishes!" There may have been no truth to the rumors, but the hostility of the embassy staff toward her, and the general low morale, were not rumors. I had never met her.

The tense roar of entrepreneurial mating filled the crowded rooms. Diplomats worked the room with swiveling heads and eyes to see where they were needed, pausing to listen tentatively at the elbows of earnest American and Arab investors, ready to inject a needed piece of advice about U.S. trade policy or the National Industrialization Company, the kingdom's joint-venture institution—itself, appropriately, half public-owned.

Besides businessmen, there were a few professionals here, including my Lebanese lawyer friend Fuad, and Aqil al-Aqil, a barrel-chested Saudi writer with a bushy mustache and stubbly chins. And there was Al Calabrese. And there was Dr. Jeanne McNett, who taught English literature at the Women's College.

She was a friend of Donna. For three years people had whispered about her hardship in facing widowhood, though her husband had died more than ten years before, in Vietnam. One day she told me that she had made all that up.

"To keep men from jumping on me. There's something about Saudi Arabia—all this sneaking around to get a glass of whiskey or read a banned book. This government is like a mother with teenagers—'I know what goes on, but as long as you're living under my roof . . .' And so many of these guys are bad enough without this place turning them into adolescents again." Jeanne was talking to a small group of women; we waved, and I felt a little surge of pride that she was from Massachusetts.

And there was Miles, Lutfallah Nasr's son-in-law from Cairo. He was no longer a diplomat. His badge identified him as a trade consultant for an illegible firm in Vienna, Virginia. He looked through me, and I moved on.

We made very slow progress through the mass of guests, all snapping up hors d'oeuvres and drinking as fast as they could (except for embassy staff) with several insisting on talking to the ambassador. He had served in the U.S. Embassy in Saigon, and many of the visitors knew him from there, or from Zaire, or from Washington. One man, wearing a name tag identifying him as VP—JVs. "PERRY" had even filched a framed picture from a bookshelf—it showed the ambassador grinning and sharing a handclasp with George Bush—and was holding it up. He wanted to tell the ambassador a George Bush story.

"Hey, guy," the ambassador interrupted him with a crinkly smile, and passed on with me in tow.

Libby was in the main dining room of the residence, encircled by a crowd of munching men. A constellation of Filipino waiters offered their trays of salmon and caviar to the men, who stubbornly placed their empty plastic cups among the crackers and asked for refills. They could not spare a moment away from this important member of the embassy harem, who was talking about Ronald Reagan. The dining room table was covered with more platters of hors d'oeuvres, candles, small plates, semicircles of linen napkins, and immense crystal ashtrays. No one sat at the piano, whose lid was rakishly aloft. A few other embassy wives were making conversation with visiting businessmen.

"It's pretty hard," Susan Dibiasi was telling one tall guest with a name tag, whose eyes were scouring the room for a free Saudi. "I have a part-time job? It's with a Swedish contractor, but when the religious police come on an inspection visit? All the women have to be herded into the ladies' room because of the laws against women working alongside men! I really wonder—"

"So you are, in fact, breaking the law," chided the man.

"Yes!" she said, her tone suggesting *Are you thick!* and *That's just the point!* Then she saw that he was serious and gave up.

"A fuckin' outrage, pal," Al De Matteis was telling another trade delegate. He was on his favorite subject: how his Saudi–American joint venture had lost the contract to build the American embassy in Riyadh. The government had awarded the job to a South Korean contractor with a slightly lower bid.

The ambassador maneuvered me in between two of Libby's listeners, and her eyes brightened as he loped back to the front door and some of the men drifted away to the bar. She began talking to me so fast that at first I did not know what she was saying.

"—Literally her oldest and dearest friend, and I didn't know you were related. She's one of my favorite columnists, and I've known her forever."

"She's no relation to me. She was married to my oldest brother."

"I'll tell her that I've met you!"

Before I could say anything more, Libby was describing how she had met my brothers Alex and Paul on the beach at Cape Cod, Massachusetts. She had been visiting the daughter of the German publisher Axel Springer, another "oldest and dearest friend." I recalled that the woman in question, a small, nervous heiress with a larger but even more nervous son, attracted very loud, status-seeking women friends. Had I been escorted the length of this house by its master to listen to this? No. Libby's dizzying monologue had slowed to a clearly enunciated lecture.

"—stupid and dumb. Now, this is my own private opinion, and my husband may or may not share it, but stupid and dumb is the kindest way I can describe it. You may be a journalist but you're still an American. And I just might remind you that you are not in America now."

I had written an article about the dedication of the U.S. Embassy, based on the accounts of a diplomat and the embassy translator. The brief ceremony had been attended by former Ambassador Murphy, then assistant secretary of state for Middle East affairs, the mayor of Riyadh, the chief of royal protocol, and the Marine guard that presented the flag to be raised. I had not described the site of the embassy; the whole length of the article would not have been sufficient to guide anyone through the tangle of anonymous streets that led to it.

"I don't see your objection at all," I answered slowly, while wondering what to say. Why was she so disgusted? The ambassador's smile came back to me. I was glad I'd had no drink; as Libby continued to lecture, I had the irrational thought that I had disliked this stranger all my life.

"We don't need you broadcasting to the world about every little thing in the embassy, and what business is handled there. There are enough threats against this country—"

"Against Saudi Arabia?"

"The United States. We can't go advertising our presence to everyone who can afford two riyals for a daily newspaper!"

"Look, Libby, there is an American military base in the dead center of this city with a plaque on the gate that says 'U.S. Military Training Mission.' There is, in all but name, an American military base in Dhahran, which also has a plaque and a flag. Vinnell has parked hundreds of American war veterans in Khurais to train the Saudi National Guard. Saudis make jokes that Reagan hired the Chinese to build the walls around our diplomatic missions. Everyone knows where they are. There are thirty thousand of us here—we're all visible."

"You need to be reminded that this is not America! We can't stand for this!"

"*You* need reminding," I seethed. "This is only one of sixty embassies in this country. Since when do embassy wives decide what they can stand for or not?"

The man who had been holding the picture of the ambassador with Bush now held another photograph—of the ambassador, his wife and Henry Kissinger—in Libby's face.

"One thing people ask me about Henry—" he began.

"Don't go anywhere," Libby ordered me.

The other embassy wives had gathered out by the pool. None of the businessmen wanted to talk to them; they had wanted to talk about themselves, and like me each had a lecture prepared on their views of this country; unlike me, they assumed everyone wanted to hear it.

Aqil al-Aqil was at the bar, very drunk. He was a talented poet, but better known as a venal columnist, drifting from the payroll of one embassy to another. After weeks of bashing Israel and South Africa, he would suddenly spring to the defense of Zairois or Greek policies, and he wrote a series of very angry articles commiserating with Idi Amin Dada, who lived in Jeddah. He also wrote a fulsome piece of welcome for Reagan's friend Charles Z. Wick. Mainly, he wrote in praise of Iraq, and meant every word, though he was surely paid for it as well. He was from Gassim Province, the son of a date merchant who had taken him along on business trips to Basra, Iraq, when he was a boy. He spoke the Basrawi dialect fluently. His hatred for Shiites, and for Iran and all its works, had helped fuel my fascination with Iran in the Sadr project, even after learning that the Iranians may have been involved in helping the Imam to disappear.

"Are you going to write about this party?"

I told him no, these trade delegations were not news; if I wrote about it my editor might think it was an insult to Saudi Arabia—if just another stupid trade delegation was suddenly newsworthy. It might imply that foreigners doing business were a rarity. "If I write about it, I'll leave you and Iohanna Mashi out of it."

"Because I have something for you to write about in your capacity as a reporter. A new book by Abdelrahman Munif, attacking the kingdom."

Where had I heard of it? Aqil was assuming that I had not read it or even heard of it yet, which was annoying.

"It will cost you as much as a bottle of Iohanna Mashi."

"Do you mean *Sharq al-Mutawasit?* I've read it—it's not bad."

"*Sharq al-Mutawasit* is nothing compared to *al-Tih*. It's six hundred pages long! It's like Dostoyevsky! Better!"

That was an intriguing title—*tih* had three distinct meanings: "desert," "labyrinth," and "lost."

"Can you lend me a copy?"

"It is a forbidden book. The government banned it because the ruling regime in the novel is no good. It's intended as an insult. It symbolizes the Saudi government."

Aqil explained that King Fahd wanted to lift the ban on Munif's books, but *al-Tih* came along and "exploded the situation." The ban would remain in place, but Fahd had invited Munif to come home. Aqil, now listing heavily, accompanied this with an extravagant "come home" wave of his arm that frightened a nearby trade delegate. Aqil had the imposing height and bulk of Rodin's jovial bronze of Balzac.

"The king seems to be getting more liberal. He's probably going to announce the majlis al-shura soon."

Aqil guffawed. The fact that plans had been announced to construct a majlis al-shura building down in Dira had not made the subject any less of a joke.

Preston Brooks was patiently explaining to the ambassador how this part of Suleimaniya had been a desert with rolling tumbleweeds just a few years ago—he used to come hunting here with some of the princes. He told him about Abdallah Suleiman, the rich merchant the district was named for. The ambassador's eyebrows were lifted—*"You-don't-say!"*—but his eyes swiveled impatiently whenever Brooks looked away. These old-timers saw themselves as the collective memory of the American community here; diplomats thought they were a nuisance and had a very low threshold for their advice. But here it came.

"You just listen to what Latifa says to me—" Brooks watched me pass with a cool stare. Latifa was one of the king's overweight, much-divorced daughters.

"Of course I can find you *al-Tih*," Fuad told me. "You and Naifa"—his wife—"should translate it into English and French. Have you ever read the Muslim histories of the Crusader wars? This is the same thing. An Arab's-eye view of the takeover of the oil fields."

"But the oil fields have always been the state property of the Al Sauds. No one has ever taken them over."

"People used to own them, *ya sheikh!* People used to live on that land. What do you suppose happened to them?"

"They were Shiites. I know they're poor—is Munif a Shiite?"

"No, no, no, no, no, no. The novel is not like that. It is about that society, of the people who were destroyed by the oil. I devoured that book!" He added that it was the first of a trilogy of novels, collectively entitled *Mudun al-Milh*—"Cities of Salt." Was this a reference to the notorious Cities of the Plain that Arabs knew as Sodoom and Omoorah? He was not sure—the next two novels weren't out yet.

Fuad was an unusual man, a Maronite Catholic married to a lovely Druze: like an Ulsterman married to a mafia princess.

There was no reason to stay, and I took leave of the ambassador. Libby was talking to Al Calabrese and Jeanne, who directed a helpless shrug at me as I went out into the prickly hot darkness. There were few people I knew, not only because it was a do for visitors, but because the turnover of foreigners in Saudi Arabia, Riyadh especially, was so high. People came on two- or three-year contracts but often left before the time was up, and the diplomatic turnover was similar. One day a hospital's corridors were busy with Lebanese, and one year later they echoed with Filipino voices, after all the Lebanese had been sent home. This was particularly striking after visits to Cairo, when the same sweepers worked on the same sidewalks, and the same waiters, shoeshine boys, and postal employees plied their trades in the same place for years on end.

Driving past the tall iron gateways, I felt lonely for Hussein, homesick for Cairo, and disgusted with myself for not working harder on the Sadr case. I had not read a novel in two months, and that had been *File #67* by Fahd Ismail Fahd, about an innocent man who symbolized Palestine, being interrogated by thugs who symbolized reactionary governments, while the terrible news of the 1967 defeat of the Arabs came over the radio, symbolizing the helplessness of the Arabs. Five years had passed since I had first set foot in Saudi Arabia, and unlike most foreigners here I was not earning a large salary. Nor had I written anything of value—I began to feel like a crony of the Saudi government because I had not done anything.

I had not published the story of Prince Faisal murdering his lover—of course, that was only hearsay. I did tell the story to a friend of the royal family, who asked the king's nephew, Prince Khalid al-Faisal, about it. Prince Khaled immediately demanded to hear the whole story, in every small detail, and when he had heard it, declared, "No. That did not happen." Which detail had been wrong? Or was it all wrong? If the whole business had been a libelous invention, why didn't the prince have a stronger reaction to it than that? In any case, it was not a news story.

I had not breathed a word of how some of the king's brothers—older ones, who were not cabinet members and had gotten bored chasing import agency contracts—had been marketing oil on their own in Europe, with two European leaders taking a cut. Of course, that had been back when the kingdom was pumping 11 million barrels of oil a day, not 3. I had been told the facts of that story by another journalist who found it too tormenting to contain. "Two governments will fall if this gets out," he warned. "One where olive trees grow, one where tulips grow."

"And no one will give a damn, where the date palms grow," I told him. There was no journalistic infrastructure for following up that story here.

I had not written about Princess Jawahir, who had worked as an artist in San Diego and enjoyed a moderate drug habit when she was hospitalized from an overdose. The Saudi consul in Los Angeles told the hospital to notify him if it happened again. When it did, Princess Jawahir regained consciousness in the King Faisal Hospital. She got her revenge by stealing flowers from the other patients' rooms and telling the nurses royal gossip. Her passport was taken away, and on being discharged she was given a house with a telephone unequipped for international calling.

Scandals were the worst way to understand other people—they were only two steps above ethnic jokes. Every time I had been tempted to write about Saudi scandals, I remembered Sheikh Muhammad al-Fassi, Fahd's in-law, whose dubious taste had forever associated Saudis, in the American mind, with plastic flowers and Greek statuary with vividly painted pubic hair. But al-Fassi's mansion on Sunset Boulevard in Beverly Hills—"Oh, that capital of subdued good taste," I would have jeered, if I were Saudi—was nothing compared to the glass house America lives in. There was no ridiculous or unfair aspect of life in any Arab country that could not be trumped ten times over by some detail of American life or history.

Of course, I had dined out on those Saudi stories. In the absence of theaters, bars, and watchable television, gossip was—as it had been for thousands of years—Arabia's chief form of entertainment. No secret was safe. Perhaps my most valuable acquisition here was the ability to keep my mouth shut. No one knew that on a trip to Cairo the previous year, I had actually gone to Baghdad; no one knew that this was my last week in Saudi Arabia, or that my next stop was Israel.

13

Reading Matter

C airo was a stepping stone to Jerusalem, but passing through the great city on the way to an important mission was also a form of knocking on wood. An aura of superstition informed this trip marking my exodus from Saudi Arabia: I could not conclude my search for the Imam without seeing what the

Israelis knew. Any Arab would have assumed that the Israelis knew everything. I assumed only that they had followed the case with interest and could provide me with reasonably good leads.

My trip to Baghdad had been a similar experiment. Like the Israelis, the Iraqis were generally thought to have been behind so much devilment in the Arab world that they might plausibly be expected to know exactly what all the other troublemakers were up to as well. More promisingly, Iraq was at war with Iran and therefore might be inclined to share what they might know of Libyan foul play in the Sadr affair. From that point of view, my visit was not a success, or rather was premature. Not long after my five-day visit ended, Ali Tehrani, the brother-in-law of Iran's President Ali Khamenei, defected to Iraq and denounced the Tehran government. A few months later, his wife, Badr, joined him in Baghdad and condemned her brother's role in Khomeini's regime. They virtually lived in front of Iraqi television cameras, eagerly describing the hollowness and corruption of the Islamic government, the insanity of the war, the staggering scale of desertions from the Iranian army, and the nearly destroyed economy. I was sure that if I had been able to see them, they would have been able to supply me with details of the cover-up of the crime against Imam Sadr, but it was too late.

So I visited the Shiite shrine cities of Najaf and Kerbela to watch the flotillas of black-turbaned mullahs drifting through the ancient streets, the gold-domed mosque-mausoleums of the Prophet's martyred grandsons Ali and Hussein, and the fiery Mesopotamian sun baking the desert. This was the tense, holy, competitive world that had formed Moussa Sadr. It had a familiar aura: academia.

Using my Saudi eyes, I saw much that was ominous in Iraq.

Baghdad was full of secular slogans, churches, and Shiite mosques (they had *O Ali* and *O Hussein* in lights on the minarets). Unlike Saudi policemen, Iraqi officers looked hard and malevolent and were everywhere. There actually were prostitutes on Rashid Street. Baghdadis swore violently and blasphemously, and got into bloody fistfights even in the city's most staid old streets. Massive portraits of the president, Saddam Hussein, throughout the capital, made King Fahd seem like a shrinking violet in comparison. Back in Riyadh a few days later, I found the Saudis' priggish adherence to prayer times and puritanism endearing. I had a new appreciation for how encircled they felt: Iraq looked like a fearsome neighbor, yet it was an ally and friend.

Riyadh had been a cold hostess, and my leavetaking was dry-eyed. The anticipation of seeing Egypt again, even for a day in transit, swamped any meditations I might have prepared on the occasion of leaving central Arabia for good. On the flight, I slept seated bolt upright and dreamed that Abdelrahman Munif had written a suspense novel solving the mystery of Moussa Sadr's disappearance. I saw written, in Arabic, the words *No foreign expertise was needed, says Munif.* I awoke as the jet bumped on to the runway, and the young Saudis around me started to slap cologne on their necks and smooth jaws.

The era of hostage taking had begun. I was sipping a martini in the fern-filled Cairo apartment of Elizabeth Colton, *Newsweek's* Middle East bureau chief, the night she announced to everyone who came through the door, "Hey! Did you hear? They got Terry!"

Terry Anderson had been walking home from a tennis match near the American University of Beirut when he was grabbed by six men who wrestled him into a car and drove off. The reaction—"the fucking bastards!"—was the same among all of the American and British journalists who were arriving for cocktails, all of whom knew Anderson. Some also knew the other hostages being held—Ben Weir and William Buckley. "Do you think they'll take him to Iran?" was Liz's next thought. David Dodge, the president of the American University in Beirut, had been kidnapped the previous year and been smuggled by his captors into Iran.

Five of us trooped down to a restaurant, where we were joined by Judith Miller of the *New York Times,* and over platters of Italian food were serenaded by three Egyptian guitarists who sang every word of "American Pie." There was nothing campy, incongruous, or stupid about this, nothing any writer could roll his eyes at and turn into a smirking sidebar. Outside El Patio, men and women, veiled and unveiled, rich and poor, crowded up and down this little lane in Zamalek and took no notice of us. This was Cairo. Scenes like this were now causing bombings in Lebanon, since the Shiites of Amal and Hezbollah had taken over West Beirut, and this became the subject of our conversation.

"They sure hate us," said the English correspondent of the *Telegraph,* generously including himself with "us" Americans to buck us up.

"Are they asking for money?" asked Judith Miller.

"Iran's behind them," said Elizabeth. "No Lebanese hated Terry. And it's not for money—the poor Shiites in Beirut don't have the resources to kidnap anybody, and the others are getting money from Iran, and from dealing hashish and guns all over Baalbek."

"I don't know how they justify it, being such big deal Muslims and everything," said Judith. "Do they even try?"

"They try," I put in, feeling on solid ground, since I had discussed kidnapping in detail with Hussein. He had told me that the Lebanese possessed nothing except chaos, but could put that chaos to use by trapping other people in it. And how else could they fight Israel and America? And followers of Khomeini knew that any action—*any* action—could be justified to strengthen the faith or punish its enemies. I outlined this to my fellow diners.

"Sounds about right," said Elizabeth.

I had also caught a glimpse of the Lebanese side of the kidnappings from the Lebanese embassies where I had applied for visas. Most had laughed at me and all had refused. In Jeddah, the Lebanese tourism attaché (!) asked me solemnly if I was sure I wanted to visit Beirut at this time. "Yes," I said unhesitatingly. "Sorry," he replied, "you just failed the mental competency test." In Baghdad, the consul got cross. "At least try to appreciate the situation from the point of view of our commercial instincts," he explained. "After the wars, Beirut is a ruined city—half the place is unemployed. Half the city doesn't know where its next meal is coming from. Our currency is soon going to be worthless. The money is in the hands of the militias, of those with foreign patrons. These Islamic Jihad people don't kidnap anyone anymore—their time is too valuable. Little thugs and middlemen do the kidnapping, then sell off the captive to the militia that supports them. Or to the highest bidder. Now look: if you, as an American go strolling down Hamra Street, they see you as a wonderful bundle of cash—say, $50,000—floating by their hand. Like a Disney cartoon. Who will resist snatching you?"

"I have friends to guard me there." Hussein and his brothers were now Amal members, and Mortada's uncle was a mullah.

"Will they protect you from a car bomb?" snapped the consul. "And do you know that three thousand Lebanese have been kidnapped by other Lebanese? Who will be responsible for you? *Allahu akbar!"* In this context that expression meant not "God is great," but "Give me a break!"

"Besides," I added after giving a lurid account of my exploits with exasperated Lebanese diplomats, "Elizabeth is right—Iran really knows how to take hostages now. They know it's a good means of publicity, but they learned, from their experience taking Americans hostage, that it's better not to do it on their own land. They do it by proxy, in another country, and hide behind a big civilian population. Who cares if the worst happens? They're a thousand miles away."

The conversation moved to the Gulf war, Libya, and the Sudanese coup of three days before. President Numiery of Sudan had been making a stop here at Cairo on his way back to Khartoum from Washington and received the news of his overthrow as he was reboarding his plane at Cairo Airport—an American gave him the news! That was the kind of detail that made Arabs edgy about the Americans hanging around their countries.

There was nothing I could contribute, except—should they ask what was new in Riyadh—"Well, Sheikh Yamani might be replaced; the religious police have got very strict about people walking around late; the king's eleven-year-old son has a new palace." All that money and oil, and yet the place was so marginal compared to a few ruined neighborhoods in Beirut, where desperate people were creating havoc for America. Then I saw that this was a dangerous thought: we took Saudi Arabia's contentment for granted. What if people in Qatif or Dhahran, instead of West Beirut, decided to teach us a lesson!

Although we were discussing Khomeini, Qaddafi, and the destruction of Lebanon, I did not mention Imam Sadr or any of my discoveries about his mystery. It was so much a part of the other problems of the Middle East—especially the kidnappings by Shiite groups—that I was afraid I would sound gloating over the relevance of my fascination with the case. It was no longer an obsession or a means of expressing loyalty or protest, only an effort to locate a point where understanding could penetrate some of the Middle East's more tenebrous regions.

The next morning I went to the Madbouli Bookstore in Talaat Harb Square, where the same glaucomic salesgirl of my AUC days followed me around with folded arms, asking, "Shall I wrap that up for you?" whenever I touched a book. "I'm looking for Abdelrahman Munif's latest," I told her, and she snatched it from a pile of books. My heart bounded when I read *al-Tih* on the spine as she folded it into a shroud of old newspaper, sealed it like a tomb, and counted my money. Saudi news seemed marginal here, but even the Egyptians had no Munif.

Taxis and buses for Alexandria, the Nile Delta cities of Tanta and Mansoura, for Upper Egypt and the flower-growing town of Fayoum departed from the crowded esplanade in front of Ramses Station, where fountains played around a fifty-foot statue of the pharaoh; public buses for greater Cairo left from in front of the Mugamm'a in Tahrir—now Sadat—Square; but the bus for Jerusalem left from a street corner in Zamalek near the Ministry of Agriculture, where soldiers, still in their black woolen winter uniforms, loitered with their machine guns behind the dusty ficus trees.

I paid little attention, on the lurching trans-Sinai bus, to my feelings on leaving the Arab world after five straight years. They were, I was vaguely aware, uncomplicated: I was both sad and happy, but more than anything frankly relieved that I was not an Arab, that I had no direct link with this part of the world, that I could walk away from it and never look back, or so I thought.

The bus was half full, and with the exception of a young Egyptian man and me, they were all Israelis in blue and white caps, energetically swapping stories in Hebrew, which, from the tone of voice and the few words I caught, were war stories of being cheated by Egyptians. *"Me and Moshe . . . Khan al-Khalili . . . I said . . . 'La, mish idfa!' . . . mamzer . . . khalas!"* The Egyptian, named Ibrahim, was in charge of the trip, for while we were not a tour group, someone would be needed to speed us through customs and immigration at Rafah, on the border of Palestinian territory: the Israeli-governed Gaza Strip. Ibrahim spent most of his bus ride shuffling several clipboards and reading four or five booklets, some of which had the Egyptian government seal on the covers; one was an Arabic-Hebrew phrasebook.

My lap was full of Imam Sadr documents, and the Munif novel was in the bag behind my feet, but I could not get to them until I'd assured myself that we were really going to Israel. Leaving on the highway east of Cairo had been very bumpy, and the Israelis had thrown fits when our white bus—an Israeli one—broke down and was replaced with a red Egyptian one. Each milestone—Zagazig, El-Qantara, Port Said—led to new bursts of conversation and even handclapping. One hairy, shirtless Israeli danced in the aisle.

"It's very nice to go to Egypt," explained the Israeli woman beside me, "but we just get tense being among the Arabs. I'm glad I came, but I'm dying to get back to Tel Aviv." She introduced herself as Naomi. "In a way I expected Cairo to be beastly, but it's just like Europe." Her father was an Egyptian Jew from Port Said, she said casually as the bus rolled on to the ferry there, and her mother was a Spanish Jew. "Now we're really in the Sinai!"

"I hope we don't spend forty years here!" I said pleasantly. Naomi sighed, got up to move to another seat, and fell asleep.

The Sinai had been returned to Egyptian sovereignty just two years before, and already hundreds of Egyptians had visited it, though they went south, to see Mount Sinai. This coastal road ran through a narrow green corridor, dense with palm trees, through which white beaches and the aqua Mediterranean were visible on the left; only travelers to El-Arish or Israel saw this. Egyptian village children in striped nightshirts waved at the bus, and some of the Israelis politely waved back. "*Yallah!*" groaned the hairy man, as if waving to the children would delay our arrival in Israel. He turned to one of friends and said, with an emphatic downstroke of his hand, what must have been, "I don't want to see *one more Egyptian!*"

The Libyans—I now read in a Lebanese intelligence report I had pried out of Adel Reza—alleged that Imam Moussa Sadr and his two friends had left Libya on Alitalia flight 881 from Tripoli to Rome on August 31, 1978. Takeoff, the report noted, had been delayed for two hours, from 7 P.M. until 9 P.M. and the plane's first-class compartment was overbooked by three. Three passengers were downgraded to economy class. Again, moments before takeoff, three more first-class travelers, all Alitalia employees, were asked to give up their seats, with no explanation given. None of the six recognized the photographs of Sadr, Yaacoub, or Badreddine shown to them later by Italian police. The flight's purser, Orlando Astolfi, also "ruled out categorically" that any of the three Lebanese had boarded the flight; so did the two first-class stewards. The sticking point was Sadr's height (over six feet), girth, and distinctive black cloak and turban, which would have made him hard to miss.

"The boarding of flight 881 at Tripoli Airport was done through the front door, and I took charge of the boarding," Lilia Cociani, the flight's senior stewardess, told the Italian police.

"During the flight I looked after all the passengers in first class, and then in tourist. In the course of the flight I did not notice any passenger corresponding to the descriptions you have given, especially since I did not remark any very tall passengers, certainly not taller than 1.90 meters, with a beard and in Arab clothes—let alone wearing a turban.

"At the time of the boarding I was positioned by the forward cabin door since I was to make the announcements from the on-board telephone located there, and thus I partly obstructed the entry to the cabin aisle. Any tall or fat passengers would have had trouble entering and would have had to ask me to move back, and I would incontestably have noticed that.

"No passenger resembling the man you describe as Moussa Sadr was among the eight first-class passengers. Had he flown economy class he would have had to be seated, due to his height, in the front row of seats or in the back of the plane near the righthand security door. All first-class passengers came on board holding red ticket stubs giving their names and seat numbers. Inside the plane, no passengers changed sections."

The immigration officers who handled flight AZ 881 deposed that they had not seen Sadr, Yaacoub, or Badreddine. The customs officer on duty, Alfredo Fedele, especially impressed the Lebanese investigators because he had lived in Egypt for thirty-three years, spoke fluent Arabic, and always chatted with arriving Arabs. He had seen no one resembling the photo of Moussa Sadr, or wearing the robes of a Muslim cleric.

Now the Israelis were all asleep, their heads nodding gently with the churning of the bus as it rumbled along the narrow road. I flipped to the testimony of the Rome Holiday Inn staff. Even the check-in time of the people claiming to be Sadr and Yaacoub gave rise to suspicion: nearly ten hours had elapsed between the touchdown of flight 881 at 11:20 P.M. and the men's appearance at the hotel.

"On the morning of September 1," one of the desk clerks testified, "at about nine o'clock, a group of Arabs came into the lobby of the Holiday Inn. I don't remember how many but there were more than two. One of the Arabs was dressed in European clothes. He came up and asked me if two single rooms were available and what they cost per night. I told him, and he went back to the group, apparently to discuss the room rates . . . the first Arab gave me two passports and I asked him to fill out the registration cards.

"I asked this Arab in English for a week's advance payment of $400, that's $200 for each room. He was dressed in European clothes, about 1.70 meters tall with eyeglasses and no mustache, and was carrying an overnight bag. He paid me from a large roll of dollars. I gave him a receipt and he headed for the elevators. I did not see him again."

The clerk confirmed that the passport photographs were those of the bearers: Muhammad Chehada was short and clean-shaven, and Moussa Asadar was tall and black-bearded; both, he judged, were in their mid-thirties. This tallied roughly with the date of birth "Chehada" gave—January 4, 1948—but the clerk ruled out that either man bore the slightest resemblance to real photographs of Sadr and Yaacoub.

Sadr, of course, had a very gray beard, not a black one, and Yaacoub had a black beard—he was certainly not clean-shaven, and always wore his robes and white turban, never a suit. The Italian police found that the genuine photographs of Sadr and Yaacoub had been removed and glued back in, with some damage to the pictures and the embossed seal. And the hotel registration cards were, the Lebanese reported, preposterously bad forgeries of the clerics' signatures, with misspellings in the names, and irregular, childish penmanship in which lower case and capital letters were arbitrarily mixed. Both Imam Sadr and Sheikh Yaacoub wrote elegantly in the Latin as well as the Arabic script.

As we reached El-Arish, I hurriedly glanced through the rest of the file. Several of the Imam's personal effects—his pocket diary and passport among them—disappeared from the Rome district attorney's office and were never found. The Italian and Lebanese authorities concluded that Imam Moussa Sadr, Sheikh Muhammad Shahada Yaacoub, and Abbas Badreddine had never landed at Rome Airport or transited through it. The two men who checked into the Holiday Inn, left the suitcases and doctored passports behind, and headed out twenty minutes later, never to return, were impostors.

A sheaf of photocopied press clippings showed how this conclusion infuriated Qaddafi. He accused Italian intelligence of laxity—"as the fate of their former prime minister [Aldo Moro] has shown." The Libyan press agency repeatedly implied, "Italy—*on whose airline the Imam travelled*—" and claimed, after the investigations were closed, that the conclusions tallied with Libya's version of events: that Sadr and his companions had got into a huff and decided to leave Tripoli unexpectedly. "How can anyone go through Rome Airport with Moussa Sadr's passport and not be Moussa Sadr?" one Libyan official asked.

The bus rumbled into El-Arish at two o'clock in the afternoon to the squawks of children selling watermelon sections and slices of poundcake in cellophane. "Twenty minutes!" called the driver, and the Israelis hustled off the bus clapping. On the ground, we stretched and walked stiffly to the restrooms of the bus depot, which resembled the little gas stations you see in out-of-the-way America, very square and small and neat. The Israelis piled back on the bus within ten minutes and immediately began to lose their tempers over the driver's delay: he was smoking a cigarette on a bench and looking out to sea.

No one's mind is orderly after seven hours on a bus, and mine was a pigpen of memories of shopping in Riyadh just three nights before, random oddments of Egyptian nostalgia I had no time to examine, five years of what I only now saw as resentment of the Arabs—or was I misreading my eagerness to get to Israel?—and my fixation on Moussa Sadr. In Saudi Arabia he had been the hope of Hussein, whom he even resembled, a wronged, even murdered saint crying out for justice. In Egypt I failed to see him that same way. In Cairo, the missing Imam belonged in the police blotter somewhere; even in the context of Libyan atrocities the kidnapping of Sadr ranked low. Egypt had innumerable more serious grievances with Qaddafi.

Most of all, the kidnappings of Frenchmen and Americans in Lebanon put Sadr in a new light. At first, I felt somehow vindicated by those crimes, since they proved that the Shiites were a potent force, that Sadr had succeeded in waking them up from their feudal complaisance. Sadr had doubted the wisdom of the PLO presence in Lebanon, and when the Israelis expelled the PLO it turned out that all the Lebanese had agreed with Sadr all along. He had backed Khomeini, and he had been right. The militias he founded now ruled Beirut. But here I was, trying to construct a case against his kidnappers, while his people were kidnapping mine. Libya had even staged an elaborate cover-up to hide their crime; the Shiites in Lebanon kidnapped and murdered people openly, and crowed about it. And how brilliant was he, really? His Khomeini gambit had succeeded, but Khomeini had done nothing to release him from captivity in Libya—may well have helped to put him there, or have him killed.

There was no doubt surrounding Libya's claims about Sadr: he had been kidnapped with two other men, and possibly killed. But why? And who was he? Events had kicked up another *toz,* an opaque sandstorm that whisked away everything familiar and rearranged what was left.

At Rafah, the Egyptian immigration officers scolded me for carrying two passports—one was valid only for travel between Egypt and Israel, and Officer Ali Shiddi wanted to confiscate it. I pointed out I could not risk having the Israelis stamp the other, since that would bar me from future travel to other Arab countries. He took both passports and disappeared behind a partition for an hour, and I began to wonder if Leon Uris had met Officer Shiddi while doing research on Arabs.

An American was arguing with a customs officer. He was carrying $2,000 for his trip to Israel, but could produce no proof of having changed that amount on entering Egypt; now Shiddi's colleague was trying to explain that he needed proof that the money was not changed on the black market.

"You need slip," the soldier said, holding up a receipt of foreign currency exchange, and then turned to me. "Did he declare his money when he came to Egypt? If not, where did he get that money?"

I translated this question.

"I work in Egypt!" screamed the American, but his loudness was panic, not anger. "Would you tell him to look at my goddamned passport? I'm not a tourist! I live in Cairo! I'm paid in dollars! I'm taking my family to Israel on vacation! We're going to miss the bus!"

Officer Shiddi reappeared with my passports.

"You must go to the Rafah passport office and have the information in your first passport transferred to the second passport." I tried to argue but he refused to say another word, and turned his attention to the other problem.

"Tell him that residence in Egypt does not exempt him from the currency regulations," the second officer told me. "He must change a fixed amount of dollars into local currency every month. I need to see those receipts."

"But why? He isn't trying to trade pounds back for dollars."

"He needs to prove that he has abided by the currency regulations."

I told the American, who said, "Fuck this. We'll just go back to Cairo. I'll have to tell my wife!"

"You are free," shrugged Shiddi, speaking in English, "but the money stay here." When the American sat down and put his head in his hands, the officer pushed $200 across the counter and said, "Take this."

"You have to give him a receipt for the rest," I told Shiddi. "That is, if you aren't a currency smuggler yourself."

Incredibly, Shiddi did not hit me, but said, "Tell him we can talk about it."

"You tell him," I replied, and went out in search of the Rafah passport office. A Gazan taxi driver took me for free. He saw very few Arabic-speaking Americans, and I was at my most rollicking, cursing the border officers as donkeys, goats, and sons of dancers. He roared with laughter when I shouted, "I should have told him to kiss my ass first thing in the morning!" This was a Syrian saying, which literally runs, "lick my ass in the ass of the morning [i.e. daybreak]." Since he was not offended, I ventured to add, "He'd tie up his own father and then fuck his mother!" and tears were running down his face as we pulled up in front of the passport office, a whitewashed shack. I knew that goofy proverbs and colorful obscenities were expected of foreigners in general and were thought to be endearing. "Is this the passport office? It's the size of a scorpion's cunt!" I gasped. Was I pushing my luck with this Syrian gem? No, he was still laughing, and led me by the hand into the office, where he told the clerk to make it snappy.

Back in the customs office there was no sign of the anguished American, and I was sent through to the Israeli side on a bus of Palestinians, mainly plump old ladies wearing kerchiefs and carrying shopping bags. We stood in the sun outside the Israeli frontier office while a bus of tourists were ushered in. About a half hour later, an Israeli soldier asked for my passport, and then crossly pushed me toward the entrance. All the Palestinian ladies, some now sitting on their bundles, cheerily waved goodbye.

Of course, Ibrahim's bus had gone on without me, and in the parking lot of bellowing taxi operators—"Jerusalem!" "Tel Aviv!" "Beersheba!"—I chose a Jerusalem taxi and five of us set off. There was a middle-aged Arab couple who slept most of the way, and an Israeli soldier beside the young Arab driver, but he was not there in his official capacity, nor was he a paying passenger. Israeli soldiers get around by hitchhiking, and road signs—here was one coming up, outside Khan Younis—urged you to pick them up. The soldier spoke Hebrew and English, the driver spoke Arabic and Hebrew, and I spoke English and Arabic. This delighted the driver, Jamal, who seemed very anxious to please the soldier. He even stopped and bought orange juice from a stand for him, and blathered at him in Hebrew for ten minutes.

"I was just telling him," Jamal said breathlessly, always looking me in the face, either in the rearview mirror or by twisting his head around, "that the juice is a gift. He asked if he should pay me. I told him, in Arabic we say, 'Two friends, one pocket.' " He slapped his heart and hip pocket to illustrate this. "That means we share. Now he's riding in my taxi. He didn't have to hitchhike—I offered him the ride in Rafeeah." Rafeeah, with a gargled *R,* was Hebrew for Rafah. "We have to live together. We *want* to be friends." Jamal went like this until the soldier began to frown, then turned back to him, obviously explaining, "I was just telling him that I told you . . ." When he was through, I asked the Israeli his name.

"My name is Deer," he smiled.

"Deer? Is that a Hebrew name?"

"Deer means Tzvi. That is my name. I speak lousy English," he added. *Tzvi* was surely related to the Arabic *zabi,* gazelle, since the Semitic 'b' and 'v' were nearly interchangeable. He did not have a lot more to say to either of us, though Jamal talked a blue streak all through the brilliant green fields and mountains of the Philistine Plain until Beth Shamash, where Tzvi got out.

I had visited Israel before, for a week's vacation in 1979, after midyear exams in Cairo. That time I had come by land from Syria and Jordan and been shocked at how ugly the West Bank was—mountains of gravel, rock piles, refugee camps, and sleek

Israeli settlements on strategic hills. Jerusalem itself reminded me of Damascus: a walled medieval city full of wonderful smells surrounded by traffic-choked suburbs. Of course, Jerusalem had much more to offer than Damascus: all kinds of restaurants, delis, cinemas, good bookstores, bars, and every profile and accent under the sun. Everywhere I turned it reminded me of Brookline, Massachusetts, though Jerusalem conspicuously lacked holiness. Reverencing this world capital of ill-will seemed like the ultimate example of simony.

Coming to the city from the west was different—this was beautiful. The Idumaean and Judean hills were as green as Vermont, and the silvery road wound through them like an illustration in a book of fairy tales. We pulled over to leave Tzvi by the sign that said Beth Shamash in Hebrew and English and Beit al-Shams in Arabic. *Shamash* was familiar to me not only as the Hebrew word for sun—as *shams* was in Arabic—but as the name of the ancient Semitic sun god; in Iraq, I had seen his statue. It was a reminder that the founder of the Hebrew nation, Abraham, was a native of Ur in present-day Iraq, and that many of the religious beliefs of all Middle Easterners shared the same pagan roots. It was evident even in such biblical names as Mordechai (from the Babylonian deity Marduk) and Esther (Ishtar).

The married couple beside me woke up as the car began the climb to Jerusalem and began talking to Jamal about a scandal involving the mayor of Gaza. They thought the Israelis had set him up. I paid polite attention for a while, then pulled out *al-Tih* and began to read. I had been saving it for bedtime reading in Jerusalem, but the sun was now dropping behind us, giving me a lovely peach-colored reading light, and I wanted to make the most of the last beautiful illumination by reading.

Unlike usual Arab novels that always seemed to introduce

their embittered heroes on the first page—"He stared at the horizon/ his image in the mirror/the impassive faces of the other bus passengers, and fingered his cracked eyeglasses/stubbly chin/the last few coins in his pocket, feeling an involuntary surge of despair. . . ." *Al-Tih* opened with a lush description of an Arabian oasis, "an outpouring of green amid the harsh, obdurate desert [*sahara*], as if it had fallen from within the earth or fallen from the sky . . . the palm trees filling the wadi and the gushing brooks surging forth in the winter and early spring. . . ." Munif went on to describe the childlike villagers of the oasis, hospitable to passing travelers and nomads, who would witness "an era of life and history that would come once and never recur, so that they could tell others of the wonders and prodigies they had seen."

This was unusual enough; coupled with the length of the book (nearly 600 dense Arabic pages), it warned that this was no typical book. Arab novels were short, derivative, and set in the present—or if not the present, then the ancient world or the Islamic golden age of conquest. Small details in this text hinted that this was the 1930s. Most remarkable of all, it was a novel about the Arabs of the desert, their tents, mud homes, and camels. These were the Arabs that Americans think of as Arabs, and yet no Arab novelist had written about them, which was odd enough—as if no American novelist had ever written about cowboys. And the pace and tone of voice rang a bell: this was how Arabs told stories. The peaceful oasis would clearly be the setting, not for a Great Story, merely a great story.

Of course, all the bucolic peace and quiet could not last. The first note of its coming destruction was sounded as a teenage boy, Fawaz, comes home late from a neighboring encampment, full of spite for his parents, who had just refused him permission to leave home and travel.

"Ibn Rashed has foreign guests," he told his father, who was still busy with the fire.

His voice fell among the coals and the clinking coffeepots as his father kept at his task, as if he had not heard or did not want to hear excuses for the delay. Fawaz spoke again, more loudly and with something of a challenge in his voice. "They're Franks, and they speak Arabic."

This was a little touch of genius. It was normal, of course, for a desert Arab to refer to a non-Arab foreigner as *Frangi*—like *Franki* in Hebrew—but in this novel it immediately recalled the distant Crusades, and that was not accidental: oil would draw more rapacious invaders to Arabia than any European king or pope had ever conscripted. Fawaz and his father ride to Ibn Rashed's encampment to look at the Franks—who, though they do not realize it (it is immediately clear to the reader) are Americans exploring for oil.

"Where are you staying?" Jamal asked. We had entered Jerusalem, and the couple, Faris and Umm Daoud, were directing him to let them off at the Damascus Gate of the old city, where they were catching another taxi to Jericho (in Hebrew, Yerikho; in Arabic, Ariha). We all alit in the little plaza by the gate, where a hundred taxis were hawking destinations in the West Bank. At first I was resentful at having my Arabian interlude interrupted, but now, in the dusk, I was walking up to the Jaffa Road and along the Turkish battlements of Old Jerusalem's walls, in the only city where, despite its sins, no one can be homesick for anywhere else, reveling in "one of those rare moments of absolute peace," as the traveler Robert Byron found in Isfahan, "when the body is loose, the mind asks no questions, and the world is a triumph."

14

Israeli Realities

$\mathcal{I}$ was immediately reminded that I was in Jerusalem with Lebanon and its Shiites on my mind. Mishkenot Sha'-nanim, the artsy Jerusalem Foundation guesthouse I checked into, was staffed completely by women, and there was no way they could get my heavy suitcase from the ferny, flagstoned lobby to my room.

"We are sorry," smiled the kerchiefed English woman in the whitewashed reception alcove. "You have to carry your own bags. All our boys are in Lebanon."

That was sad; something in her face told me that her own son might be there. Then I remembered that it was infinitely sadder for the Lebanese than for the Israelis, frowned at her, and asked, "Is that reflected in the rates?" She looked down and did not answer, but it had been a long day and I did not bother to wonder how awful it sounded.

How odd it was to see Palestinians selling juice, sweeping streets, and driving taxis. In the Arab countries where another million Palestinians lived, you saw them practicing law, medicine, and business. Few of these poorer ones ever made it out of the occupied territories, and the ones who did were generally refugees in squalid camps in Lebanon, Jordan, and Syria. (I had not seen the camps in Gaza, but they were said to be as dire as any ghettoes on earth.) Yet here was the full spectrum of Palestinian society, though whether running shops or hawking lemonade they had something in common. They were the underclass and looked it. They had the same tired, wary look of Palestinians in Egypt and the Gulf, and finally did look like the "Jews of the Arab world" now that they were outnumbered by Israelis wearing that spring's biggest-selling T-shirt: a Kfir combat plane with the legend "Don't Worry, America, Israel Is Behind You."

I walked down the Jaffa Road the next morning, savoring the thrill of being in this forbidden city—that is what years in the Arab countries had made it. Official Arab propaganda dwelt on the inevitable return of Jerusalem to Arab sovereignty, and ruled it absolutely out of bounds in the meantime. An Israeli stamp in your passport barred you from every Arab country except Egypt. Just gazing at the lemony sunlight on the old and new beige stone of the walls, buildings, and streets in West Jerusalem gave me a certain feeling of triumphant, science-fictional criminality, as if I had alit on Krypton itself.

But it was not just "me." There was a special aura in Jerusalem apart from this thrill and the religious aura: it was tension, the same feeling of *anything can happen* that fills a bar where a fight is about to break out or a crime is unfolding or bad news—an assassination or catastrophe—comes over the radio. Unlike Cairo, whose appeal came from sexiness, grandeur, and the sheer glorious weight of its history, the adrenalin that Jerusalem released arose from barely contained violence. Arab men and women tramped past stone walls covered with blue and white posters of a crude fist and two Hebrew letters spelling KACH, a racist movement seeking to promote anti-Arab pogroms. Arabs walked by these signs urging their expulsion from their country, not meeting the eyes of their Jewish neighbors, who may or may not be in sympathy. Soldiers and guns everywhere enhanced the ugly, electric thrill of danger.

Even Israelis must have found it claustrophobic here. Their radios—I had fiddled with mine before collapsing the night before—easily brought in Damascus, The Voice of the Masses from Baghdad, and some of the loonier Beirut stations where oratorical editorialists raged against "Zionist usurpers" and urged violence against them. The reception was even better than it had been in Riyadh. On the other hand, Radio Amman from next-door Jordan had a Hebrew-language service and sounded no threats. None of these stations was jammed. Of course, Israel Radio's Arabic service never seemed to be jammed in Egypt or

Saudi Arabia, and no matter how much the Arabs boiled at hearing the occupied territories referred to as "Judaea and Samaria," Jerusalem (al-Quds) as Ur-Shalim, and nearly all Palestinians as "terrorists," they were often captivated by the cool-headed decoding of Arab politics.

Reading faces on the Jaffa Road, now turning into King George V Street, was spellbinding. In Saudi Arabia, it had helped me to look at the Jews as Arabs and the Arabs as Jews: how would I—how would the world—look at Qaddafi if he were Jewish? Or if Begin or Shamir were Arabs? In Jerusalem the hypothetical was real—you did not have to ask hypothetically, would the world allow Jews to be put in camps like Deheisha? Would we allow Arabs to suffer the isolation Israel endures?

Semitic cousins or not, it was impossible to mistake one for the other, and not only because the Arabs looked Jewish while the Jews looked Russian and German: the Arabs looked beaten and the Jews looked awake, alert, faintly roosterish—they knew the tension of the city even more than I did. What a contrast to the plump, innocent, indulged Saudi Arabians. The Israelis shared the sidewalk with their "terrorist" foes while, for most Arabs, but especially the rich ones, the obsessive cold war with Israel meant the adoption of fastidious taboos against everything Jewish—encyclopedias had all references to Jewish history, Israel, and the Hebrew language obliterated with black markers. They tried to make this country they detested invisible, not knowing there was nothing more devastating than an invisible enemy.

I turned into Agrippa Street and its messy rows of clothes vendors, barbershops, arguing women, and children tearing around holding toy planes in the air. As in the big shopping streets, people stared at me straight in the eye as they walked past.

Did they think they knew me? For the tenth time I wondered if there was a wanted poster out for someone who looked like me.

You got the feeling that everyone here was thinking the same thing. They were confident and defensive at the same time, and proud of the nerdy machismo so evident in their Foreign Ministry building: a series of nondescript prefabricated buildings full of narrow corridors, grimy counters, and tired-looking officials. Shimon Sassoon was one of the most harassed-looking of all; but then, he manned the Lebanon desk.

A huge map of greater Beirut—actually a composite of dozens of black-and-white aerial photographs—took up almost a whole wall of his little office, showing every street, building, car, and bus, with street and neighborhood names overprinted in Hebrew. His little metal desk was strewn with that day's Lebanese newspapers.

"Actually, Moussa Sadr was not a Savak agent, but they did subsidize him because he was advancing the cause of Iran, of Shiism, in the Arab world. But he took Lebanese nationality and had a very bad time with the Iranian ambassador in Beirut, Mansour Qadar, who was a very hostile Savak official."

Sassoon was actually reading his newspapers as he spoke to me. I had been able to impose on his time only because David Kimche, a former agent of the Israeli Mossad currently serving as director of the Foreign Ministry, had asked him to see me, at the request of Lord Weidenfeld, the British publisher of the Moussa Sadr book. Still, he did not seem rude or unfriendly, or even busy—he gave the impression that he often did two or three things at once. He did not offer me tea or coffee—something told me that officials here had to make it for themselves.

"The Imam is most certainly dead. To document that you

would have to refer to the press, particularly the Arab press in Europe. The Arab press in the Arab countries, as you know better than I, is rarely put in the service of solving such cases unless there is a motive to defame somebody. To prove it, you would need to talk with Colonel Qaddafi, and then I am very much afraid you will yourself be the subject of a book!"

I did have all the press clippings, of course. They were mostly from Saudi and Iraqi-backed magazines published in London and Paris, and all told the same story with slight variations: Sadr and his two friends were summoned to a meeting with Qaddafi on August 31, 1978, and got into a terrible argument with Qaddafi, who then had them taken away, and then they were shot to death. The most reliable account, in *Jeune Afrique,* included the most chilling detail of all: Qaddafi had barked an ambiguous order to his men to end the meeting, which could have meant, "Enough!" or "Get rid of them!" or "That's it!" (The order must have been *"Khalas!"*), and his men took it to mean: Get rid of them for good. I tried to imagine the kind of entourage Qaddafi reigned over—where his men had to wonder, "Now, does he mean I should take them back to their hotel, or execute them?" When the mistake was discovered, Libyan agents flew to Rome, disguised themselves, planted the suitcases in the Holiday Inn, left a false trail for Abbas Badreddine, and flew back to Tripoli the next day.

There was a witness, too. Ali Nizar, a Lebanese electrician on a job in Tripoli, had spoken to the Imam as the three men left the Al Shatti Beach Hotel for—Sadr said—an audience with Qaddafi. His deposition was reprinted in Reza's book.

All the Shiite organizations in Lebanon and Iran rejected reports of Sadr's death, even though a half dozen defecting Libyan intelligence agents routinely confirmed them. The line they put about was that he was alive and imprisoned, and that they were working toward his release.

"First of all," Sassoon responded to my question, still skimming *al-Safir*, "Khomeini must pretend that Sadr is alive, because he badly needs his alliance with Libya and could not maintain it if it were known that Imam Sadr had been murdered in cold blood by Qaddafi's closest men. Secondly, some very cruel and opportunistic people, by no means all Iranian or Lebanese, keep tantalizing Sadr's family with supposed proof that he is alive, that they can make a deal, and that they need a little more money, to get him free."

Rabab, Sadr's devoted sister, was constantly publicizing new information she had that "shows my brother is indisputably alive. I have never thought for a single second, since I heard of his abduction, that anyone could dream of harming him." Yasser Arafat was one of the biggest braggarts when it came to claiming special knowledge of Sadr's captivity, even though the PLO had accused Libya of murdering the Imam (Libya responded by accusing the PLO of murdering him; both eventually withdrew their accusations). Now Sassoon looked at me intently for the first time.

"I am from Iraq, you know. Thousands of Iraqi Jews left Baghdad after Palestine was partitioned, because we were made the targets of extreme violence. Many escaped through Iran, but many came through the desert, through Syria and Jordan, using guides. Those were often killed by treacherous guides or common robbers, though they had left most of what they owned in Iraq. To this day, my mother in Tel Aviv is waiting for one of her nephews. Of course, we don't know what happened, but . . ." He shrugged. "You can't tell *her*."

Sassoon was very much up on the remnants of Sadr's Amal

militia and the Harakat al-Mahrumin, the Movement of the De-
prived, which had split up into groups working under the names
Islamic Amal, Hezbollah, and Islamic Jihad. He had a directory of
photos and biographies of Hussein Moussawi, Abbas Moussawi,
Rabab Sadr, Muhammad Hussein Fadlallah—had the writing not
been all in Hebrew, it would have looked like a high school
yearbook of the Shiite movement. He gave me the phone number
in Tel Aviv of Ziama Devon—the number two to Uri Lubrani,
Israel's commander in the Lebanon war.

I was not sorry to leave Jerusalem, in spite of all the history and
the opportunities to talk to Palestinians. I used a trick to get their
attention: when they tried to pull me into their shops to buy
mother-of-pearl and olive wood *objets,* I refused with polite but
very "country" thanks: *"chathar Allah kheirak!"* "You speak peasant!" they glowed, and hauled me in for tea and a thorough
debriefing. I enumerated the Arab countries I knew, but they
were only curious about the Iran–Iraq war (they hated it and
knew that Israel was helping Iran) and what other Arabs were
saying about the occupied territories. They often shook their
heads sadly at one another but never commented on what I said
until I mentioned my interest in Moussa Sadr. They detested him,
of course, for turning against the PLO, but admitted only to
being confused about Lebanon.

"Are they out of their minds?" asked one old shopkeeper who
told me his name was Adib Seif. "How can they kill one another?
I have never wanted to kill even a Jew, but they kill their own
kind with such a passion! How can they stand themselves! Well,
that's why they do it, I suppose." The Israeli-Lebanese massacre of
Palestinians (and southern Shiites) at Sabra and Chatilla three

years before had left Palestinians with a vivid bitterness toward Lebanon. "Do you know, I took my honeymoon there?" Adib laughed. "A bicycling trip around southern Lebanon. In those days the Lebanese liked us. And the hills and mountains, the orchards, the sea! It was like a vision of Paradise!"

When I mentioned Syria, Seif made a *Haj*-like face and spat five feet into the street, muttering, "God damn them!" Yasser Arafat had been chased out of Syria one year ago, and Syrian forces had all but leveled two Palestinian refugee camps in northern Lebanon in an attempt to destroy the PLO, which they had tried to replace with a new pro-Syrian PLO based in Damascus.

I could never afford to buy anything after these talks, but my stories about Iraqi veterans who had machine-gunned waves of invading children, of Saudi religious zeal and Libyan intrigues, seemed to put them out of the selling mood, and I was usually sent on my way, full of tea, with a complimentary olive wood rosary in a baggie. The rosary may still be sitting on the window sill in the *New York Times'* little Jerusalem office on Rivlin Street, where I tied up the telex machine for an hour sending a valedictory Saudi article to the Sunday Magazine, much to the annoyance of the Pulitzer Prize-winning bureau chief, Tom Friedman.

Before leaving Mishkenot Sha'ananim, I had a Moroccan Jewish dinner with a Dutch-Israeli scholar and his wife. His name was Van Creveld and his books on military strategy were published by university presses in America. They would be visiting the U.S. soon. I told them about my Sadr project and mentioned that after visiting Tel Aviv I would head back to Cairo and then to Paris, to interview exiled Iranian politicians. This was, I told them, the end of the Middle Eastern period of my life.

"Lucky you—Cairo and Paris!" the woman smiled.

We talked of local matters. The professor hated the Palestinians and thought Jerusalem needed a Berlin Wall between its mainly Jewish and mainly Arab halves. When I reminded him that it had just that until 1967, when Israel obliterated the dividing line, his wife broke in with a little story from work. She had a job at the Yad Vashem Museum of the Holocaust.

"We have a custodian, you know, at Yad Vashem, an Arab. He used to own land round there, but lost it. One day he told us that we should have refreshments for visitors—a sort of cafeteria. Well! we thought—refreshments at Yad Vashem? It didn't seem right, not at a shrine to the Holocaust, but at the same time it made sense, because we offered nothing to visitors. So he does it now—he sells coffee and sandwiches. He's a total outsider, of course, being an Arab and a menial worker, but one of my co-workers said it made her think, to see him selling his coffee and sandwiches and looking around, you know, like someone is going to thrash him. Risa said, 'My God, the poor man, he's playing the part of the Polish Jew in Poland!' "

I enjoyed her story, and took the point of it to be that the old Palestinian selling coffee had once been a landowner—perhaps even of the land upon which the Holocaust museum stood. She herself was from Lima, Peru; she and her husband were both Israeli citizens; the Palestinian Polish Jew she chuckled about was a Jerusalemite. American history was too full of parallel injustices for me to bring that up for discussion. I would be leaving Jerusalem the next day, and had no wish to open the world's biggest can of worms.

On the bus to Tel Aviv, I read in the *Jerusalem Post* that as of that month fifty-one percent of the land in the occupied West Bank had been expropriated from its owners by Israel since 1967.

The figure was confirmed by Meron Benvenisti of the West Bank Data Project. I felt sure that this historic statistic would definitely not be reported in most Arab countries, where it would be seen as mortifying proof of their failure to resist Israel.

The editorial pages carried the latest jabs in a running feud between readers on opposing sides of the "rudeness issue." A recent letter from an Israeli who flew TWA from New York had sparked the trouble by praising the American airline's polite service. Why, he appealed, couldn't the El Al cabin crews be that nice? They were always shoving passengers around, ramming dinner carts through the aisles and jostling people without ever saying "Excuse me." For days, the hapless writer was pilloried by enraged subscribers who pronounced their scorn for the "plastic smiles" and "phony-baloney 'courtesy' " rampant in America. Mannerly Israelis were now counterattacking with "we must be *direct,* yes; rude, *never!*"

Direct, yes. In a matter of a week in these streets I had been unmercifully asked uncounted dozens of times where I was from, how I earned a living, how much I earned, whether I was married, why was I not married, and why I didn't speak better Hebrew. I was often able to understand people asking directions, but when I provided the directions in English I was reprimanded and sometimes given a short Hebrew lesson on the spot. And Jerusalem pedestrians had an unnerving habit of maintaining unbroken eye contact as they marched by me on the street, or broken only when they gave an equally frank stare to my crotch. I must have checked fifty times a day to see that my fly was zipped.

Tel Aviv was full of young people sunbathing and shopping and reading, half naked, at crowded cafes. It suggested to me what Beirut might once have been like, and certainly differed from

Jerusalem much in the same way Arabs contrasted Beirut and Damascus: while the coastal city was all blue and white, permissive and fun-loving, the inland city was dust, stone, gates, and women with covered heads. The same comparison held true, on a far dustier and less permissive scale, of Jeddah and Riyadh.

Admiring the Chagalls in the Tel Aviv Museum of Modern Art, I laughed at the memory of the carefully surreal offerings you saw in Riyadh, and the rubbish in the Damascus Art Museum. While both Baghdad and Damascus were noted for their wonderful talent and excellent galleries, somehow only the junk made it into the national museums. I would never forget the oversized *Evisceration,* the centerpiece of a Syrian revolutionary art exhibition. A supine, cruciform figure erupting in blood was surmounted by a daubed vulture with a valentine in its beak. Emblazoned on its chest was a big blue Star of David. "This masterpiece," ran the caption in English, French, and Arabic, "interprets the martyr's collapse as a malignant force (Zionism??) eviscerates his heart."

Shmuel Devon—"Ziama" was his Russian nickname—had a long military career, from the pre-Independence Jewish forces of the Haganah to the failed war in Lebanon. He met with me in a small Defense Ministry cubicle that made Sassoon's office look palatial by comparison. I assumed it was not his office, just a handy corner in which to answer the questions of a nosy foreigner who would otherwise be trying to peer at his maps, files, and radios. We were joined by two of his aides, Moti and Shimon— neither of them spoke English, only Hebrew and Arabic.

I asked Devon about the recurrent rumor that Qaddafi used radical PLO figures to help cover up the murder of Sadr; it was even said that they may have killed him.

"I doubt that the Palestinians had any role in the Moussa Sadr disappearance," said Devon. "Moti?"

Moti and Shimon agreed. "Don't forget," said Moti, "that the radical groups friendly to Libya, such as Sa'eqa and Ahmed Jibril's people, were also friendly to Syria, and Sadr was an ally of Syria too." It seemed clear from their accents that while Shimon had learned his Arabic here and in Lebanon, Moti was Iraqi.

"Being a Syrian ally doesn't exclude being killed by Syria, still less does it exclude Syria's acquiescence in Libya's action." I pointed out. "Look at Kamal Jumblatt." This luckless Syrian ally in Lebanon's civil war, the father of Druze chieftain Walid Jumblatt, was assassinated by Syrians when he had outlived his usefulness.

"Of course Syria acquiesced," said Devon. "Libya is important to President Asad, and he's not a sentimental man. Sadr legitimized Asad's regime by assuring everyone that Asad was Muslim —Asad is Alawite, of course, to the extent that he is anything." That move of Sadr's, angrily disputed by Syria's own Muslim clergy, glossed over the esoteric and heretical nature of Alawite belief. "And Sadr was an ally of diminishing value—in 1978, Amal was down to two or three thousand men. But this doesn't mean that radical Palestinians were involved."

Devon thought the likeliest non-Libyan role might have been played by the Iranians—by Savak.

"When we went into Lebanon in '78, the Shah's government managed to get their soldiers into the observer forces. This was entirely to watch Moussa Sadr and the Iranian opposition figures he was working with. They had Savak agents all over him but could not do anything. I met some of those people in Tehran in the summer of '78 and all they wanted to talk about was Sadr—of course, we barely knew who he was, we never paid attention to the Shiites. Savak showed a disproportionate interest in him. 'Why don't you do something about him?' they asked us. They were more worried about him than about Khomeini! Khomeini was like a nut—but Sadr was liked by everybody. But we were no better than the foreign ministry, really. We didn't see the Shiites coming. And we had no contact with him."

That made Sadr unusual. Southern Lebanese Shiites often did not share the Arab allergy to Israel for several reasons: their religious ties tended to be with Iran rather than the overwhelmingly Sunni Arabs; they resented the PLO's occupation of southern Lebanon; and simple proximity. Because of the job discrimination they faced in Beirut, some Shiites sought work in northern Israel instead. The blundering 1982 invasion changed that, however, and Israeli public opinion now bitterly regretted their squandering of the Shiites' good will—already Amal, rejuvenated by adversity, had inflicted terrible losses on the Israeli army and forced the Israeli Defense Forces to retreat—a first. It was common to hear Israelis complain, "The goddamned Christians—we should have made the Druze our allies," "We should have cast our lot with the Shiites," "We should have used the bomb"—there was a lot of directionless recrimination. They managed to keep a presence in the south and had chased the PLO to a new base in Tunis, but they had been whipped by the Shiites and now had to worry about the Palestinians learning from the Shiite success.

"Would you like to go to Lebanon?" offered Devon.

It was easy to forget that southern Lebanon, all but cut off from the rest of the world, was less than an hour's drive away from here, and that the Israelis controlled much of it. They were the ones who had cut it off, after all.

"Where to, for example?"

"Tyre, Marjayoun, I don't know. Wherever you can talk to local people there. We can find someone to take you. Bint Jbeil. Khiam. Naqura."

Why did Khiam sound familiar? I considered Devon's generous offer—he probably had people going back and forth twenty times a day from Lebanon, not to mention special trips to bring journalists. Even from Beirut the south was inaccessible because of Israeli roadblocks. I recalled the pictures I had seen of Jebel Amel and the little Shiite villages in the foothills of Mount Hermon, the turquoise sea and pine forests. Fuad had told me about it, and the olive wood merchant in the Street of the Chain in Jerusalem, not to mention Hussein. Ah—that's why Khiam rang a bell; Hussein's brothers were being held in the Israeli prison camp there.

Shimon and Moti escorted me out of the Defense Ministry in single file, since the halls in that particular building were not much wider than library stacks. On the bus back to Cairo, some American and Israeli students were getting into a frantic argument over a hot new issue: an increased travel tax on Israelis that amounted to nearly $200 just for the privilege of leaving the country and returning. Backers of the plan said that people traveling abroad could afford it, or else they should stay at home. The trouble was that the frequent travelers, like so much of Israel's Jewish population, were from somewhere else and were now using their original passports rather than Israeli ones. What had put the issue in the headlines was the fact that Israelis of German origin now preferred their German papers to Israeli and were renouncing their Israeli citizenship in favor of German to avoid paying the travel tax; as Jews, they did not lose their right to reside in Israel. Now, according to these shouting students, members of the Knesset on opposite sides of the issue were calling each other "Nazis," which had led to a whole new crisis.

"Do you think one Jew should lose his temper and call another Jew a Nazi? In the Israeli Knesset?" the boy seated in front turned around to ask me. He had heard me laugh at the argument.

"In America we have special radio stations for problems like this," I told him. It struck me as ludicrous that non-Israelis should bother with it.

"What were you doing in Israel? Just hanging out?"

I wanted to tell him about my Imam Sadr project, but caught myself thinking: why am I bothering with it?

"Pretty much." I pulled out *al-Tih.*

Seventeen days later the Americans left and took their two guides with them, but this time they headed deeper into the interior rather than going back where they had come from. Miteb al-Hathal, who was not convinced by this departure, regarding it instead as an even greater cause for alarm, said in Ibn Rashed's encampment one night, before many of the men of Wadi al-Uyoun, "They're after something."

Now the bus was sputtering through Gaza, and at the sight of the ocean of plywood, aluminum, and cooking smoke through which thousands of refugees thronged, everyone fell silent. By the time we got to Cairo it would be midnight. I made a note to go back to the Madbouli Bookstore the next day for a good dictionary.

15

The Exile

$\mathcal{S}$yrians talked about the new bridges and flyovers swerving through Damascus as if this city, the world's oldest, had entered the space age, but the grimy concrete structures carried very little traffic, only battered red buses spewing blue smoke, tiny knock-off Fiats from the USSR, and vans with portraits of Ayatollah Khomeini pasted against the side windows. (Iranian families were sent here to visit the tomb of the Prophet's granddaughter Zeinab as a consolation for losing loved ones in the war with Iraq.) The asphalt and auto metal glimmered with rainwater. Winter in Damascus is stormy and bitter cold, and the lurching buses plunging through brown puddles splashed Ali's Newsstand's plastic-draped rows of *al-Baath* and *Tishrin* and *Pravda* fastened with clothespins to his display racks, and the stacks of Khomeini's *Islamic Government, Al-Quwa al-Sawda* (Black Power) by Stokely Carmichael, and the *Collected Odes* of Mustafa Tlas, Syria's defense minister.

"It adds something to the hotel," Riad, the doorman, assured me. He gazed at the huge disfiguring arch of dripping concrete with almost paternal pride from behind the swinging glass doors of the Semiramis Hotel. "And it makes the lobby a lot quieter now that all the traffic doesn't go roaring by." The staff of the Semiramis—I joked with the manager that I could not afford fully ramis accommodations—liked to talk about the flyover, but it had been there for at least ten years. I had seen it in 1979 on a visit from Cairo, the first time I had seen Damascus. At the time, you could not find a hotel room because of the influx of Iraqis: Syria and Iraq had just proclaimed unity, sealing a new friendship based on common enmity for Egypt, and the border had been declared open.

Now nearly every headline on display at Ali's corner sneered at Iraq's success at having fought Iran to a standstill; Iran had sued for peace, despite Khomeini's reckless boast, displayed in all his embassies, that "We Shall Fight This War Even Should It Last 200 Years." Syria had supported Iran all the way, and Riad's friend Mazen the janitor told me with a wry smile, "We're going to get our asses kicked." This wry fatalism was typically Syrian; it was hard to imagine that remark coming from an Israeli or Egyptian or American tongue. This attitude, it occurred to me, had helped this struggling country to achieve its geopolitical success: small egos make for sharp eyes.

Other headlines denounced recent Israeli aggression in Lebanon, praised daring Palestinian commando actions in Bethlehem, and mocked American government contacts with "the Zionist stooge, Yasser Arafat." It was hard to believe that almost four years had passed since I had left the Middle East "for good," but the proof was in the new Damascene fashions (bellbottoms were out, jeans were in) and my spoken Arabic, now hesitant after four years of American hibernation. When the book about Imam Moussa Sadr was published, I was in California, toasting its (otherwise unnoticed) publication day with the *Los Angeles Times'* former Middle East correspondent David Lamb.

Even before the final chapter of the Imam book was complete, I was drafting a proposal for an American publisher ("As yet, no Arab writer has won the Nobel Prize for Literature. Abdelrahman Munif will be the first . . .") to bring out a translation of *al-Tih* under the title of the trilogy of which it was the first volume, *Cities of Salt*. I spent one year translating the novel into English, and it was published in 1988, shortly after Naguib Mahfouz won the Nobel Prize for Literature, with a doctored endorsement from Graham Greene on the jacket. (Greene had written that this "excellent" novel "opened strange new vistas to the imagination" but the publisher struck the "strange".) The book had a gold palm tree on the spine and a tinted and hand-lettered title page with more palm trees. I was proud to be transporting three plump copies of this translation to Munif himself, whose latest migration had brought him here to Damascus; his wife was Syrian.

By coming to Syria I was taking a break from translating the second volume of the trilogy, *al-Ukhdoud.* Where the first volume described the shock of the oil discovery to the desert folk whose pretty oasis towns became vast oil fields and smoking refineries, the second followed the intrigues of the oil kingdom's royal court and rather doltish government. Munif and I had discussed the trilogy in detail in a lively correspondence between 1986 and 1989, and since I wanted to meet him, and could now at last face the Arab world as someone besides an aimless imperialist swept away by visions of dunes, sarcophagi, and the French Foreign Legion, I persuaded the great author that I needed to know more.

Crown Prince Abdullah of Saudi Arabia was also in Damascus, meeting with President Asad and "hailing Syria's tough stances," "calling for Arab steadfastness"—it made them sound like they were looking for taxis—but (and this was the real truth) he was here mainly to demand that Syria now reestablish diplomatic relations with Egypt. What this cost Saudi Arabia I could only imagine, but it must have been astronomical because Syria actually attended, much against its will, the Arab Summit in Morocco the following week. On seeing the front-page photos at Ali's, I felt a little surge of pride that I had come to Damascus to meet someone of far greater importance than Abdullah or the cruel Asad.

Jebel Qasioun, a looming orange hill, hangs over central Damascus like a guilty conscience. The snowy top was barely visible in the driving rain and heavy fog—or were those low thunderclouds? The other buildings were all darkened—no one seemed to be working today, and the air of desertion gave a free hand to the violent weather. The streets were almost empty except for three Iranian mullahs in brown cloaks and black turbans sweeping down Salhier Street toward the National Hotel, where at least 200 windows displayed identical posters of Khomeini.

I looked out at this cold, ramshackle city with true love. Some Middle Eastern cities embrace you (Cairo). Others try to impress you with their suavity (prewar Beirut) or callousness (Baghdad); most, one way or another, ask understanding for their still-tender traditions (Riyadh), and quite a few demand adoration (Jerusalem, Bethlehem, Mecca, Kerbela—lots of those). Only Damascus could not care less. It makes little capital out of its Street Called Straight, Omayyad Mosque, and the wall where Saul was let down in a basket. Even tour guides will not bother to tell you that Damascus was founded by Noah's grandson Uz.

I spent my first morning getting reacquainted with central Damascus. The iron balconies of old stone apartment buildings still carried signboards proclaiming the offices of the exiled Communist Party of Iraq, the National Salvation Movement of Somalia, the Popular Front for the Liberation of the Arabian Gulf, the Islamic Movement for the Liberation of Bahrain, the Voice of Arab Egypt, and a dozen more malcontent groups, including, until recently, al-Assifa, headquarters of the notorious Abu Nidal. All are leftist organizations, representing what the Saudis call, with a shudder, "imported ideologies." Syria thrives unashamedly on imported ideologies, including some (Islam, pan-Arabism) they share with the conservative Arabians, and others, like Baathism ("Unity, Freedom, Socialism") which they do not. For the most part, though, the presence of these groups gives Syria a sort of control panel with which to turn up or decrease the pressure on semi-friendly countries.

Hafez al-Asad's face is so omnipresent that after a week I was almost surprised not to see it in the mirror: with and without sunglasses, looking kindly, scowling, smirking, or meditating; in a suit or in military uniform and beret, but always with the same legend, "Hafez al-Asad, Our Leader Forever." And there was something new since 1979: the "I [heart] [Asad's face]" bumper sticker. I first saw one on a jeep in front of the Kuwait Airlines office and actually screamed; the soldier on guard glowered.

Up Abu Rummaneh Street the embassies were all drab in the rain. The Yugoslav and Libyan missions were big and boxy, their sodden flags slapping against the poles. The Saudi Embassy, very neat and paranoid, with all its green-shuttered staff housing right there inside the wall. There were police and soldiers all over the place.

At the Baath Newsstand I browsed among the Snickers bars, aging *International Herald Tribunes,* and postcards, finally selecting a view of Saladin's tomb on which I scribbled a note to Hamdan in Saudi Arabia. He had visited me in Long Beach in 1988 on his last "drugs visit" to America before settling down with his new wife and baby in al-Mursilat, and even newer and more westerly suburb of Riyadh. He and his brothers had turned antimonarchical and fiercely religious; they had read Naser Saeed's *Tarikh Al-Saud* and now believed that the royal family were American agents descended from the Arabian Jewish tribe of al-Qainuqah. (That was not to be his last visit; a few months after this Syrian trip of mine he made a wrathful telephone call from Miami to scold me for compromising him with the Saudi postal authorities by sending him a card from "communist Syria.")

As the street became an uphill climb toward Jebel Qasioun, a Middle East icon came into view on the left: nearly a hundred people of all ages huddled in the rain outside the American consulate. There was even a joke about it, popular in Egyptian, Sudanese, Ethiopian, and Libyan versions. Asad (Sadat/Numeiri/ Mengistu/Qaddafi) hears that there is a line of his citizens waiting to apply for U.S. visas. "Impossible!" he shouts. "Who could want to leave this beloved country and my wise rule?" Next morning he sneaks out to the American Embassy, sees the incredible line, and stalks up to the window. "What's going on here!? What are you telling all these people?" "What people?" asks the clerk innocently. The fearless leader looks around to an empty street—empty except for one peasant. "Where did everyone go?" he snaps. "Well," answers the peasant, "if *you've* come to emigrate to America, we'll all stay here!"

There it was. My favorite Damascene monument was still standing: the Egyptian Embassy, on the west side of this elegant, sloping plaza also bordered by a tall mosque and two or three buildings of the American Embassy. The modern Egyptian edifice, made of the big beige blocks so favored for public buildings in Damascus as well as Jerusalem, has a grand metal gate and five stories of black iron balcony railings and tinted glass panels, and at first glance outshines even the U.S. consulate to the south, across a shady lane along a brook. Take a second look: behind the plane trees, most of the windows are smashed, broken glass, overturned filing cabinets and disemboweled easy chairs litter the floors inside, and there is no sign of any attempt at repair. The embassy was sacked by a government-sanctioned mob when Egypt signed its treaty with Israel, and no Egyptian has been allowed to return here since. Broken gutters spewed rainwater under the gate and down the tilted sidewalk.

It is not a garrulous city and Damascenes have nothing to say to foreigners, unless they are soldiers—a fixture of every downtown corner, bank, embassy, and government office. Some look dark and central Asian, some are apple-cheeked and blue-eyed but a good half of them look barely old enough to shave, and there are thousands in uniform, male and female, who are actual children, carrying schoolbooks. All public school pupils wear a military uniform, and swarms of children in green fatigues and corfam shoes mob the sidewalks for half the day.

It was nearly ten o'clock, and I hurried through the tearing wind to the hotel lobby and its lugubrious coven of five men in overcoats on the big sofa. A newcomer to Damascus and its hundreds of watchful soldiers, omnipresent Asad faces, and relentless propaganda might assume them to be idle spies or informers, but there were men drinking tea and doing nothing all over the city and I had the feeling these might be salesmen or middlemen waiting to do a deal, who considered this faded lobby the height of power chic.

I ordered Turkish coffee *saadeh,* sugarless, and opened *Tishrin.* Asad had received the French and Albanian ambassadors, the Syrian Orthodox Antiochian patriarch, and cables of support—why was not mentioned—from citizens of the Raqqa region. Perhaps there had been a massacre there which he was now demonstrating had not happened, or met with local approval. He had sent a cable wishing a speedy recovery to Emperor Hirohito, who was said to be dying. The United States had committed aggression against Libyan planes over international waters. I sipped my coffee with a neutral scowl on my face, in imitation of the five men on the central sofa, and gazed out the glass walls at more soldiers and clerical tourists from Iran battling the whipping wind. A small boy tried to sell a pack of Marlboro Lights (he kept his stock under his pants, tucked into his baggy socks) to a pair of mullahs, who ignored him and climbed the shattered steps of a concrete pedestrian bridge, looking like warlocks in their whipping cloaks. A swarthy man with iron-gray hair and sunglasses parked his newish Japanese car and looked up at the hotel.

Abdelrahman Munif pushed open the glass door to the lobby looking both ways, as if crossing a street. Unlike the other Arabs in the street, the Saudi Arabian did not look out of place in his heavy parka and scarf: long exile in Eastern Europe and France had accustomed him to this kind of weather.

Upstairs, on the edge of a sofa on the mezzanine, he smiled at the American and British editions of *Cities of Salt* I had brought and riffled through the pages. He nodded his agreement to my awkward explanation of the title (it had been four years since I had talked at such length in Arabic): Yes, *al-Tih* was a difficult title—it would lose too much in translation. Better to use the title of the whole trilogy, *Mudun al-Milh,* which was alliterative in English too. He wondered if the meaning was less obvious in translation—"to dissolve like salt in water" was a common Arab expression, easily suggesting the transitory nature of what the oil had accomplished, but I had read it so many times in keeping up with the Sadr press ("he vanished like salt in water" cropped up in every article) that I could no longer remember whether we had the same saying in English.

"It's not a conventional novel, actually," he replied to my next stuttered question. "It's not entirely history, either. It's a parallel history, in novel form but involving in one time period events from fifty and twenty years ago, and the present, to give the truest picture of the country."

"What country?" In the 582 pages of the novel, the words "Saudi Arabia" were never used.

"Well, everyone knows," Munif beamed. "Not that that's so important. Our history—modern Arab history, that is, our version of it—is not too honest."

That was putting it mildly. While it was understandable that the Arabs needed more time to process the religious revival that had plagued the region since the late 1970s, there was no excuse for the absence of the major Arab event of this century—the discovery of oil—from their literature. It was a delicate subject because most Arabs were without oil and felt that the oil countries were misusing their wealth. It was impossible to write about oil without writing about politics, so that was that.

Cities of Salt—al-Tih—described an Arab country making the hard transition from nomadism to oil, but with little reference to politics or government—which, after all, hardly existed for the bedouin. They had an absentee government, one which showed not the slightest interest in them until oil was discovered by the mysterious American invaders, and then forced them from their land. Invaders was putting it kindly. From the simple bedouin's point of view, the Americans were terrifying aliens, and scenes such as the ones describing the installation of the power generator in the desert, its deafening noise, and the blinding light from the lamps it powered, read like science fiction.

Later on, there were less ominous scenes of misunderstanding the aliens: the Arab's bumpkin emir trying to use a radio; wondering if a telephone can connect him to all absent people, even the dead; and asking about the Americans' big metal steed ("How long did Ford live? Would he respond to different riders? Did he need training, or was he naturally tame?").

The book contained not one malevolent American, though—in fact, for a political novel it had virtually no "us" and "them."

We were all "us" in shifting permutations, misunderstanding one another in new and different ways, kept from communicating by primitive fear and arrogance.

The absence of Americans from Arab novels is an intriguing example of the presence of absence, explicable, perhaps, in terms of the constant nagging presence of American food, appliances, music, and politics even in the remotest Arab town or oasis: when an Arab novelist sits down to write, he shuts it all out. They wish we were invisible. Edward Said has pointed out that while the Arab and Islamic worlds are earnestly studied in the U.S., there are no institutes or organizations anywhere in the Arab world for studying the United States, "by far the greatest economic and political influence in the region." It is common for educated Arabs to plead eloquently for a more subtle American under- standing of their countries but to show, at the same time, no interest at all in the forces that make the U.S. work. I blamed the Arab and Islamic tendency toward cultural arrogance.

"Why did you translate it?" Munif asked.

I told him a truthful story.

"I have a good friend who spent five years in Kuwait, as I did in Saudi Arabia, and when he went back to the United States he wanted the Arab world to be part of his life still. He had no way—his feelings for that part of the world were inarticulate. He didn't speak Arabic so he couldn't keep up with the literature or movies. He couldn't visit every now and then because the Kuwai- tis don't give tourist visas. So he joined the Arab-American Anti- Discrimination League."

"That was good," said Munif, lighting his pipe.

"For him. You see, Arab-American groups like that put their energy into protecting Arab rights in Israel, the occupied territories, and the United States. They don't get involved in human rights abuses in, for example, Iraq, Syria, Libya, or Saudia Arabia—least of all, Saudi Arabia. That means taking sides in a certain way. I wanted to keep in touch with the Middle East, too, and to repay all it taught me. But my way was to translate your novels."

"That's even better." He puffed away. "But it's the last thing I ever imagined an American wanting to read. It's very local: the history, the people, even the dialects. Especially the dialects! I wrote that book for Arabs to read. I can see my other books in translation, but that one? I never thought I'd see it!"

Most of his books were translated into Eastern European languages, in Poland, Yugoslavia, Czechoslovakia, and the Soviet Union. He had studied in Belgrade, not Moscow, as the Riyadh rumor had it, and spoke Serbo-Croatian perfectly; French, too. He spoke English but I never heard it. This was Damascus, and we spoke only Arabic. It was a shock to my badly jet-lagged system and malfunctioning memory, but it was a compliment and I graciously accepted it.

As we left the hotel, it became clear from his questions that I was being adopted for the next ten days. What was my program? Was I free to come to Aleppo with him and his wife? He would be giving a lecture there, at an Armenian cultural club. What did I want to do here? Meet writers? Artists? Politicians? Go shopping? Or should they plan my time for me? We discussed it strolling through some handicraft markets, where he forbade me to buy anything just yet. "We'll come back with my wife— you'll get better prices."

"Are you expert hagglers?"

"She is. I hate haggling—I can't tolerate it. It's just a bother, these unfixed prices. Foreigners, above all, get robbed blind." In *Cities of Salt,* the people of Wadi al-Uyoun, the innocent oasis that gets blown to bits by oilmen, also despise haggling for its cynical greed.

That was not typical. Nor was his dislike of Damascus. He plainly loathed the crowds and shabbiness of the city, and hated driving through the chaotic traffic that was nearly as mad as Cairo's. He repeated several times that I had to see Aleppo. "Everyone prefers it to Damascus. It's full of Armenians—wonderful people."

Munif lived in al-Mezze, a suburb of Damascus on the road to Beirut, in a ground-floor apartment with busy walls of books and paintings. He was an art collector, and some of the excellent artwork from the covers of the Arabic editions of the *Cities of Salt* trilogy hung on his walls along with Arabian pottery, casts of Ugaritic texts, and modern statuary. His two beautiful teenage daughters, Aza and Leila, were energetically setting the table for lunch when we came in. His two sons gravely shook hands with me.

"Hani and Yasser," said Munif. "Take Peter's jacket."

Mentally I saw his children in robes and veils; all four teenagers looked very Saudi. But they were dressed in sweaters and tight jeans, and speaking French among themselves.

"We spent a year in Paris," Munif explained. "I wrote *al-Tih* there, and the children go to the French School here."

Mrs. Munif appeared, short, dark-eyed, fair-skinned, with no makeup, a Damascene beauty, to shake hands and retire back into the kitchen to finish up lunch. Munif asked if I preferred whiskey or arak.

In the two hours before the jet lag destroyed my thinking processes and I was driven back to the Semiramis with my eyes beginning to cross, we established several things. Munif's father was Saudi, his mother Iraqi. He had been stripped of his Saudi citizenship in 1963, and now carried a South Yemeni passport. The Saudis had offered him a temporary passport so that he could visit Riyadh, conclude some business, visit family members, and leave; he refused, demanding nothing less than the restoration of his nationality. The third volume of the *Cities of Salt* trilogy would be published in Beirut in a few days. Because of economic restrictions, there would be separate Iraqi, Syrian, and Egyptian editions of the book—identical text, but locally manufactured, well below the still very high standards of Lebanese book production. (I recalled from my visit to Iraq that, with few exceptions, only books manufactured in Iraq could be sold there. This policy, disguised as protectionism, was actually an ingenious form of blanket censorship.) Tomorrow we would visit Maaloula, one of the last remaining places on earth where Aramaic, the language of Jesus, was spoken.

"Oil is the first and last and only chance for the Arabs to do something for themselves," fumed Munif as we sped north out of Damascus. "It is incredible that they throw it away the way they do!"

I was almost human after a good night's sleep. This was a cold, bright day, and we were leaving the city's straggling suburbs behind us while the winding road through the brown, snow-littered hills made the landscape shift with every curve.

"Do you find this pretty?" asked Mrs. Munif from the back seat.

"It looks like a world without maps!" I immediately replied. That was the title of one of his books, and I had determined to make puns on all the titles whenever possible. They both laughed, but Munif immediately returned to the subject of Saudi Arabia.

"Look at the young Saudis you see in Paris. You've seen them in Riyadh, of course. Eating hamburgers—as fat as balloons! I feel sorry for them! They're being weaned off of their way of life and what are they given in return? They're told to take Western technology but look down on the West. Respect the Arab traditions that they're encouraged to forget. And look what they're building in Riyadh and Jeddah!"

The car drew to a stop to allow a shepherd in jeans and a baseball jacket to drive his flock of goats across the road, then surged forward.

"Twenty stories of glass walls—in that climate! Do they think they'll have oil forever? They want to be American. America is a very good place but there is only one America. If they want to be like America, why not adopt a constitution." He pronounced that word, *dustour,* lovingly. "Anything can go wrong in America, any crook or fool can get into the White House, but there's always the Constitution there to protect the people. That's what the Arabs need. Constitutions that are worth something."

I asked him if he had been to the United States; I was fairly sure that he had not. He laughed.

"Where do you think I got the idea for *Cities of Salt?* I visited New York, Washington, San Francisco, and Atlanta. What a place! America,"—he turned to his wife—"America is a *continent.* California made the greatest impression on me. Americans are adventurers, especially the people in California. They'll just pick themselves up and move huge distances to grasp a new opportunity. They have no fear of change, or challenge, or of adapting. In some ways they closely resemble the Arabs, and in other ways they do not share some of our negative qualities."

"How did they provide the idea for your novel?"

"Oh, not that. It was the abandoned gold mines in northern California—my friends took me there. You see how the gold, and especially the people flooding after it, molded California, and the country as a whole. And the mines are empty now. Someday the oil wells in Saudi Arabia will look like that. Does anyone in the Saudi government realize that?"

I pointed out that because of the kingdom's gigantic reserves of petroleum, the post-oil era could be generations away, and that in any case they were diversifying intelligently into petrochemicals and downstream industries. Still, Munif had his doctorate in petroleum economics and in 1973 had published a book entitled *Principles of Partnership and Arab Oil Nationalization* in Beirut, so knew whereof he spoke.

"They'll have oil for a long time—or maybe not so long, at the rate they're going now—but they won't be millionaires for that long. They've been pumping it too fast, only to fund their development, much of which isn't even development, it's just projects to keep the family"—he did not have to say which family—"rich, and the people complacent. They have to adapt, to evolve politically sooner or later, but they're using the oil wealth to resist change. And selling off the future to do so. There is never a good excuse to waste money or deplete a nonrenewable resource—especially when we have nothing else! Look—enemies of the revolution."

There was a rather small prison set back from the road, with a narrow yard behind the tall chain-link fence. Munif shook his head sadly.

Munif's sensible oil views conformed with those of the Arab Baath Socialist Party, to which he had belonged in Baghdad twenty years before. The anti-imperialist party preached Arab unity and restrained use of oil resources. Saudi Arabia had become a huge oil power through its partnership with the American oil companies in Aramco, and pumped at a dizzying rate to fund its development. Iraq built its oil industry slowly, wanting to use only Iraqi manpower, and vowed to husband its resources carefully. "Of the last two barrels of oil produced on earth," the party had said, "one will be Iraqi."

We arrived, amid overhanging cliffs and narrow caves, in Maaloula, and drove up a steeply sloping lane to park in a little square. Children playing on the cobblestones chattered in Aramaic, and a church loomed on the peak of the highest hill. The next thing I saw was a good-sized mosque with a metallic dome. This town was known for its ancient Christian population: their language had survived only here and in two neighboring villages, and no Muslims spoke it. Munif followed my gaze and smiled.

"Muslims settle here because they don't like the idea of there being a place that's exclusively Christian."

We walked through a winding cave, open at the top, to reach the Church of St. Sarkis at the top of the hill. A priest who led us around to examine the icons of Near Eastern saints and narrate the history of the church visibly lost patience with Munif's innocent but persistent questions.

"If you'll just wait until I finish," he smiled menacingly. He had delivered his spiel how many thousands of times, and there was no room for spontaneity. Munif—who later told me that he did not like churches—strolled outside, and when we joined him he was listening closely to a long story from an old man on a bicycle.

"Then I remarried," the man was saying. "We moved here because I didn't like the way things were going in Damascus. The Defense Squads"—belonging to the president's brother, Rifaat al-Asad—"were harassing women who wore the veil. They thought their own shadows belonged to the Muslim Brotherhood!"

"Abdelrahman talks to everybody," said Mrs. Munif with a smile. "And he can talk to strangers for the longest time!"

Over lunch in the tiny hamlet of Mnin, Munif asked about my book on Imam Moussa Sadr—how was it for an American researching that book? Did I believe anything I had been told? I briefly described what I had learned in the Middle East, and subsequent meetings, in Paris, with two Iranian politicians, Abolhassan Bani Sadr and Shahpour Bakhtiar.

"At the end of the day," I said, "everyone tells you what best suits their own interests. My conclusion was that the most obvious scenario, that Sadr was executed in Libya, was fact, but not provable. Certainly Khomeini could have prevented it, or exposed the whole affair, but didn't."

"Why not?" asked Munif.

I responded with a joke an Iranian photographer told me in Paris: A businessman divorces his wife to marry his beautiful young secretary, and the new couple goes away on their honeymoon. "I guess I'll have to hire a new secretary when we get back, dear," he tells her. "I've already taken care of that," she tells him lovingly. "Darling, you think of everything!" "Yes," she says. "He starts Monday." Khomeini had exploited religion to the fullest to make himself ruler of Iran, and he was the expert on how much trouble a clergyman could cause. He did not want Sadr as a rival, alive or dead.

"I thought the case would shed light on some of the problems of the region," I confessed, "because they all intersected in the Sadr affair. In fact, though, the story of Sadr shed light only by exemplifying them. It's so knotty and so obvious at the same time, so surrounded by myths and strong emotions. There are no clean hands, and no objectivity."

"We used to live in Beirut," sighed Mrs. Munif, but then smiled brilliantly. "It was heavenly! The weather was nice, and there was so much life, so much tolerance. It couldn't last, of course."

"Did you live there during the war?" I asked. "Lots of the Lebanese praise the place so much, even now, that I've never taken them seriously."

"We left," said Munif. "I haven't been there in almost twenty years. What is there left to see? Horrors. Atrocities."

A young waiter served the platters of salads, dips, chicken and beef kebabs, bread and fresh beers, and retired to the far end of the restaurant. Under the influence of the beers I told Munif that I had been disappointed to see Naguib Mahfouz win the Nobel Prize for Literature; I had hoped that he, Munif, would be the first Arab recipient.

"If anyone deserves it, he does," he insisted.

"He writes very good novels but they're not great, and they don't have the originality yours have," I explained with no trace of embarrassment because to me these were facts, though it was a pleasure to see Munif's admiration for Mahfouz, who had fought the Arab left as grimly as Munif had promoted it. I went on to say that it would have woken up the Saudi government to have a son they had disowned win international recognition of that kind. When the first Olympic gold medal ever won by an Arab went to a woman—at the Los Angeles Olympics in 1984—the Saudis were crushed, but learned to be proud. "I thought you could be the Nawal Mutawakkil of Arab literature," I told him.

We talked about Baghdad; they had lived there, too, and Munif had collaborated on a novel there with the famous poet and novelist Jabra Ibrahim Jabra. "It started almost as a joke," he said, "but we saw the possibilities and followed it through." Did he enjoy collaborating? He laughed. "Never again! Never!" They were surprised that I had liked Baghdad; Arabs considered it an oppressive, lifeless city, and the climate was, if possible, even more infernal than in Riyadh.

"I didn't find out anything useful about Imam Sadr," I admitted—Sadr had studied in Iraq—"but Baghdad was so closed off for such a long time that it has stayed different." Actually, I could never explain adequately why I liked Baghdad so much. Since I had not lived there, I could only list what attracted me. It was hot, there was good shopping, lots of history, and above all they had a bewitching dialect, with a very pretty accent and quaint loan words from Persian, Turkish, even English. Baghdadis expressed "ice cream cone" with a phrase consisting of one Turkish and two English words: *glass-biscuit-dondirma,* ice cream in a glass made of cookie. People there were very courteous. It was the Fertile Crescent.

There was a statue in Saadoun Street that summed up Baghdad for me: Murjaneh, the wise servant girl from the story of Ali Baba and the Forty Thieves. She was portrayed pouring out her big bronze jug into a vast array of tall jars, and a fountain splashed water from the statue day and night. Only after gazing at the splendid, romantic monument for a moment did you remember that she was pouring boiling oil onto the hiding thieves, to scald them to death. I got the same thrill being there that many other people got from Jerusalem.

"Was everything fine?" asked the waiter, suddenly reappearing, with a special smile for me. "What do you say—is the cooking better here or in America?"

"You see what big ears they have!" whispered Mrs. Munif when he had gone.

That was our last meal in a restaurant. On every subsequent day, the subject turned to food at least once, and we discussed the good points of certain dishes versus others. The one I preferred always appeared for dinner the next day. Munif showed up at the Semiramis every morning, with his boys, his girls, or his wife, and we toured the city and shopped until lunchtime. Every day we passed on Shukri Kuwatly Street the al-Kindi Cinema's huge poster of Faye Dunaway as Joan Crawford, and the title *Habeebti Moomie* ("The Romantic American Film"), and, on a nearby wall, a sample of government graffiti that was a full block long: DOWN WITH THE IMPERIALIST AMERICAN-ISRAELI CONSPIRACY: BOY-COTT AMERICAN GOODS! This embarrassed Mrs. Munif, who assured me, "We buy *lots* of American goods."

We had just done all of my shopping, or rather she had, because she did not want me to be overcharged, so we were carrying bundles of embroidered Damascene tablecloths, pottery dishes and statues, chocolates, books, a bottle of arak, pumice stones, and a parchment of Kufic calligraphy. Later, they refused to be paid back; all my souvenirs in Syria became gifts from them.

"Syrians give America the benefit of the doubt," observed Munif. "Their government, which is not tender with their lives, uses up half its energy slandering America, so the people get curious about the United States, and rather sympathetic. When you see traces of anti-Americanism here, it's the hand of the government."

"It's the opposite in Saudi Arabia," I said. He might have thought it ungracious to point this out himself. "We're all over them, the government is almost slavish toward Reagan—at least Fahd is. They think they know everything about us. If only we weren't such ardent suitors they'd like us better. I think the world needs a vacation from America."

"But everybody wants American money," laughed Mrs. Munif.

Munif was extravagant in his praise of the physical beauty of America, the kindness of Americans, the sheer size of the country, and our wise constitution, but never alluded to U.S. politics, so I assumed he hated them and Reagan.

"What's that?" asked Munif. His car had a Denver boot on the front left wheel; we had parked illegally. The device was half the size of an American one—flimsy, mended with wire, its red paint flaking off, like some old toy. A young policeman with a pencil mustache squeezed through the crowd in front of these shops and waved a ticket at Munif.

"I'm foreign here," Munif explained. "How do I know I can't park on a corner?"

"I'm sorry," said the officer, pointing to the amount of the fine. Munif grumbled and paid; it was about $2.

" 'Foreign,' " said Mrs. Munif, and made a face at me. "Really, Abdelrahman."

"Foreign," said Munif stubbornly, but smiled. "From someplace else. By the way," he added, looking concerned, "you are most likely blacklisted in Saudi Arabia for translating the book. You realize that?"

We were momentarily separated by a pack of old Iranian ladies who had provided martyrs for the lost cause, in white wimples and patterned chadors. Each carried string bags of cigarettes, gum, and kleenex, and one had a green box of dates from Medina—a hot item for visitors getting no closer to the Holy Land.

I wanted to tell him that if that were my biggest worry, I was a lucky man, but it would have been slighting to his country; every word he had ever written was informed with love of its people. I could have joked that we were both exiles now; but for some reason I suddenly felt too sad to say anything.

16

The Moral

When the sun came out, shiny Damascus smelled like roses and eucalyptus trees, and the hundreds of streams generated by the Barada River could be heard rushing under the city's little bridges and through the sunken canals that ran along residential streets in the Arnouss and Abu Rummaneh neighborhoods. The piercing notes of thrushes could be heard among the honking horns again. This was my last day in Damascus. Munif and I were meandering toward the center of the old city, veering around Islam's most famous building outside of Mecca, Medina, and Jerusalem.

The Omayyad Mosque is built on the site of the Aramaean temple of Rimmon, where the biblical commander Naaman deposited two mule loads of earth from Samaria so that he could worship Yahweh on Israelite soil. In the first century A.D., a columned Temple of Jupiter was constructed over the House of Rimmon, and in the fourth century the Emperor Theodosius built a Christian cathedral over the Roman temple. When the Omayyad dynasty converted the Church of St. John the Baptist to a mosque in 705, they spared the magnificent reliquary of John the Baptist's head: "Iohanna al-Ma'amadan" is a saint to the Muslims, too. The edifice standing in the heart of Old Damascus, whose old stone is adorned with green and gold mosaics, contains elements of all its past lives; minarets (the first in Islam) have been added and some Roman columns remain outside its walls, where the city's biggest bazaar, the Souq al-Hamidiya, debouches.

The mosque is a tourist attraction, too; like many historical mosques, such as al-Azhar in Cairo, it charges admission to non-Muslims. I had gone in on my first visit to Damascus, mainly to complete a certain devotional symmetry, since ten years earlier I had seen the burial place of John the Baptist's headless body, in an Egyptian monastery in Wadi Natroun. Now there was no reason to go in; no longer a reporter or a member of a Muslim society, I did not have the curiosity or sense of obligation to see how things were developing in there.

There were no Iranians here. They harbored a grudge against

the Omayyad caliphate, and cherished much more feeling for the Shiite Abbasid dynasty, whose black banners had flown not here but in Baghdad. The Iranians were all across town at the gilded tomb of Sitt Zeinab. Zeinab's tomb was Syria's prime Shiite attraction, and it was an important meeting place for Iranian and Lebanese Shiites, mobbed with mullahs, festooned with anti-American banners, and plastered with posters of Khomeini. Now there was a place I had wanted to visit, but Munif preferred to take a stroll through the old town.

It seemed a shame to pass up a place where I would see Moussa Sadr's picture on display, and could soak up such a lavish Shiite atmosphere; most of all, I was faintly disappointed when I realized that I really did not mind missing it. Five years earlier, there had been a certain thrill in the militancy of Arabia's Shiite minorities, and in Iran's tireless pillorying of conservative Arab regimes. Khomeini's unrelenting ridicule of Saudi Arabia's royal theocracy had been a great comfort in Riyadh, but Damascus was another story. The ranting of Iran's Islamic government was no joke here—it was part of a paranoid, militant, theocratic-imperial hatred for the Arabs, accepted here because the heartless genius of Syria's politics saw Iran as a useful ally against its current enemies, Iraq and Egypt. My feelings at passing up Sitt Zeinab were complex but not strong: on the whole, I preferred to shop for an inlaid box for my parents and talk to Munif.

In front of the Omayyad Mosque, German tourists were pulling off their shoes and stepping into rented wooden clogs. This was awkward to do standing up, grasping one another's shoulders for balance. One elderly man was pulling off his socks as well as his shoes. The squatting Syrian clog purveyor tapped the man's knee and motioned for him to keep his socks on. Apart from the

Iranian war tourists and Lebanese refugees, these seemed to be the only visitors in Damascus: European bible tourists zealous enough to want to see the few, mostly Pauline sites. After Damascus they would take buses south to Jordan and then to Jerusalem and the West Bank.

An old German or Swiss lady crossed herself piously before clomping into the grand mosque on her clogs.

"John the Baptist is known in Arabic as Iohanna to Christians, but Muslims call him Yahya," I remarked. "We call Jesus Iesu but Muslims call him Isa."

Munif nodded. Religion was not a topic that stirred him up, so we sloshed through the Street Called Straight and talked about names. *Cities of Salt* was full of odd names, and the second volume of the trilogy was even more perplexing.

"Fanar, Rakan, Khureybit—are they Arabic names?"

"Yes, they are! Not very common names—they're rare, like Mufaddi in the first part."

Munif referred to the novels of his trilogy as "parts." When he said "the novel" he meant the whole cycle, though each could, he claimed, be read independently of the others.

"But I've actually known a Mufaddi, in Saudi Arabia; he was from the north, from al-Jouf."

"You wouldn't find a Mufaddi from anywhere else!"

It wasn't just that these were unusual names; they were downright unattractive or even ugly. When I put this as politely as I could, Munif laughed.

"It's partly superstition. Arabs from the peninsula want the evil eye to take no interest in their children, to be intimidated by them, in fact. So they name a boy Raad." It meant thunder. "Or they name him for a fierce animal—Fahd or Osama." Panther or lion. "Or Kleib." Little dog. "Even Jahsh." Donkey. "They wouldn't do that with girls, of course—girls have names that suggest piety or beauty. Perhaps it is thought that the evil eye would not be as interested in a girl child, or that it would have fewer opportunities to reach her." In Iraq, Munif said, revolutionary names were always in vogue: Thawra, "revolution," was popular, as were Nidal, "struggle," and Intishal, "uprising" or "uplift." These secular names also fudged the bearer's religion.

I commented that in volume two of *Cities of Salt* there was a slave named Surour. It seemed to me that every slave in Arabic literature had that name: the *1001 Nights* was littered with them.

"Hah—you're right! It means pleasure. Slaves always have pretty names—people wanted to be surrounded by pleasant associations. Slaves didn't have names such as you would give an animal, as I think was often the case in America in past centuries. In Arabia slaves were more ornamental, they didn't support the economy. Slaveowners in Arabia gave them names like Surour, Marzouq, Mabrouk, and so forth. The rich liked to say, 'Come here, Pleasure,' 'Come near me, Gladness,' 'Listen to me, Blessed One.' Some slaves were named for flowers, or got names that suggested their sweet personalities—Tayyib, Zein"—both these names meant "good"—"or even 'Beauties.'"

I reminded Munif that when Saudi Arabia outlawed slavery in 1964, an elderly princess of King Faisal's family was said to have refused to free her slaves. "The king cannot forbid what is sanctioned in the Koran," she reasoned, "unless I am a criminal, and he chooses to confiscate my property. If that is not the case, my property is still my property."

"Brother!" A young Syrian in an army jacket pulled at my arm and unraveled a wad of paper in my face. An address was scrawled on it. "Please tell me where to find this shop."

"It's near Bab Tuma." Thomas's Gate was not far from here.

"He thought you were Syrian!" Munif thought this very funny, but I was used to blending in among the Damascenes, until I opened my mouth, and told him so. "Not at all!" he generously insisted.

We found a shop selling inlaid boxes, chessboards, picture frames, and end tables, and I instantly selected one. Even Munif, with his intense dislike of bargaining, groaned at the folly of letting a shopkeeper know precisely what you wanted—this at least tripled the price. The shopkeeper, Jirjis Kateb (he had an inlaid nameplate on his desk) would accept no less than 200 lira. Munif insisted on paying, but wanted it polished. While Jirjis' son searched for oil and a rag, I asked Munif if he had heard of the novel *The Satanic Verses* by Salman Rushdie, which was due to be published in the U.S. the following month.

"Banned in India, and all the Muslim countries, but that's all I know. That, and the fact that it has created a certain fear of novels in the Arab world. Kuwait has banned the rest of the *Cities of Salt* trilogy."

That must have hurt: Kuwait, though tiny, was one of the few Arab markets rich and free enough for Munif's books to be sold openly and in large quantities, and it was an important outlet for offshore sales to Saudi Arabians. Kuwait had substantial communities of expatriate Palestinians and native Shiites and liked to demonstrate its independence from Riyadh, frequently infuriating the Saudi government with slightly radical or permissive policies—just such things as allowing Munif's novels to be sold. It was interesting that a confused fear of fiction had accomplished something that the might of Saudi Arabia had failed to do. Or perhaps several years of depressed oil revenues had damaged the self-confidence of the Gulf. Or perhaps in literature religious extremists had found a battleground that Arab governments did not care to defend. (In Egypt, Naguib Mahfouz would be sentenced to death by Sheikh Abdelfattah Ahmed of the Islamic League of Egypt just seven months later.)

The woodworker's boy ducked back into the room holding out the now glossy hexagonal box, which smelled strongly of polish, and when they had painstakingly wrapped it in brown paper and then newspaper I tucked it into my pocket. The bell on the door clacked as we set out, Munif with his hands in his coat pockets, clenched his pipe in his teeth, still musing over the new relationships between authorship, censorship, and death. I reminded him of an American actress's comment on modern times: "No matter how cynical you become, you can't keep up." He had to abruptly rescue his pipe from falling while he laughed loudly.

"You must know about that from trying to follow the fate of Moussa Sadr!"

It was true. For months and years after my Imam book was published, reports abounded that he was alive and about to be freed. The Iraqis circulated rumors, through magazines they owned in Paris and London, that Syria and Libya had everything to fear from the Imam's freedom and were trying to prevent it. The Syrians used the Lebanese media to suggest that they were on the brink of arranging Sadr's release—they did this whenever they needed to get the Shiites off their back. Most of the rumors, though, came from Iran, and were clearly part of a struggle between social-climbing psychotics (the "radicals") and totally amoral opportunists (the "moderates").

Throughout 1988, one Ayatollah Mahdi Rouhani in Tehran pitilessly tantalized the Sadr family and the Shia of Lebanon with his stories that the Imam would reappear, in Cairo, within four weeks; eight weeks; very soon. He was in contact with "all relevant parties"; success was assured; "one of the superpowers" was intimately involved, much against its will. As it turned out, Rouhani was playing two games: one was to prevent the election of a new president of the Supreme Shiites Islamic Council of Lebanon, a post Sadr held at the time of his disappearance. Retirement from the job was automatic at age sixty-five, and Rouhani was trying to scare off more moderate rivals for the position by reviving the notion that Sadr was still alive. He did so on behalf of the Iranian government, which was trying to ensure that "its man" would be the best placed for the battle in 1993, when Sadr would have turned sixty-five. Rouhani's second game involved cash gifts he was receiving from a consortium of European insurance companies which had insured Imam Sadr's life for $5 million, and which also appreciated rumors that their client was still alive.

"The Muslims always call him *al-imam al-hadher al-ghayib*, the present-absent Imam," I said, and Munif nodded. "When you think of it, it's very useful—he's not dead, but not alive to dispute them. Everyone tries to threaten everyone else with his return. It's a sort of vampire status." It was also fitting in a religious culture like the Middle East's that dealt so freely in Messiahs, Twelfth Imams, and Second Comings. A few months later, Khomeini himself would be gone, and would usurp Sadr's title of *al-imam al-hadher al-ghayib*.

It seemed especially appropriate that the ambiguous Sadr, with his two nationalities and tandem loyalties, ended up both living and dead. I had not cracked his case, and it was fair to assume that no one ever would, but his mystery, a perfect emblem for his life, had been a pillar of cloud leading me through Arabia, Egypt, and

Israel, and the journey had been more rewarding than any documented solution to the whereabouts of his bones. I had learned to see myself as a foreigner, and in the process become something of a native. I suddenly thought: what a surprise Munif has in store for him, when his Saudi citizenship is restored, and he tries to move his daughters back there.

"You are smiling!" said Munif. He was smiling, too. He did not look like an exile: he looked like a magician who had sent his kingdom into exile and was waiting for it to come around.

We emerged from the old city at the Bab al-Sharqi, the eastern gate, an arch with a stained-glass fan set in a block of the old city wall. *Bab,* of course, meant door or gate, Munif said, and was an extremely ancient word. It was an eastern Semitic word, identical in Assyrian and Babylonian. In fact, the word "Babylon," or "Babel" in Arabic and Hebrew, came from *Bab-Ilu,* meaning the Gate of God. *Ilu,* of course, had evolved into El, Elohim, Allah, and other forms. As he unlocked the door of his car to head back to al-Mezze for our last lunch together, I listened closely to his thoughts on the ancient Near East. Harran, an Arabian city in the trilogy, was named for the biblical Harran, where the patriarch Abraham had stayed while en route from Ur of the Chaldees to Canaan.

"One of my next projects," said Munif, "will be to tour ancient sites in Syria and Iraq with a photographer, and produce a beautiful book. Look at the traffic," he sighed. "I hope we won't be late for lunch. And you have a plane to catch. What a short visit! Next time, we'll all pick up and go, the family and you, to Palmyra. It's breathtaking!" He touched the horn gently to warn a wobbly bicyclist working crossways through the almost stopped traffic. Five disorderly lanes of bleating buses and tinny

Soviet-made sedans were nudging into a nearly blocked rotary by the city's west wall.

"Take your time," I told him, looking out at Damascus's winter brightness, the golden, moss-dotted wall of the old city, and mobs of schoolchildren in olive-drab uniforms swinging their black briefcases at one another. I was looking forward to seeing his family, but did not want to be asked, *What time is your flight? Are you packed? Did you reconfirm?* I was grateful for the traffic jam, and wanted it to last.